Mr. Dunn Browne's Experiences in the Army, edited by noted Civil War writer Stephen Sears, provides a candid, often witty, behind-the-scenes look at the Civil War. A collection of battlefront letters composed by Browne (pseudonym of Captain Samuel Wheelock Fiske of the 14th Connecticut Volunteer Infantry), this book is unique in the literature of the Civil War. Fiske was at once a fighting infantryman and an experienced newspaper correspondent, and no one in this war, on either side, wrote better accounts of a soldier's experiences in battle and in camp. From Antietam to the Wilderness, readers of the *Springfield Republican* had Dunn Browne to explain to them just how it was in the Army of the Potomac. In addition, he was an investigative reporter (before that term was invented) who delved

(Continued on back flap)

MR. DUNN BROWNE'S EXPERIENCES IN THE ARMY

Yours

Dunn Browne.

Mr. Dunn Browne's Experiences in the Army

*The Civil War Letters
of Samuel W. Fiske*

Edited by

STEPHEN W. SEARS

Fordham University Press
New York
1998

ISSN 1089-8719
The North's Civil War, No. 6

Library of Congress Cataloging-in-Publication Data

Fiske, Samuel Wheelock, 1828–1864.
  Mr. Dunn Browne's experiences in the Army : the Civil War letters
of Samuel W. Fiske / edited by Stephen W. Sears.
    p. cm. — (The North's Civil War ; no. 6)
  Includes bibliographical references and index.
  ISBN 0-8232-1833-3 (hardcover).
  1. Fiske, Samuel Wheelock, 1828–1864—Correspondence.   2. United
States. Army. Connecticut Infantry Regiment, 14th (1862–1865)
3. Connecticut—History—Civil War, 1861–1865—Personal narratives.
4. United States—History—Civil War, 1861–1865—Personal
narratives.   5. Connecticut—History—Civil War, 1861–1865—
Regimental histories.   6. United States—History—Civil War,
1861–1865—Regimental histories.   7. Soldiers—Connecticut—
Correspondence.   I. Sears, Stephen W.   II. Title.   III. Series.
E499.5 14th.F57   1998
973.7′446—dc21   98-14100
                                                                        CIP

Printed in the United States of America

CONTENTS

INTRODUCTION

During the years of the Civil War, the *Springfield Republican* un-blushingly described itself as "The leading journal of New England," and aspired to even more: to be the voice, indeed the conscience, of all New England. Springfield, in southwestern Massachusetts, was centrally located for this self-proclaimed role. The *Republican*'s flagship weekly edition, published Saturdays, had a circulation of 12,000 across the Northeast, which its publisher claimed was "greater than that of any other interior journal in the country" and exceeded by "but few of the city papers."

In these years the weekly's eight pages were crowded with political news from all across the North, with local news from all the New England states, with reviews of books and the arts, with stories "original and selected" from literature, with news of business and the farm, with "six to eight columns of leading editorials, and editorial paragraphs," and, most extensive of all, with reports of every sort from the war. An important feature of this war coverage was column after column labeled "Correspondence of The Republican"—letters from the paper's special correspondents. "Van" reported from Washington, "Periwinkle" from New York, "Warrington" from Boston, "R.W.B." from the 10th Massachusetts in the field, "E.S.S." from the 37th Massachusetts. The most prominently displayed of these special correspondents, with a letter almost every week, was published under the heading "Dunn Browne at the War."

The use of a nom de plume was common newspaper practice in mid-nineteenth-century America. The tactic was said to allow the correspondent to speak his mind without fear of retaliation or repression. For Dunn Browne, on those occasions when he unleashed what he termed his "grumblings" against army bureaucracy or commanding generals, his nom de plume was surely a comfort. The *Springfield Republican* would reveal Dunn

Browne's identity only on May 16, 1863—in decidedly odd circumstances, to be described shortly—but even then there was no pulling of punches by the writer of these observant, witty, sometimes angry, frequently profound letters from the battle lines to the folks back home.

In the guise of Dunn Browne was a man of manifold talents—Samuel Wheelock Fiske, captain, 14th Connecticut volunteers, Army of the Potomac. Fiske was not at all the typical Civil War soldier, or even the typical officer. That he had joined up at all, and then in the infantry, was the mark of a man to whom the Union cause was simply the Cause.

Samuel Fiske, born in 1828 in Shelburne, Massachusetts, had entered Amherst College at age sixteen, slight of stature, charmingly personable, and very bright. Coming from a family of slight means, he worked his way through college, mostly by laboring in a book bindery. That he flourished in the atmosphere of a classical education of the time was evident at commencement in 1848, when he delivered, in the words of one of his professors, "a salutatory oration as full of fun as the grave and stately 'lingua Latina' could be made to carry." Two years of teaching in academies and three of studying theology followed. In 1853 Fiske returned to his alma mater as a tutor. Then, in 1855, he set off for Europe and the Middle East, acting as "a kind of guide and historiographer" for a party of a dozen fellow travelers embarking on what was called in that day the Grand Tour.

It was during these travels abroad that readers of the *Springfield Republican* first made the acquaintance of Dunn Browne. Fiske's letters sent back to the newspaper, over the signature of his newly adopted nom de plume, made him, it was said, "one of the most racy, witty and spicy of all our newspaper correspondents" (surely "racy" and "spicy" being relative terms in that more innocent age). He was described as a model traveler, "inexhaustible in wit, never at a loss for an expedient, master of himself, and more than a match for Greeks and Jews, Arabs and Turks, believers and infidels. . . ." In 1857 these travel letters were published as *Dunn Browne's Experiences in Foreign Parts.* In an author's note, Fiske, carefully remaining offstage, remarked that Browne had not always been his name. It was originally Greene, he explained. Over time the salutary lessons of life's experiences had "scorched as it were his verdancy into a sober russet hue, in consequence of which experience the writer has, in the lapse of years (without once applying to the legislature for a change), gradually come to be called Browne." As to his chosen Christian name he was silent; of course his readers knew dun to be a shade of brown.

As his profession Fiske had elected the ministry, and he became pastor of the Congregational church in Madison, Connecticut. At age thirty he married nineteen-year-old Elizabeth Foster, the daughter of a minister, and a year later their first child, a boy, was born. At the time of Fort Sumter, then, Samuel Fiske was nearly thirty-three, married and a father, and a full-time pastor to a Congregational parish. It appeared to him, in those heady days of 1861, to be a younger, less-obligated-man's war; and it was from that pool of manpower that Connecticut filled its first quota of volunteers in expectation of putting down the rebellion in short order.

By the summer of 1862, however, the scene had changed, and darkened. McClellan's massive Peninsula campaign against Richmond was a failure, and Mr. Lincoln was obliged to call for 300,000 more volunteers. "I stood it just as long as I possibly could & then caved in," Fiske wrote his brother Asa; ". . . I do not despair of the republic." He had just turned thirty-four, with a family and his wife eight months' pregnant, and if he had to go to war at all he most properly ought to have signed up as a chaplain—brother Asa, also a minister, was chaplain to the 4th Minnesota—but he spoke of a greater obligation: "I want to fight for my country." Raising what he described as a squad of men from among his neighbors, he signed his enlistment papers on August 8, 1862, and was made a second lieutenant in Company I of the newly authorized 14th Connecticut regiment. By August 25 the raw new Connecticut 14th was on its way to the seat of war. Fiske found time to make an arrangement with the editor of the *Springfield Republican*, and in less than a week after starting for the front he had the first of his ninety wartime Dunn Browne letters on the way to the *Republican*.

Ten months and some thirty-five Dunn Browne letters later, Fiske sought to explain to his readers what he was about in his reporting. Of a battle, he wrote, "Your correspondent can only give the impressions of one soldier, who is acting his own small part somewhere under the smoky cloud." His scenes were necessarily fragmentary, "because they are genuine, such as they are—daguerreotypes, and not fancy sketches." However modest they may be, Samuel Fiske's daguerreotypes have the same qualities as Brady's—great clarity and striking depth. His account of his green regiment's baptism of fire, at Antietam, is one such example. To understand what that holocaust of a battle was like for an entire untrained regiment—the officers knew as little as their men—meeting hostile fire for the first time in their lives, one need look no farther than Fiske's letter. Another example is his reporting from Gettysburg—an eyewitness, on the firing line, writing virtually contemporaneously with events, and far more perceptive than any newspaper correspondent on that field of battle.

In his reporting of events, whether they be battles, skirmishes, or marches, Samuel Fiske represented a unique combination—an experienced correspondent conscientiously reporting to an audience, on the one hand, and, at the same time, with no choice in the matter, an infantry soldier undergoing the actual minute-by-minute, often very deadly experience. There is nothing comparable in Civil War literature.

It was just this sort of circumstance that led the *Republican* to reveal Dunn Browne's identity prematurely. In the confusing woodland tangle at Chancellorsville, in May 1863, Captain Fiske disappeared and was presumed killed; so stated the first reports. In fact, in the deep woods, Fiske had stumbled on a band of armed Confederates and been forced to surrender—a scene he renders with his usual ironic humor—and this fact did not make its way back to Springfield before the paper had printed the obituary of Samuel W. Fiske, "our Dunn Browne." Much would be made, of course, after Fiske's exchange, of Dunn Browne's reading his own obituary. Alas, his good luck was not to be repeated.

In the Army of the Potomac during the twenty-month period of Fiske's service—Antietam to the Wilderness—the fighting was of course not continuous. Consequently, Dunn Browne took the opportunity, between battles, to explore numerous military questions and issues for the people on the home front. He acted, in the terminology of the modern press, as an investigative reporter, and investigating in uniform, from the inside. He was boldly candid—breaking the story, in effect—when he revealed that his fellow Yankee soldiers coursed through the Maryland countryside like a plague of locusts. That was not what other papers were reporting. Frequently, too, he found the army bureaucracy a fertile field for exposé. When issues at home promised to affect the troops on the firing line, Dunn Browne responded righteously. In the spring elections of 1863, for example, Connecticut Democrats put up a peace candidate for governor, and Fiske's avowal that the Copperhead credo was a stab in the back of every fighting man at the front surely helped influence the electorate to vote down the Democrat.

One of the most interesting of Dunn Browne's crusades was launched against the abuses of conscription in the North. To most readers of the *Republican*, the draft and its evasive provisions must have seemed more theory than practice. Then, in a series of letters from the banks of the Rapidan in Virginia, Dunn Browne provided the practice. He vividly described the fruits of conscription: the scum-of-the-earth substitutes and the duplicitous bounty-jumpers coming into the army—and into the Connecticut 14th in particular—prodded into the ranks at gunpoint, their every effort focused on the first opportunity to desert. Fiske aimed a variety of tactics—cajoling, appealing to patriotism, shaming—at draft-age New Englanders, urging them to sign up voluntarily and help finish the job. There is no knowing how effective he was, of course, but at least he contributed strongly to the public discourse on the thorny questions of conscription.

The *Springfield Republican* was a staunch supporter of the administration, and an influential one, although, like Fiske, it recognized much room for improvement in Washington's war policies and practices. The paper was both willing and able to showcase Fiske's efforts to educate and influence and inspire the home front on the great issues of the war. *Republican* editorials frequently echoed Fiske's crusades; the editor might position a Dunn Browne letter as obvious support, from the firing line as it were, for some stance of the paper's. For example, the Dunn Browne letter castigating the Copperheads as betrayers of Connecticut's gallant fighting men was prominently displayed in the *Republican* just days before the state election.

Numerous Northern newspapers carried letters from the battle fronts, some sent to family and then passed on to editor, others written deliberately for publication. But Samuel Fiske stands well ahead of the crowd on several counts. First, he had perfected the art of newspaper correspondence with his prewar travel letters to the *Republican*—and in the process gained an audience for his later work. Second, his choice of subject matter was varied, yet always focused on the interests and concerns and morale of those on the home front. Finally, Fiske had mastered the art of the small essay. He clothed his sharply aimed purposes in wry, self-effacing humor, and he had perspective and a point of view. It would be hard to find another soldier, on either side in this war, who was more consistent, and more eloquent, in expressing just what it was he was fighting for.

It is soon obvious, in reading these letters, that Captain Samuel Fiske was a good soldier as well as a good essayist. He believed in his cause—the Cause—and as the spring campaign of 1864 approached, he elected to stay on in the army and see it through. He was not obligated to do so—his original agreement with his parish was for a one-year leave of absence, and he had already exceeded that—but he felt his true obligation was to the men with whom he had enlisted. Leadership was a rare commodity in the Civil War; good leadership at the company level required constant risk and exposure to enemy fire. Captains of companies—good captains—perforce led from the front, not from the rear. So it was that Captain Fiske was at the front in the Battle of the Wilderness, May 1864, and so it was that he was wounded there. He was shot through a lung, a type of wound all too often fatal. He lingered sixteen days and, on May 22, 1864, he died. He was buried at his birthplace, Shelburne, Massachusetts. At the funeral it was said of Samuel Fiske, and of Dunn Browne, "Not one of his talents will be lost. Not one of his sufferings and sacrifices will be in vain. They are all a part of the price that must be paid for the redemption of the country."

Of the ninety-two letters reproduced here, ninety were printed in the *Springfield Republican*, and one appeared in a newspaper serving Fiske's Connecticut parish. The opening letter, written to his brother Asa Fiske, is included for its explanation of Fiske's decision to enlist. In 1866 the letters to the *Republican* were collected by Asa Fiske and published as *Mr. Dunn Browne's Experiences in the Army* (Boston: Nichols and Noyes). For this volume, the letters have been transcribed just as they appeared in the *Springfield Republican* and arranged in proper sequence. Headings are those of the *Republican*'s editor or supplied by the editor of this volume. The editor has also supplied the chapter headings and headnotes for the letters.

The headnotes utilize material drawn from the columns of the *Republican* accompanying the Dunn Browne letters. Additionally, extensive use has been made of Samuel Fiske's wartime letters to his family, and of letters by Asa Fiske, in the John Aldrich Stephenson Collection of the Papers of the Hand, Fiske, and Aldrich Families, in the Library of Congress. The editor wishes to acknowledge the assistance of Jeffrey M. Flannery at the Manuscript Division, Library of Congress, of Thomas Knoles at the American Antiquarian Society, and of Janice Pruchnicki, Madison, Connecticut, who is preparing a biographical study of Samuel W. Fiske.

STEPHEN W. SEARS

1

DUNN BROWNE GOES TO WAR

The 14th Connecticut was mustered into Federal service at Hartford on August 23, 1862. A few days previous, newly minted 2nd Lieutenant Fiske wrote his brother, a chaplain with the 4th Minnesota who had been in service since the previous fall, to explain his decision to join up and to give his view of the critical plight of the Union. Granted a year-long "vacation" by his congregation in Madison, he rented his house there and sent his wife, Elizabeth, and their son George to stay with her parents. Overnight, pastor Fiske became soldier Fiske.

Samuel W. Fiske to Asa S. Fiske

Camp Foote, Hartford Conn.
Headquarters 14th Regt. Conn. Vols.
[August 1862]

2nd Lieut. Fiske to Chaplain Fiske, Greeting
My Dear Bro.

I stood it just as long as I possibly could & then caved in, got a year's vacation from my people & went to recruiting.

Got a squad of some 25 men from Guilford & came in as a 2nd Lieut. under Capt. Bronson of the Foote Rifles (Co. I) 14th Regt. to start in a few days probably for the seat of war. The Madisonians are here alongside with a whole Co. (the Scranton Guard) of which sixty are from the town. Guilford has about one hundred & fifty men now in the field & other towns in proportion. Old Connecticut is finally rousing up. We of the reserve are coming down to help you who are in the advance. Give us room. Let us hope that the administration is beginning to come up a little to the demands of the people that this war be carried on in earnest. If they do waste & fritter away the resources of the nation in property & in life as they have done hitherto, it will be the most astonishing instance the world ever saw of a country ruined by its government & will prove indeed the failure of democratic method. I will not believe it possible. I do not despair of the republic. I am going to do what I can that it receive no detriment.

I think I may be offered the chaplaincy. But shall hesitate strongly about accepting it. I want to fight for my country. Do not know that I can pass muster as to military knowledge, but shall study all I can.

Expect Lizzie & George to go up to Shelburne Falls to board. Rice takes my house for a year & will see to my affairs more or less.

We are in a great hurry making out our muster roll & so I cannot write you at much length. Willard is Capt. & Wm. Hart 1st Lieut. with a railroad chap by the name of Sherman as 2nd Lieut. in the Madison Co.

God bless you & keep you. Your aff. bro.
SAMUEL FISKE

This is the first of Fiske's "Dunn Browne" Civil War letters to be published in the Springfield Republican. *His regiment had left Hartford on August 25 and traveled by steamer and rail to Washington, going into camp in nearby Arlington. As he wrote, the armies of the Potomac and of Virginia, under Pope, were streaming back from the disastrous battlefield of Second Bull Run. There was great uncertainty in the ranks—particularly the ranks of a raw new regiment like the 14th Connecticut.*

Dunn Browne in Camp

Near Washington
Sept. 1, 1862

Your old correspondent has been able to restrain his warlike inclinations, and remain in the quiet performance of his professional duties, until this last grand rally of his countrymen to the field of battle. But, when the 300,000 additional volunteers were called for, it was no use for him to stand it out any longer. One 300,000th of that call was for him undoubtedly. So professional engagements were at once split open by the wedge of a year's vacation, wife and baby hastily disposed of at father's house, property of a movable kind supplied with wings, and put to a hasty flight; and three weeks from the time of the first decision sees the peaceful citizen clad in military costume, and quite at home in the life of a camp—yes, even now within the sound of booming cannon, and with a regiment that sleeps on its arms every night, expecting an attack.

News, of course, you cannot expect from me, except by an occasional favorable accident. What you may expect in the letters I mean semi-occasionally to send you are some impressions of life in camp; some random sketches of things that seem most striking, most *uncivil*, and out of the way of our ordinary peaceful life.

The first observation every man would make, judging from my brief experience, is that the soldier's life is an eminently dirty one. Our boys, on their way to the field, slept on the dirty decks of a steamer, lying together as thick as rows of pins on a paper; were packed in dirty, close cars, like sheep in a pen; and marched through dust so thick and fine, that, mixed in proper proportion with the perspiration caused by the intense heat, it formed a good plaster cast of every man's face and form. Water is often too precious to waste in ablutions; linen gets dirty; washerwomen are scarce; clothing of every kind grows ragged; and, on the whole, dirt steadily and surely prevails, till a regiment of veterans appears to one uninitiated like a regiment of ragamuffins. Experience has already shown us, also, that a soldier's is sometimes a pretty hungry and thirsty life. For three days together, in our first week, we had nothing to eat but a few hard crackers, and once a morsel of cheese and once a slice of ham served round; and for one night and part of a hot day we had no water in camp.

And again: ours is an amazingly uncertain life. Two nights ago we were in comfortable tents, with luggage and knapsacks all around us; last night and to-night we are far away from both, lying on the cold ground, in rainy weather, with nothing between us and the open sky but a thin rubber-blanket. One night the camp is all alive with lights, fires, songs, and shouts of laughter; the next all is silence, fires are out, men talk almost in whispers, and lie on their arms, expecting a momentary attack. The soldier knows least of all men what a day may bring forth. His to-morrow may hold in its bosom for him starvation or plenty, the shout of victory, the shame of defeat, the pain of wounds, or the closing scene of death.

DUNN BROWNE

Fiske writes now embarked on the pursuit of Lee's invading legions. General McClellan was back in command, absorbing the Army of Virginia into the Army of the Potomac, reorganizing and reinvigorating the defeated Yankee troops. The 14th Connecticut had been assigned to a new brigade in a newly assembled division under William H. French in Edwin V. Sumner's Second Corps. After their months of campaigning in alien Virginia, the troops regarded Maryland as a land of milk and honey and, to Fiske's dismay, foraged in this supposedly loyal state "like a cloud of locusts." His candor in reporting this was unusual in the Northern press. Fiske's knowing reference to the Crimean War and the army of Egypt is a recollection of his prewar Grand Tour of Europe and the Middle East.

The "Sovereigns" as Soldiers

Near Rockville, Md.
Wednesday, September 10 [1862]

An army is a big thing, as anybody will realize who sits on a high hill as I do and sees the ground it occupies. There are about a thousand acres of soldiers visible from this point, and we have passed miles and miles of army wagons on our way up the Potomac, to reinforce Burnside, or cut off Jackson, or whatever business it is that we are going upon, which you probably know a great deal better than any of us do. It is a tremendous big thing, of which we are a part at this present time, I assure you. We move on up the country, through woods and vales, on roads and on byways, in three long parallel anaconda lines, no one of which is ever all visible at once, and which seem absolutely interminable, and of whose numbers we here can scarcely form an idea. And when we double up and crowd together at night for a bivouac, we cover the whole face of the country round about like a cloud of locusts, as thick and as destructive. Acres and acres of soldiers, but not an acre of corn, or potatoes, or fruit, or anything else eatable within a circle of two or three miles I suppose, and that too though we had been here only over night. A crop of soldiers kills out any other crop in the quickest possible time. Our orders against plundering are very strict, too, and guards generally placed over property. It seems to be impossible to keep an army from destroying everything through which it passes.

The orders are strict enough, but a strict enforcement of the great principle of obedience seems to be utterly repugnant to the spirit of our citizen soldiers. I am sorry to acknowledge it, and yet more sorry to see and believe that our soldiers very generally are or soon become a set of lawless plunderers, and the older the regiment the more bold and expert in petty larceny. And the older the regiment, too, the more undisciplined and disorderly, and the less inclined to go into a battle or perform the duties of a soldier any way, so far as I have yet seen. Hundreds of men and dozens of officers in the old regiments of McClellan's and other armies, have told me that their long marches and servant's work in the trenches, and lack of food and privations had constantly demoralized our men; that they had grown neglectful of discipline and yielded to dirty and disorderly habits. I hope this may not be universally or generally true. But I must say that of all the armies I have ever seen, including the 300,000 allied and Russian troops in the Crimea after their tremendous campaign, and hardly excluding even the army of the Pasha in Egypt, that which is entrusted with the defense of our United States government, is in appearance the dirtiest and the least orderly. I suppose the rebels are even superior to us in these respects, but cannot yet speak from observation. Our new levies I am sure ought to be good material to make efficient soldiers out of, but even a sovereign American citizen must condescend to obey orders and consent to discipline in order to become a valuable soldier.

Your correspondent personally is getting hardened famously

to camp life. Last week he ceased to scrape together leaves on which to lay his blanket for the night. Last night for the first time he didn't take the trouble to pull out the sticks and stones for his bed of earth, and henceforth the nearest spot on the bosom of his mother earth will be his chosen pillow.

DUNN BROWNE

This letter, printed in the Republican *on September 27, was composed on the eve of the Battle of Antietam. McClellan had found Lee's army at Sharpsburg, in western Maryland, drawn up behind Antietam Creek. At this writing, Fiske's regiment was posted on the heights across the creek, to the east. McClellan had determined that the seventeenth would be the day of battle.*

Under Fire

State of Maryland, on a Hill
September 16, 1862

That is not very definite, dear Republican, to be sure; but we are within a few miles of Harper's Ferry and about the same from Hagerstown, and in the midst of a most tremendous cannonading on all our march for the last two days, the meaning of which I presume you know, but we do not very well. Our batteries, however, are pitching shot and shell into the enemy at a deafening rate about a mile on our right, and the enemy are responding very nearly as rapidly, and many of their missiles come over our heads and among us. One lieutenant has just stepped out from a regiment adjoining ours to get a nearer view, and a solid shot struck his foot and crushed it. A lieutenant colonel's horse is torn all to pieces on the other side of us, a moment since, leaving the bridle hanging to the fence. A pair of artillery horses just behind us have just been grazed by a ball, which knocked off the pommel of a saddle from the back of one and cut the crupper strap clean from the other, without hurting or scaring either of them. About a dozen shot and shell have passed over our heads and struck in the midst of us (Gen. French's division, a few regiments of it) within the past fifteen minutes. I suppose they are not really intended for us, but for our batteries which are playing on them. Still I don't know that it would be any great consolation to your correspondent, having, for instance, one of his well-shaped legs taken off by a rebel shot to think that it wasn't done on purpose. Our boys stand the fire on the whole I should say nobly. A few squat or crouch when they hear the whistle of the shot or the screech of the shell. A few stand quietly and watch the field to see where the missile strikes. Some shout, some swear, some I hope pray. Some would skedaddle if they dared to I doubt not. I hope it will be long before any one in our ranks will dare to do that.

Now don't suppose from what I am writing you that we are in the midst of a battle. It is only a small artillery skirmish so far as we here are concerned (though there are plenty more big guns firing far away in the distance); but as it is the first time I have been actually under fire I have spoken of it more particularly. The situation is not, I confess, to me a pleasant one. (The firing is over for the present.) I had no disposition to run away, and indeed didn't see any very favorable place to escape from shot which fell in front, on both sides, and as much as a mile in our rear. But the feeling of being exposed to the mangling effects of those murderous messengers of destruction is far from an agreeable one. You can calculate the probabilities as being a thousand to one or ten thousand to one against your being struck, but somehow the one chance looms up rather disproportionately in your view. However, your correspondent is happy to be able to close with the assurance that as yet, though having been under fire, he has not been hit.

Dunn Browne

Antietam, fought on September 17, was the bloodiest single day in the Civil War; indeed, in the nation's history. Fiske's letter, written the next day as the two exhausted armies lay facing one another, is a graphic account of the savage fight for the center of the battlefield. What appeared to Fiske to be a ravine was the so-called Sunken Road—or Bloody Lane—running along the crest of a low ridge. French's division made the first charge on Bloody Lane;

Dwight Morris's brigade, which included the 14th Connecticut, comprised the second line of the assault, as Fiske reports. The "stray general" who took them in hand was Winfield Scott Hancock, replacing the mortally wounded Israel Richardson in that sector of the field. The final count of the 14th Connecticut's casualties in its first battle came to 20 dead, 88 wounded, and 48 missing. "I had some rather narrow escapes, but wasn't touched," Fiske wrote in a private letter. "One soon gets used to the whistling of shot & the screech of the shells. . . ."

Dunn Browne in a Battle

Battle Field, Maryland
Sept. 18 [1862]

Well, dear Republican, I have at last turned over a new and bloody leaf in my experience and seen a battle; and am now writing you, sitting in a newly-plowed field, all strewn with the dead of our gallant Union soldiers, still unburied, lying as they fell; 14 of the 88th New York, of General Meagher's Irish brigade, lying for instance only two or three rods behind our present position, all in one line as they dropped at one deadly volley poured in upon them as they rushed forward on the gallant charge which did so much to win for us yesterday's hard fought day.

It has been a tremendous battle we have passed through, and one in which victory has crowned our arms, for we hold the whole field, and have taken many prisoners; but of the precise results, or even of the forces engaged, or of the probabilities as to a renewal of the contest, you will know ere this reaches you a hundred times more than I can yet tell you. It is astonishing, the ignorance of us who are actually playing the soldier's part here, of what is going on around us. We cannot get any information anyhow. The most absurd and contradictory rumors circulate through the camp. What we see with our own eyes is all that we can believe, as a general thing, and sometimes scarcely that. The battle itself was a scene of indescribable confusion. Troops didn't know what they were expected to do, and sometimes in the excitement, fired at their own men. Generals were the scarcest imaginable article, plentiful as they are generally supposed to be. We neither saw nor heard anything of our division commander after starting on our first charge early in the morning, but went in and came out, here and there, promiscuously, according to our own ideas through the whole day.

The part I saw of the fight was something like this: The enemy held a very large corn field, surrounded on the three sides (on which we were obliged to attack) by a steep and difficult ravine. On the north, east and south we advanced to the attack, our batteries playing over our heads. Our regiment came in from the northeast to attack on the north, being the second line, the first line a few rods before us being composed of a Delaware and one other regiment. As we came along even with the east line of the rebels, we also entered a cornfield, and at once were opened upon by a raking fire of musketry, and a good many of our men fell. The north end of our line pressed on till we came round facing the enemy on the edge of the ravine, and we opened fire upon the enemy across the ravine, firing into the corn which concealed them from our view. After a few minutes the Delaware men, who had tried to cross the ravine before us, broke and came running back upon us, crying out, some of them, "Skedaddle, skedaddle." Some of our men tried to stop them, and a few of them, it must be confessed, joined in their flight. But in the main, for green troops, I think we behaved well, the men firing with precision and deliberation, though some shut their eyes and fired up into the air.

Finally, after a straggling and confused scene of about an hour's fighting, advancing and retreating, carrying off the wounded and cheering each other on, some of our own troops came up between us and the enemy on the opposite side of the ravine, so that it was dangerous for us to fire any longer, and we retired and attempted to advance on another side, but could get no place and so drew off and supported a battery two or three hours till all its horses and ammunition were shot away, we exposed all the while to a fire of grape and canister. (Here we saw and helped away Gen. Richardson, wounded.) And finally, towards evening, the enemy being driven from all their positions, we were picked up by a stray general, and ordered to hold an advanced position across a plowed field where we were within reach of the enemy's skirmishers, who have been practicing on us ever since. In which dirty and uncomfortable place I must bid you good-bye for the present. Our regiment loses 75 to 100 killed and wounded; others, many more. The fight raged many hours. Old officers said the musketry fire was the hottest they ever heard. Yours truly,

DUNN BROWNE

After standing in place on Thursday, September 18, defying Mc-Clellan to renew the battle, Lee led his bloodied army back across the Potomac to Virginia. McClellan's half-hearted pursuit allowed the Confederates to make good their withdrawal. In a letter to his family written the same day as this one to the Republican, *Fiske remarked, "We suppose the enemy to have retreated beyond the Potomac. I think if we had followed up our success on Thursday we might have annihilated him but things are not managed with a great deal of energy according to my notion." In reporting to the* Republican *enemy losses in Maryland of 40,000 to 50,000 men, Fiske was accepting camp rumor. In fact, for the campaign as a whole, the Union loss was 27,000 (including the captured Harper's Ferry garrison) against 14,000 for the Rebels.*

After the Battle

Field of Battle, near Sharpsburg, Md.
Saturday, Sept. 20 [1862]

The excitement of battle comes in the day of it, but the horrors of it two or three days after. I have just passed over a part of the field, I suppose only a small part of it, and yet I have counted nearly a thousand dead bodies of rebels lying still unburied in groves and corn-fields, on hill sides and in trenches. Three hundred and fifty I was told by one who helped to bury them, were taken this morning from one long rifle pit which lay just in front of where the 14th (among other regiments) made their fight, and were buried in one trench. The air grows terribly offensive from the unburied bodies, and a pestilence will speedily be bred if they are not put under ground. The most of the Union soldiers are now buried, but some of them only slightly. Think now of the horrors of such a scene as lies all around us, for there are hundreds of horses too, all mangled and putrefying, scattered everywhere. Then there are the broken gun carriages, and wagons, the thousands of muskets and all sorts of equipments, the clothing all torn and bloody, and cartridges and cannon shot and pieces of shell, the trees torn with shot and scarred with bullets, the farm houses and barns knocked to pieces and burned down, the crops trampled and wasted, the whole country forlorn and desolate. And yet I saw over all this scene of devastation and horror, yesternight, one of the loveliest double rainbows that ever mortal eyes looked upon. It was as if heaven sat serene over human woes and horrors, and crowned all the earthly evils with the promise of ultimate most glorious good. I took it as an emblem of success to our blessed Union cause, that out of the horrors of battle shall arise the blessings of a more secure freedom and stable system of liberal government.

The enemy has retired in disgrace from his bold invasion of the North with at least 40,000 or 50,000 less men than he entered upon it—and after all our disasters and blunders and waste, let us hope that the successful end is beginning to draw nigh. The waste of this war is tremendous beyond all conception. It would take a long time to reckon that of this one battle. Thousands and thousands and tens of thousands of muskets, stacks of guns, piles of guns like big piles of rails, muskets laid up against rocks and trees and muskets scattered yet over the ground and choking up water courses, muskets rusty and broken and dirty, spoiled and half-spoiled, that a few days ago were bright in the hands of living men, are only one item of the waste. Whole regiments threw away their overcoats and blankets and everything that encumbered them, and they were trampled in the rush of conflicting hosts, and so with equipments and stores and ammunition and everything else. Waste, waste, ruin and destruction. Why, I saw a whole immense stack of unthreshed wheat, big as a barn, scattered in a few minutes over a hundred acre field (the same I think from which it had been reaped) just as bedding for the soldiers for a single night. Much of this waste is unavoidable. Much of it might be helped. Just as it is said that out of the waste of an American kitchen a French family would live comfortably, so it might almost be said that out of the waste of an American war a European war might be carried on. But I must make no more waste of ink now. Yours truly,

DUNN BROWNE

Following Antietam, during fine campaigning weather in September and October, McClellan encamped his army in the vicinity of Harper's Ferry and engaged Washington in a contentious debate over supplies and equipment and reinforcements. Lieutenant Fiske's letter reflects this debate at the company level. Lee, meanwhile, positioned his Army of Northern Virginia in the Shenandoah Valley for refitting and renewal.

Camp Fare and Other Things

Camp of Bolivar Heights, near Harper's Ferry, Va.
September 24 [1862]

Dear Republican: Did you ever see a brigadier general riding along on his splendid charger, with a string of sweet corn ears hanging on his left arm, and onion tops peeping out of his saddle-bags? I did, yesterday, and observed his look of triumph in the possession of the aforesaid articles, greater than if he had gained a battle. And I saw a colonel chuckling over a plate of peaches which he had in some way captured for his mess table, and a major spurring joyfully into camp with a couple of live chickens tied to his saddle bows. I also can speak from experience of the rapture of a starved and generally-used-up lieutenant over the possession of a loaf of real bread—the first that had made his heart glad for weeks. I tell you, Republican, you haven't any idea of the blessings of a decent meal of victuals. You don't know the treasure you possess in a boiled potato, bursting its tight jacket and revealing its hidden mealiness as it comes smoking upon your dinner table. Such a sight would bring tears to the eyes of thousands now crunching their hard crackers and drinking their decoction of beans which Uncle Sam passes off upon us as coffee, on this barren hill. As for myself, I should faint at the very smell of a delicate chicken broth or a barley soup, and at the thought of a bowl of bread and milk—

Oh, dear me; it is too much. I must change the subject. I was out with a brother officer, the other day, washing in a muddy brook. We had hung up our checkered woolen shirts on some bushes, while we plied the soap and sand in scouring our outer man. A little group of old soldiers passing by espied the shirts, and one exclaims to the others, "Oh, gorry, boys, come and take a look at the clean shirts these chaps are going to put on!" I assure you, Republican, on my honor as a United States soldier, we had worn those same shirts over a fortnight, and yet to the eyes of those veterans in rags and dirt they seemed the very *ne plus ultra* of cleanliness. Things are all comparative in this world.

I suspect we are to remain in this vicinity a little while and refresh ourselves and get reinforcements and be ready to sweep the rebels down through Virginia a few weeks hence. I should think the most of McClellan's army was in the vicinity, and the rebels are hard by. But it must be that we can get reinforcements and munitions of war faster than they. Our troops are in very fine spirits and courage, but weak with diarrhea from insufficient and improper food, and fatigue and exposure. The management of the commissariat department of our army must be very defective or very dishonest. And indeed the want of thorough organization and a system of checks and of strict responsibility is the great and almost fatal curse in every department of military affairs. I wonder how we gain any success when I compare these things with what little I have seen in other countries in the same line. We couldn't if we hadn't the best materials for soldiers the world ever saw. Yours in haste,

DUNN BROWNE

2

IN CAMP IN THE FIELD

By adopting a pseudonym, a favorite journalistic device of the day, Samuel Fiske could write critically of the army and its generals and the management of the war and feel secure from retribution by his superiors. Nor did the Springfield Republican *provide any clue to his identity. In this letter Fiske offers a coy hint with the proposition that anyone utterly unable to stem an outpouring of words, as he was, must be an editor or a minister or a lawyer "or anything of that kind." Fiske's concluding remark, that he believed his letters had been stopped in the mails, was apparently unfounded. This letter, and the three written during the previous week, all appeared in the October 4 issue of the* Republican.

Dunn Browne Must Write—Let Him

Bolivar Heights, near Harper's Ferry, Va.
September 26 [1862]

Dear Republican: Do I bore you with my letters without news, and confused accounts of things very partially seen, and occasional soldierly grumblings about lack of food and the mismanagement of superior officers? Well, set it down partly to indigestion and partly to the necessity of writing that a man is under who has once allowed himself to fall into the habit. Fault-finding is the easiest kind of writing to which one can turn his hand; and write somehow and somewhat a man must who has ever been an editor or a minister, or a lawyer, or anything of that kind, as you well know. I don't want to write. I don't mean to. I never sit down to it but I wish I was done. And yet by the strange necessity of which I have spoken, no sooner is a halt ordered, be it at sultry noon-day or in the shades of evening before the twilight is gone; no matter how weary the limbs, nor how inappropriate the place; sometimes sitting on a fence with my ink horn stuck into a rail (by the way, I mention as a strange circumstance that I haven't yet observed in the state of Virginia a specimen of that style of fence known as the Virginia fence); sometimes in the front seat of a baggage wagon with the horses eating their hay from between my feet; sometimes on a stone by a brook with my bare feet cooling in the running water; again, squatted on a furrow of a plowed field with bullets whistling all around, or sitting by the flickering light of an unusually bright camp-fire at midnight; in health or in sickness, in battle or on the march, so long as the ink holds out and a sheet of paper can be begged or borrowed, the old habit holds its power, the stream of correspondence doesn't run dry, complacent friends pretend to be pleased with one's faithfulness, newspaper columns are burdened and after-dinner readers perhaps keep awake. So look out for more of the same and many like them, and even if you should read in the bulletin that Dunn Browne has fallen in a heroic charge upon the enemy's battery, waving his sword and cheering on his men, &c., &c., you may still expect one more farewell epistle written perhaps in red ink and showing the ruling passion strong in death.

This region where we are, the scene before us from these heights where we are encamped, does really seem too lovely to be the seat of a horrid war, a paradise too sweet for the devil to enter with his polluting presence. But the devil of war is a mighty fiend, and he is laying his strong hand of desolation heavily on this particular region, sweeping down the noble forests and groves, and crowning these hills instead with frowning batteries, trampling down the crop-laden fields, burning farm houses, stacks and barns, and leaving villages in ruins. Harper's Ferry itself, occupied and given up so many times by each army in turn, is a woeful picture of ruin and destruction, but romantic and picturesque to the last, more interesting perhaps in its ruin than in its former beauty. All the public works and most of the private buildings are a heap of rubbish and cinders. But I must suddenly stop, as I have an opportunity of sending this by a private hand, and have reason to suspect that many or all our recent letters have been stopped. Yours truly,

DUNN BROWNE

A Congregational minister in civilian life, Fiske might well have entered the army as a chaplain, but had elected to fight in this war rather than preach. He retained, however, a close interest in the religious well-being of his fellows, as this letter suggests. He earlier described the regimental chaplain as "a Baptist clever fellow. . . ."

Sunday in Camp

Bolivar Heights, Harper's Ferry, Va.
October 1, 1862

Who dare say that there is no Sabbath day to the soldier, no worship of God in the camp? Let him come and see a regiment of eager men gathered together under the rays of a burning sun at noonday, after a week's hard marching and drilling, to hear the word of God preached and join in prayer and praise; *standing up* too through a service of nearly an hour. Tell him how generally the regiment came together to service in that splendid white oak grove near Sharpsburg on the Sabbath after the battle. Show him the earnest groups that assembled for social prayer two or three times a week at any chance resting place in any spare hour that can be so improved. Aye, soldiers' prayers are short and often interrupted, but the Lord has a place for them, an ear to listen to them, a strong right hand to work in answering them. The Christian, God-fearing men of our regiment are a leaven of good working in the whole lump, shirking no soldierly duty, and to be depended upon in any emergency. And many of our boys that have been called wild and reckless at home, show that the associations of the holy Sabbath and the influences of God's word have a deep hold upon their hearts.

It is letter-day at last in our camp. The long, long delayed mail has at last arrived from Washington, the first tidings for four weeks from the loved ones at home, four long, crowded, eventful weeks. Oh, it would have done your tender and sympathizing heart good, my dear Republican, to have stood before that long line of anxious, eager soldiers, *falling* in to receive their letters; to have seen the eye light up and the hand stretch forth to grasp the missive of affection (very likely ill-spelled and directed in crooked lines, with no capital letters, down into one corner of the envelope) as the name was called off, and the company's "orderly" handed up the document. And it would have done you good too, albeit somewhat to the dimming of your eyes, to have seen the delicacy of emotion manifested, the hushed murmur of sympathy that passed down the ranks as the name of one of the dead comrades was read, and the loving reverence with which those unread epistles were tied together and laid carefully away to be returned to the bereaved friends.

Oh! it has been a most eventful day with us, a whole month of life, as it were, compressed into one short afternoon. I can't however expect to compress it, or very much of the interest of it into one brief letter to you, so good bye.

DUNN BROWNE

In writing to his sister at this time, Lieutenant Fiske recorded (as noted in the letter above) that his regiment had just welcomed "four or five bushels" of long-delayed mail, and on the evidence of the following letter to the Republican, *it appears that he had received a backlog of Northern newspapers as well. His reaction to the array of gammon—a Britishism for "blather"—they contained sent him reaching for pen and paper to explain to the people back home how it really was in the army.*

How the Soldiers Feel

Bolivar Heights, near Harper's Ferry, Va.
[c. October 2, 1862]

News of army movements, &c. I can't tell you, but how the soldiers feel here in camp and in battle and on marches I can tell you, for that I see and know. When you read from newspaper correspondents and "reliable gentlemen" that the army are "full of enthusiasm" and "eager for the renewal of the conflict," that they "have entire confidence in their generals" and "rush joyfully to battle under their guidance as to a feast," I doubt not your common sense teaches you just about how much such gammon is worth. The simple fact of the matter is that the soldiers universally, every man of them so far as my observation goes, dislike war and dislike battles, as all good citizen-soldiers should, dislike to be killed with shell or minie bullets, or to be starved to death or to be marched to death, just as much as other men do. Indeed, they are all *other men* than soldiers by profession or preference. But they have come to war reluctantly from the pressure of urgent necessity and a strong sense of duty, and they want the war over within the quickest possible time. And they are not satisfied with their generals, because they have common sense enough to see that, with some few exceptions, our armies are not well-managed, nor well-provided, nor well-led into battle; that their strength, their energies, their lives are to a very great extent wasted.

The soldiers are aware however that this state of things is hard to remedy. They endure it, they bear the privations, a great part of which they know to be unnecessary, with less grumbling than the people of any other nation under heaven would utter. They go into battle, aware that it is pretty much a chance whether their bravery and endurance will be of any avail, with a cheerful resolution that does them the highest honor. I glory in our common soldiers. I do not despair of the country when I see the materials that compose the army for her defense. The government may dally with the foes and difficulties it has to encounter. Greedy contractors and corrupt officials may eat up our resources. Incompetent and traitorous commanders may waste our tremendous armies. All the more credit to the unbroken and unconquerable spirit of our people that is carrying and will carry our cause through in spite of every obstacle and at the cost of whatever sacrifice.

Of course I am saying this of the men in general of our armies. Some of them are poor enough material for anything, too poor to waste good powder and ball upon; utterly unworthy to fight in behalf of our glorious cause. Probably it was from a consciousness of this unworthiness that so many of them *skedaddled* from our big field of battle at Sharpsburg. The vile, obscene, blasphemous swaggerers of our regiment, the thieves and drunkards and rowdies of the regiment generally, to the number of seventy-five or a hundred, were found wanting in that fatal corn field, and came sneaking back for days after the battle, with cock-and-bull stories of being forced into hospital service and care of the wounded.

DUNN BROWNE

Here Fiske, now a veteran of six weeks in the service, directs sage advice to others among the 300,000 answering the President's call—volunteers, nine-month militiamen, and those drafted or paid bounties to meet state enrollment quotas.

Soldiers' Luggage

Bolivar Heights, near Harper's Ferry, Va.
Oct. 6 [1862]

Dear Republican: Have all those three years men and nine months men, who have volunteered, or been drafted, or been bought with extravagant bounties into the service of the United States, yet started off and left you desolate? If there are still a few left who may be benefited by my advice, I wish to speak a word, especially to the officers, in reference to outfits and equipments. As old a campaigner as your humble servant happens to be; though he has traveled over a good part of the world with no other luggage than a small carpet bag, he is compelled with shame to acknowledge himself in the present instance to have acted as foolishly, in respect of baggage, as the greenest young lieutenant, who has just donned his brilliant uniform with its shining buttons and entangled his legs with the awkward sword.

Your correspondent having dropped the peaceful toga from off his shoulders and sprung to arms in his country's defense, went into this military toggery and outfitting business utterly regardless of expense, and filled up a trunk, right up to the eighty pounds or 12 cubic feet allowed by Uncle Sam's army regulations. That same costly trunk, stored with magnificent apparel, wherein your humble correspondent expected to appear in due time before his regiment, like Solomon arrayed in all his glory, when he came out at the head of the Jewish militia, came into his possession about one week after he left the good old state of

Connecticut, and remained within his reach precisely five days, at the expiration of which time, he received with his regiment, orders to march without baggage or knapsacks, and so shut down the cover and buckled up the straps with a sigh of regret, and—has never seen it more from that day to this; and, what is worse, has many doubts as to whether it ever will bless his eyes again. In case he should ever have it in his power once more (which will only be by his getting it expressed on from Washington at an exorbitant price as private freight), his first measure will be to drag out of its depths that same little despised carpet bag before alluded to, put in it a clean shirt, a bible and toothbrush to take with him, and his next measure to send by express the three-feet-by-two evidence of his dotage back to Mrs. D.B. in dear old New England.

For learn, oh you foolish generation of military novices, that when Uncle Sam says you are entitled to so much transportation, he means that you are welcome to it, if you can get it; that he will gladly forward the 40 trunks, more or less, of the officers of a regiment, provided they can conveniently be carried in the three or five wagons allowed, together with the company chests, the stores of various kinds that *must* go, &c., &c. Moreover, the wagons are always many miles in the rear of a marching army, and in case of danger from the enemy do not come up, often for days and even it may be for weeks together. What the soldier or the officer (except the field and staff officers, who, as they ride horses instead of having only themselves to attend to, cannot be expected to carry much, and so have a trunk in the wagon)— what the soldier or the line officer can carry on his own back, that he is reasonably sure of (till somebody steals it or he throws it away in battle), and the less he relies on any other government transportation than his own legs, the less likely to be disappointed.

Get your things for use, oh my friends, and not for show. Be not deluded by the asseverations of military tailors and outfitters. Use your common sense if you have any; if not take a little of mine, which not having been used by myself remains for me now freely to offer unto others. Go into a harness-maker's and have a good strong strap of homely leather made for you into a sword belt instead of investing in the costly, varnished-without and pasteboard-within article that glistens before your eyes in the shops, and other things in like manner. And as to quantity get the least possible. Trust to Providence, reduce your wants to the smallest compass, and have great regard to the weakness of your poor human legs. For when their stiffening shall have been reduced by the moderate diet of crackers and water to which you may sooner than you think come, your tottering knees will have their full burden, in *toting* enough to keep your back warm and your stomach full. Take these remarks to heart, oh military tyro, for though homely and perhaps a little dampening to your first military ardor, they are rich in truth and sense, and come from one who has "been there" and who was and is glad to be there, and who without much romance in his ideas of war, yet rejoices every day to be permitted to share in the hardships and the dangers of his country's defenders. Yours truly,

DUNN BROWNE

As a comparatively late arrival in the Army of the Potomac, Samuel Fiske did not share the admiration many of the veteran troops felt for General McClellan. He seems to have shared Mr. Lincoln's view that the general had the "slows." On October 1–4 the President visited McClellan and the army, the occasion for the review Fiske mentions.

Dunn Browne Resolutely Reticent

Bolivar Heights, near Harper's Ferry, Va.
October 12 [1862]

Dear Republican: I have nothing to say. I am not going to say anything. If the date of my letter speaks for itself, as hinting for instance that the tremendous army of McClellan is still lying in its tracks now for almost the full month after its victory at Sharpsburg, in the most precious part of the whole year for active military operations, and seems to be repeating its masterly inactivity of last year over again with the utmost precision; if, I say, my date itself be a tell-tale, blot it out, knock the types on which it is set up into *pi,* for we must have no fault-finding with

our generals or our government; agitation must be suppressed
and incendiary opinions promptly choked down. The grand army
of the Potomac, I am happy to inform you, anxious Republican, is
safe (and so are its enemies). Evidences of a great contemplated
onward movement thicken before our wondering and admiring
eyes. For didn't the great general himself, with a tall president in
train, and many splendidly dressed officers and a long mounted
retinue, did they not actually appear before us a few days ago,
and make a tour of the whole army, and bow very sagaciously to
us as we received them in line with "present arms," as much as
to say, "look out, boys, for a jolly march to Richmond, as soon
as the fall rains, which we are patiently waiting for, shall have
placed the roads in their normal condition, of two feet in
depth"?

Lest, however, I should violate my opening premise and say
something, which might betray still further the imminent plans
of the impetuous general, and, published in your columns, bring
you under government censure as affording contraband information to the enemy (who is fully three miles away from us, all
around our western and southern line of encampment), I will
pass away from the dangerous theme at once, and turn to one of
more personal interest to myself and to yourself, also, in speaking of the joy with which I hailed the appearance of a stray copy
of the Republican the other day in our camp. The young man in
whose hands I saw it (and whose name has since been handed in
with strong recommendations for the next vacant corporalcy)
takes it regularly, so that I am now able to reflect with a spirit of
comparative independence upon your failure to comply with my
request that you should forward a copy of your weekly sheet to
my address, Washington, D.C. Did you refuse that request,
tender-hearted Republican, that I might not be pained with the
knowledge that my lucubrations remained unpublished, and
found an ignoble end in your waste paper box? Or do the D.B.
letters create such an increase of subscribers that there absolutely doesn't remain paper enough to print a spare copy on?
However this may be, I read that stray number through even to
the guessing out the mysterious "e o p t f" &c. directions at the
corners of the advertisements, and it had so strong a scent of
the old Connecticut valley and home associations that I have
hardly had the heart to look in a "Baltimore Clipper" or "Phila-

delphia Enquirer" since, although they are cried in our ears (at
the low price of ten cents a copy, and sometimes a day old at
that) from morning till night. The dear old Connecticut valley!
When this terrible war is over with what joy shall I carry back
whatever may be left of me to the chosen spot! Talk about the
danger to our country from its citizens becoming enamored of
military glories and in love with standing armies. I assure you
that our soldiers will be the ones of all others to rejoice with joy
unspeakable over the return of peace. War, certainly as conducted on the principles of the present one, proves its own best
antidote. The man who has seen its horrid face fears it most.
There is only one thing that is worse, and that is our country
destroyed, our liberties lost, our precious institutions perished.
Yours truly,

DUNN BROWNE

*In a private letter dated September 30, Fiske explained how the
officers of Company I had fared before the crisis he describes
below: "We selected the most enterprising man in our company,
took off his musket & every encumbrance, released him from duty,
got him a pass (with some finessing), gave him an unlimited supply of money & a big bag, two canteens & several bottles, & sent
him out . . . & he has done nobly." It was the illness of this expert
scrounger that threw them back on their own resources. The
rumor Fiske records about the 14th Connecticut being transferred
out of Sumner's Second Corps proved to be just that—a rumor.*

Cooking in Camp

Bolivar Heights, near Harper's Ferry, Va.
October 15 [1862]

Dear Republican: Shall I draw the curtain from before our
kitchen and let you into the secret of some of the domestic and
culinary arrangements of the officers of Company I? The fact is
that the man whom we have detailed to forage and cook for our
mess, has been sick for a week, and not being able to provide a

suitable substitute for him we have been cooking and hunting up our own provisions. In other words our masculine Bridget having caved in, we have been obliged to take to the basting ladle and toasting forks ourselves.

At the first scene, then, oh Republican, behold your correspondent at the hour of half past three this misty, drizzling morning, issuing forth from his tent with a cluster of canteens slung over his back, a demijohn in one hand and a huge coffee pot in the other, on the laudable errand of procuring water for our small crowd, which he obtained by sliding, walking and stumbling down our steep hill, at an angle of about 45 degrees, over rolling stones and fallen trees and among stumps, to a spring some three-fourths of a mile distant, whence he returned after the space of an hour quite refreshed with his morning ramble. See next the captain himself, with overcoat on and eyes half open at work a little back of the line of tents kindling up a fire under the smouldering edge of a big oak log which constitutes the back of our fire place and afterwards burying sundry sweet potatoes in the ashes, whereupon ceasing from his efforts and retiring upon his dignity and sundry woolen blankets for another morning nap. The third actor upon our culinary stage is our other lieutenant, slender and graceful, who, rising a little later and spending a little more time in his ablutions, is now to be seen preparing tea and taking the mackerel out of the mess-pan where it has been soaking over night ready for a broil over the coals (on two disabled ram-rods) to constitute the relish for our morning meal.

Meantime the first mentioned, having recovered from the fatigue of his water-detail and leisurely completing his morning toilet, bathing arms and face in a whole pint of water poured out by an obliging corporal from a cup of that capacity (for wash basins we have none), proceeds to a neighboring tent to borrow a loaf of bread, returns with half a loaf, which he has found frequently in his recent experience to be a great deal better than no bread, and the trio assembles, each man with his contribution to partake of the frugal meal. Seated in Turkish style upon the straw-covered (ground) floor of our tent and our smoking viands placed upon a low box between us, with a big newspaper for a table cloth, we make a very hearty and satisfactory breakfast. We have a paper of salt, a box of pepper (holes pricked through the top with a bayonet), a jar of pickles, a little tin can of butter, another of sugar and another of solidified milk, tin cups to drink our tea from and one spoon to stir it withal. (We confidently expect a new supply to-morrow of tin spoons and knives and forks.) The delicious potatoes quickly disappear, the buttered mackerel leaves only his skeleton and fins behind him, the "half loaf" becomes "no bread"; the first lieutenant reaches his hand into our box to bring out two or three bunches of fresh grapes left over from our yesterday dinner's dessert, but searching in vain, is evidently disposed to suspect the captain of having appropriated them in the night. Then comes the usual discussion as to who shall wash the dishes, which ends in your correspondent's volunteering to perform the task on condition that his brother lieutenant shall go down to the village and do the catering for the day. Bearing in mind the uncertainties of our market, he is instructed to procure for our dinner a chicken, *or* a bit of beef, *or* ham, *or* a can of oysters; to carry a canteen and bring us a quart of milk, if love or money, his brass or his good looks can obtain it; to be sure and bring us some more of "those grapes," or any other fruit he can find; and not to think of seeing our faces again if he doesn't come with a bottle of vinegar, that we may use the noble cabbage that we bought yesterday.

Now, dear Republican, do you think that it is trifling and foolish to write and have printed in a paper these little, every day matters, to devote time and ink to these things that are of no comparative consequence, in the midst of the grand and solemn realities of war with which we are surrounded? No. You do not. You can have ten descriptions of a battle or plans of a campaign sooner than one glimpse at the little un-thought-of details of a soldier's life. It would make a more interesting column in your paper just to set down a minute detail of one day's doings of one of our privates in camp here, to picture him to you as he sleeps and wakes, prepares his meals and eats them, drills, mounts guard, cleans his equipments and clothes, writes his letters, does his duties, and takes his ease, &c., &c., than to describe the grand course of a campaign, or give you the most vivid account of a military parade or battle scene. The greater part of the soldier's life, as well as anybody else's life, is made up of these little things. Accordingly, though it is harder writing than the grand descriptions of the thunder-and-lightning battle scenes, I am going into the commonplace details a little. I am not proud, personally, of cooking my own dinner or washing dishes, but I think your readers will like to hear what the soldiers of the people's grand army can do in case of an emergency, and that they will also share in our joy at having anything to cook and eat.

To change the subject at the last moment a little, there are rumors this morning of our being attached to Burnside's corps (and detached from Sumner's) and under marching orders. So there is no telling how soon I may have stirring news enough to write about and have little leisure to speak of or engage in culinary processes. Well, I trust, in God's strength, that we shall take up our march or enter into the smoke of battle, if it be His will, as cheerfully and coolly as we sit down to dinner. Yours in feast or fray,

DUNN BROWNE

How badly the army was managed, in ways small and large, is demonstrated in this report by the observant Lieutenant Fiske. And this, be it remembered, was under the regime of General McClellan, who was supposed to be, if nothing else, a skilled administrator.

The Worry and Waste of War

Weverton Hotel, Knoxville, Md.
(8 miles below Harper's Ferry), Oct. 17 [1862]

This is a fine large hotel and we occupy one of the best rooms in it, the parlor or drawing room, I think. It is the best ventilated hotel, I believe, I ever was in, unless perhaps I except an Eastern Caravansary in which I once spent a night and which had no roof at all. This building has a roof (minus a good many shingles) but not a whole window from cellar to garret. The place had been turned from its legitimate purposes and occupied by the government for headquarters of the quartermaster's department, and like everything else used for Uncle Sam's service, is decidedly the worse for the wear; windows smashed, piazza and steps broken down, furniture entirely demolished and removed, walls defaced by charcoal inscriptions, ceilings dropping in, and the whole establishment decidedly resembling one of the Herculaneum and Pompeii houses that have been digged out from the lava of Vesuvius.

The way we happen to be here is this. Our regiment at Bolivar Heights received orders yesterday noon to come down to Harper's Ferry for 24 hours' guard service. So we fell in and came down the hill a mile or two to the Ferry, waited there in the sun an hour and then were told that it wasn't exactly there that we were wanted but about a mile up the Shenandoah River to protect commissary stores and forage. So off we marched up the Shenandoah till we came to the end of the railroad track and saw a vast pile of some 10,000 boxes of hard crackers and 2,000 barrels of beef and pork, whereupon we halted again in the sun and waited another hour for orders. At the end of that time came the news that only two companies of the regiment were needed there, and the rest must go back to Harper's Ferry and perhaps over the Potomac to Sandy Hook. Accordingly we countermarched, dropped off the last two companies of our long column and traveled back to the Ferry. There we learned that two more of our companies were needed, but the rest were to be marched over to the Maryland side of the Potomac and down to Knoxville, three miles. So the remaining six companies of us came on through Sandy Hook, over hill and dale to this place, arriving at about 5 p.m. Waited here an hour, and then received orders to leave three of our companies here on guard, and send back the other three to Sandy Hook, two miles and more, over the road that we had just marched in coming, some of the boys so weak and feeble, too, that they could hardly stand. But finally, as a shower was coming on, we all stayed here over night, and sent the other three companies back to Sandy Hook early this morning. Whether they remain there, or are still "marching on," like the soul of John Brown, I know not.

I don't mention this as a matter of any great consequence, for the march wasn't a very long one, altogether, and it made no particular difference when we arrived at our destination, as the whole way was lined with regiments of soldiers, enough to guard all the property a hundred times over without any of our help. But I speak of it merely to give you an idea of the way everything is managed hereabouts. I have scarcely seen a march or movement of any kind executed in any cleaner or more direct and definite style than that. Nobody knows what he is to do, or when he is to do it, or how. I have already told you of the vexations and needless delay in getting our mail to us. Now our regiment is receiving every day dozens of boxes by express that have been on their way from four to six weeks, and whose contents have been nearly all spoiled by the delay in transmission. And all the soldiers' knapsacks and officers' baggage that were left stored at Washington, during our march through Maryland, remain there still, although it is nearly four full weeks that we have lain here at Harper's Ferry, sixty miles from Washington, with communications two or three times a day each way by rail, and we are all suffering for our indispensable articles of wearing apparel and obliged to replace them by now. Just these comparatively trivial personal matters, mismanaged, wouldn't ruin the country, but this is only a fair specimen, yes, only a fair specimen, of the general way in which everything, and especially the great things of the war, go on. Why, through the hard rain of last night, thousands, and I guess tens of thousands, of bags of oats and corn lay out here under our guard by the side of the track, soaking through and through. And so all along the track for miles, boxes of hard bread (which only needs to get a little wet to mould and grow musty and breed worms and be condemned) and every kind of provision and forage and baggage. Men, horses and property of every kind are all alike neglected, improvidently managed, scattered and wasted in this extravagant war. Yours economically,

DUNN BROWNE

Parson Fiske offers a sermon to his fellow soldiers—and to the people back home—as he sought, like so many others of his day, to find some meaning in the all-too-often senseless conflict. This topic was much on Fiske's mind in these weeks. "I suppose the Lord is working even through such instruments as our stupid generals & Cabinet officers," he wrote his brother, "but it is hard to believe it." The Mrs. Partington he mentions was an invention of the English clergyman and satirist Sydney Smith. Fiske's concluding reference to the 150,000 Rebels they faced was the wildly exaggerated figure that General McClellan fed to the newspapers.

Sunday on Picket Duty

Army of the Potomac, Harper's Ferry
October 19 [1862]

Dear Republican: Lying here under the edge of a wheat-stack at four o'clock this misty morning, my head wet with the dews of the night and feet cold with the chills of the damp straw that covers them, I was inclined to take gloomy views of things and agree with Mrs. Partington as to the disagreeableness of "sleeping on a picket" as compared with "sleeping on a post," and hold the world as a dreary kind of a place to dwell in, especially the out-of-doors part of it, and to be low in spirits generally as to the war and the country and the universal moral system of things, and more particularly as to my own prospects for a pleasant Sabbath. But when the glorious sun showed his cheerful face over the ridge of Loudoun Heights, and the hosts of mist and fog and cloud could not abide the sight of his countenance, and the crests of the hills began first to appear and then the tree-tops, the farm-houses, the orchards and groves; as I now write, with the dew dried up, the earth (and my toes) warmed in the sunbeams, the delightful notes of the quail whistling up from the valley below us, and the whole bright, fresh and bracing autumnal morning throwing its influences of cheer around me; why the mists begin to clear away, before my mental and spiritual vision too, my views of philosophy, morals and religion partake of the brightness of the fair morning. The world, the country, even this grim war, assume a softened aspect, and arrange themselves in their harmonious place in God's grand plan of operations. For better than the morning sun driving away the mists have been the blessed words of Holy Writ to my spirit; the glorious Psalm of David to which I opened at random, which has for its frequent refrain, "Oh that men would praise the Lord for his goodness and for his wonderful works to the children of men." And again the sweet words from Christ's own mouth that I found in reading my Sabbath morning chapters in the Gospel, where we are assured that the sparrow falleth not to the ground without Our Father, that the very hairs of our head are numbered, &c. Yes, God's word is the best recipe for promoting cheerfulness and patience, and enabling a man to take things as they come, believing they all come from Him who doeth all things well. Surely it is just the book for the soldier to get his daily comfort from, and I rejoice to see how many of our soldiers do make it their continual solace.

I think I closed my last letter to you with some foolish, common-place remark about the waste of men, blood and treasure of this war. Whatever it may have been I take that all back. That was said from a low, merely human point of view. In the sight of God, in whose great name I trust, we set up our banners in this war, not a drop of blood, not a sigh or a groan uttered, a hardship or a danger passed through, not one of all the sacrifices made by an individual citizen however humble, through the length and breadth of our vast country, has been wasted. The tired soldier has fallen out of the ranks and died by the wayside before he has had the opportunity of striking a blow for his country, but not in vain. The brave, enthusiastic patriot has rushed to the defense of his country without looking for position or counting the cost, and has sacrificed his life to the blunder of some incompetent officer, or the corruption and treachery of some scoundrel, but the eye of God has seen and accepted the sacrifice. The large-hearted wife or mother or sister, has stifled her sighs as she bade adieu to the loved one and bravely endured his absence and the sad tidings of his wounds and death, and man hath thought little of it outside of the circle of bereaved ones, but God's eye hath taken it all in. There is no waste of patriotism or sacrifice in this great plan. The mismanagement of His human agents is all provided for; it is a part of the allowance for friction in the running of His machinery. There is no such thing or word as mistake with Him. And so all this blundering, wasteful, extravagant war is an economical, well-ordered part of His system, and shall promote the great general progress of virtue and liberty in the world and the glory of His own great name.

This is the way I muse to-day, spending my Sabbath on picket duty, stationed under the lee of a wheat-stack. We shall have out here under the sky a short service of worship and praise to God, though there be no other than myself to lead therein, with the sword girt on my thigh and the enemy's pickets in sight before us. God will help us to keep His day holy though we are clad in the panoply of war and obliged to do many military duties. He will accept our praise if we offer it in sincerity. He will feed us with His word, though we have it only in a few copies and can only snatch now and then a moment to peruse or listen to it. He will listen to our prayers though they be brief and broken. For He is our strength and our refuge, our strong fortress and our high tower. He is the God of the soldier and the soldier's loved ones at home, the God of battles, the God of our country and our fathers. We will have him for our God, and pray that He may be the God of our children and our regenerated, repurchased country unto all future generations. Thus much from yours, immediately in front of a hundred and fifty thousand rebels,

DUNN BROWNE

P.S. We surely expected a fight two or three days ago. A few thousand of us were ordered to the front (though our regiment, being absent in the rear on guard duty when the order came, couldn't go), expecting the whole army to follow. But having looked the enemy in the face and had a sharp skirmish with artillery in the vicinity of Charles Town, and "the whole object of the movement having been successfully accomplished," to use the cant military phrase, we are all called back again to our old quarters, the enemy's pickets come up as close as ever, and "all is quiet along the Potomac" for another month I fear.

The Springfield Republican *had normally published its "Dunn Browne at the War" letters on the seventh of its eight pages, with other correspondence and newsworthy notices. This outburst of outrage, however, ran as a full column on the front page of the November 1 issue of the* Republican, *and an editorial lent support to Dunn Browne's plea that "the voice of an outraged people" be heard in the land. Fiske's anger at these abuses had been building for weeks. On September 30 he had written privately, "I did pitch into the Col. till I was almost ashamed, about our men lying out so exposed, & we have finally gotten a . . . nearly tolerable supply of shelter tents. . . ."*

Cruel Abuses in the Army

Bolivar Heights, near Harper's Ferry, Va.
October 25 [1862]

Dear Republican: Behold your correspondent at the head of sixty-six men, out on a wood-chopping excursion of a few days, our swords not exactly turned into plow-shares, but our rifles transformed into the clumsiest axes that were ever put into human hands to wield; and the giants of the forests groaning with an almost human agony as their trunks are mangled with their cruel strokes. We are sweeping clean of its shade and forest trees a most lovely little valley along up the Baltimore and Ohio railroad to the west; letting the glaring sun into shady dells, choking up the bed of a clear-running stream with the corpses of many a stately oak and sycamore and elm and hickory and maple, noble fellows, four, five and six feet in diameter; and leaving many a cottage and mill bare of its ornamental shade. It seems a villainous business, a sacrilege against nature in her holiest mysteries. But our cannon are pointed in this direction and whatever interferes with their sweep and destructive efficiency must go down at whatever cost. The trees must fall that men may the more readily fall if they should come to take their places. Pitiless war spares nothing, carries devastation and desolation to houses and fields, forest and mountain-sides, cities and great communities. Considering in our business of to-day how far the range of our heavy batteries extended, I thought, oh what a tremendous, infinite range all this array of war-artillery possesses. Not one little valley like this, but all the valleys through the length and breadth of our land; not these scattered houses in our sight, but the homes of the nation have the dreadful guns bearing directly upon them. The cannon pointed from one of these hills may take effect on the shores of the Penobscot or the Rio Grande. The musketry discharge in Virginia may fill graves in Connecticut and in Georgia.

But I am not going to moralize or sentimentalize. "We came out here to fight and not to chop wood" was the disgusted remark of one of my boys as he held up to me his blistered hands after a combat of about an hour and a half with a huge sycamore by the brook-side, in which he had succeeded in encircling the old monarch's body with a girdle of barely perceptible scars; "We came out here to fight and not to chop wood." And this sets me off to thinking again in spite of my resolution not to moralize. We don't object to chopping wood for once in a while as occasion may serve, or doing any other little extra work that Uncle Samuel may require. But *we came here to fight.* We expected and wanted to fight weeks ago. We haven't been permitted to fight. The weather in which we can fight comfortably is well nigh past for the season. And the soldiers are treated in such a way that they are fast losing their disposition to fight. Our brigade and others so far as I can judge are not in any respect in so good a fighting condition as they were three or four weeks since. Nothing pains me so much as to hear the expressions of the men on every side, of discouragement and complaint, of regret for having enlisted, and wishes that they were home again, and curses on the government and on the generals, &c.—ad infinitum.

The few who came from a mere sense of patriotic Christian duty stand their ground and bear everything without much murmuring, and doubtless half the grumblers don't mean all that they say and would come up to the mark in a battle manfully. But I should do injustice to my honest belief if I said otherwise than that the spirit of the army is going down and backward every day. The men feel that they are treated like dogs, and are out of patience with it. And there is too much ground for it, as I say to you, and wish I could say to the governors of all the states and to the president of the United States. Their wants are not attended to, their feelings are not regarded. They are neglected when they are sick, and are left to die with little care or sympathy manifested in their behalf. I tell you again, as I have told you before, the knapsacks of the men and the baggage of the officers of this and at least one other adjoining regiment still lie in a storehouse at Washington, 60 miles from here, with railway trains running three or four times each way every day, now tomorrow five weeks since we came to Harper's Ferry, and all the remonstrances we have sent in, all the messengers we have dispatched, and orders and telegrams with which we have burdened the wires, have failed to obtain that which was indispensable to our comfort. Men have died, not one but many, to my knowledge, from no other apparent cause than the exposure of sleeping night after night and week after week on the ground, without overcoat or blanket, and sometimes without any kind of tent shelter these cold October nights, on these bare exposed heights. And yet, when we sent in to our division or corps commander, for permission to one of our officers to go to Washington to get these things, the permission has been constantly refused; and when we have written or telegraphed for them, or sent special (citizen) messengers to bring them, the answer has been returned that they would only be given up to one of our commissioned officers. So have we been beaten about from pillar to post for weeks and weeks, and our sufferings contemptuously disregarded and our lives needlessly imperiled.

In the smaller matter of our mail conveniences, the same disregard is shown to the soldier's comfort. Irregularity and irritating delay are the rule, order the exception. A full week has now passed away since we have received any mail from Washington (where all our letters are directed) and as to-morrow is the Sabbath with no mail, the ninth day at least must come and that with no more than the hope of relief to us. Yet there is a mail train and a mail agent running over the route every day. Our hospital arrangements are very little better. Little rooms and crowded with the patients; scarcely any pleasant delicacies such as the sick receive at home; physicians who are tired and over-crowded with cases till their manner is harsh and stern, and their pills and potions become doubly bitter to the poor fellows who receive them. And when death comes, as it does oh so frequently, then a brief funeral service, a rough coffin, a shallow grave and a wooden headboard are for the worn-out soldier of the Union, laid down to his last rest, a true hero perhaps who has come forth with the exalted motives of a Hampden or a Washington to lay his life a sacrifice on the altar of his country: a true Christian perhaps, in whose behalf the Judge shall say on the great, final day, to many now high in civil or military position, "Inasmuch as ye did it not unto one of the least of these, ye did it not unto me." I speak seriously because I speak from the side of freshly-opened graves, and death makes us sober and thoughtful, but I speak inside the truth when I say that the needless privations and hardships and losses of this war are greater and more numerous than the necessary ones. And now if we must expect a continuance of the same incompetency, waste, heedless cruelty and general mismanagement which have characterized the conduct of this war hitherto, may we not at least bring a strong pressure upon those that guide our affairs, through the voice of an outraged people who have furnished men and treasure enough to have crushed this rebellion a dozen times over, to hurry up the final struggle and let our soldiers die if need be in manful battle with their enemies and not in the continued hardships and exposures of such a life of inaction as ours? If we cannot conquer, in heaven's name let us find out and make peace and go home. And if we can conquer let us do it, before, in a general bankruptcy and wreck of things, victory and defeat become of equal value to us.

"Come, boys, that last sycamore clears the valley. Fall in, Fourteenth. Shoulder—arms! Forward, toward Bolivar Heights. Quick—march!" Yours, &c.,

DUNN BROWNE

3

A WINTER CAMPAIGN

On October 26, 1862, the Army of the Potomac began crossing the Potomac into Virginia as McClellan at last embarked on a new campaign. With his company assigned duty in the rear, Fiske was concerned he would be left behind. However, he cherished the recollection of his night's stay in the Harper's Ferry engine house where in 1859 John Brown had attempted to lead a slave uprising. Old Brown, he thought, had put up a better fight than did Colonel Dixon Miles, who surrendered Harper's Ferry to Stonewall Jackson on the eve of Antietam.

Dunn Browne in John Brown's Headquarters

Maryland Heights, near Harper's Ferry, Va.
[October 28, 1862]

Dear Republican: Who can tell what a day will bring forth? Last Sabbath noon, or a little after, as we had just finished our lunch and were about sitting down, a few of us, to get a lesson in God's Word together, congratulating ourselves that the Lord's day did not find us on picket duty as one week ago, and that the cold, driving, pitiless rain did not fall upon us unsheltered, the sergeant major came rushing in to our quarters with orders for Company I to strike tents, pack up everything and be ready to march in fifteen minutes to Harper's Ferry and report to the provost marshal for orders. Away goes our heavy baggage, in the shape of potatoes, onions, cabbages and various kinds of provisions, to whomsoever would take them; the lighter articles are thrust into haversacks; blankets rolled up; overcoats, equipments, bundles and various light portable goods, such as frying-pans, kettles, tin cups, &c., are suspended about the person; then stakes are pulled up, tents taken down, rolled together and put into a wagon to follow us, and we take up our line of march, amidst a pouring rain that changes the ground under our feet into a slippery pudding, and greatly hastens our locomotion down the steep heights to the Ferry. Sprawling, splashing, soaking and dripping, we draw up in two lines (in a puddle about six inches deep) before the provost marshal's quarters, and send in our commanding officer to report for orders. The provost marshal, who is a regular United States officer, and so much less inclined to military delays and punctilios than the volunteers, does not keep us waiting many minutes, takes pity on our forlorn condition, and sends us round to quarters for the night before ascending the steep Maryland Heights which he tells us are to be our new camping ground. And those same quarters for the night proved to be no other than the old engine house which John Brown and his 17 men defended against the sovereign state of Virginia and the United States government, in the old time when he held Harper's Ferry, and made much more of a fight before yielding it up than did miserable Miles with his cannons and twelve thousand men. A huge fire soon blazes on the brick floor of the chief apartment of this memorable building and sixty men proceed to make themselves as comfortable therein as circumstances will permit. Your correspondent occupying for a seat an inverted flat-bottomed iron kettle is conspicuous as the only sitting member of the circle, and dries his stockings with serene complacency, as not forgetting present duty even while surrounded by strange historical memories. The loop-holes through which Brown fired upon his assailants are all built up, but the breaches he made upon the institution and the ideas of the South have been widening ever since. This little, low, plain building remains about the only one in decent condition in Harper's Ferry, and it may be that the memory of the humble, obscure old man, who was hung for treason, will remain the deepest and most indelible of Harper's Ferry historical associations. I have at least the memory of one pretty comfortable night's rest on the brick floor of the old building, without any disturbance from the old man's ghost.

Dried and refreshed by our night's rest and the rain having ceased, we climbed with comparative ease the precipitous Maryland Heights, and pitched our camp in a little open space amid the forest, with running water on either side, the noble trees sheltering us from the winds, the high mountain rising up for our protection on the east. Here our duty is, with three or four companies from other regiments, to guard, and keep at work some hundreds of deserters and stragglers from the Union armies who have been picked up by the provost guard and assigned to labor here on fortifications for punishment—a sort of state's prison business, while all is again movement and bustle around us, indicating approaching business with the enemy, which your correspondent for one doesn't like. The whole army is again really on the advance, and, late as it is, perhaps great things will yet be accomplished before the fall campaign closes. The roads are choked with wagons, and black with thronging men clad in the livery of war. Trains of artillery, squadrons of horse, ambulance corps and all the constituents and accompaniments of a tremendous army are going forward in majestic movement. And it may be that your correspondent, left behind in this sudden and most unexpected manner, will not be permitted to share in the stirring events before us. But what happens to the individual matters little so the great cause goes forward, the noble people's will be accomplished and the grand blow be struck for our national preservation and unity. So mote it be.

DUNN BROWNE

Fiske reports here the announcement to the army that McClellan had resigned, but in fact he was removed on November 7 after Lincoln finally lost all patience with his dilatory general. "I believe the army is satisfied with the change," Fiske wrote privately, but for many of the veteran troops the change was a wrenching one. Warrenton, where this letter was written, was some thirty-five miles from the Rappahannock, behind which the Confederate army was gathering.

On the March

Near Warrenton, Va.
Nov. 10, 1862

Dear Republican: "General McClellan has resigned and Burnside has taken his place." This may be old news to you, or old long before it gets to you, but it is quite fresh to us, and the sight of the big body of troops drawn up to exchange farewell greetings with their long-time commander, and the booming of the cannon and the shouts of the troops as he passes and the martial music that fills the air, comes with quite a startling effect upon us as we enter camp from our early morning march and rest up and breakfast in this beautiful grove, while our captain goes to report us at headquarters and find out where our regiment lies. For our company has been marching these last four days from Harper's Ferry out into the bowels of the land to join our regiment. Our road has seemed anything but the route of an advancing army. No troops moving forward or backward, no supply trains or ambulances or baggage wagons to obstruct our passage, but the whole way to ourselves, all indicating that the army gets its supplies over some other route.

It has been a beautiful country over which we have passed, and doesn't show very many traces of the desolations of war either. The huge stacks of wheat, the full barns, the cattle, sheep and hogs that everywhere abound do not look much like ruin. And from some experience in the prices demanded for all manner of produce by the inhabitants, as well as the sight of big bundles of Uncle Sam's money in their possession, I have my suspicions that the passage of the army has been of more profit than damage to the people of this part of Virginia at least. Our march hither has been nearly without incident save the common ones of blistered feet, grumbling at the shortness of rations and the length of marches, some little ludicrous occurrences at our bivouacs, &c., and the very uncommon personal incident to myself of spending one night in a civilized manner, actually sleeping on a feather bed (for the first time of sleeping on a bed and taking off my clothes for it since leaving New England) and sitting down to a table at supper and breakfast like "white folks." Blessings on the head of that amiable Quaker (his name is Beans) who extended his hospitality to us-ward, and blessings on the head of the pretty Beans girl who brought us the smoking muffins and honey and coffee and chickens for our meals with her own fair hands.

An incident occurred to us, however, before we left Maryland Heights which was of very great moment indeed to those who were immediately concerned. The baggage and knapsacks of the 14th regiment arrived at the Ferry from Washington on Sunday, just eight weeks from the time we lost sight of them at Fort Ethan Allen, opposite Washington, and after nearly six weeks of lying within sixty miles of them at Harper's Ferry those necessaries actually came by rail; and when we looked thereon we rejoiced, though we could scarcely believe the evidence of our senses as to their presence. The men, having no other transportation, carried them, heavy trunks and all, two miles up the steep Maryland Heights, on their own backs, to our camp, coming in at about 10 a.m. Was it a desecration of the Sabbath? Verily it looked to me, and so I instructed the men that it was a work of necessity and mercy, always provided it was followed by a work of ablution and personal cleanliness. For my own part I made, as I think, a really religious and devout use of the next two hours of that Sabbath in thoroughly putting off my whole old, dirty, outward man, and renovating myself entirely from head to foot, so that I seemed to myself and presume appeared also to my friends a totally new person. Then we all gathered together at a little after noon under the shade of an old oak, with clean clothes and grateful hearts, for divine service. I think the work of the morning aided and not injured the praises and prayers of the afternoon.

And now in a few words I will finish up this baggage topic, and I trust not allude to it again. The day we (one company of the regiment) received ours, the whole regiment moved from Bolivar Heights right through the Ferry, past their baggage, on to the front. The next day wagons put the knapsacks on board and carried them forward to the camp of the regiment for the night, reaching it a few minutes after the regiment had started again in the morning, and emptying them out on the ground to take on other loading. They were finally packed away in an old empty house without any guard and in a few days entirely plundered and destroyed by stragglers. Fitting consummation of the whole transaction! The 14th will have no more trouble and anxiety about its knapsacks. The officers' trunks may remain to be still longer an encumbrance to their owners, as the last I saw of them was in a big heap out in the open air where they had been lying two days and may be now.

The country here is very beautiful; the style of architecture consists of a great many variations on the common basis of the log, such as the log house simple, the log house chinked, the log house chinked and plastered, and even the log house stuccoed and painted in imitation of stone. Then the log house without windows, the log house with holes cut for windows, the log house with framed and glazed windows, and so on.

As for movements, we are expecting any moment orders to march, orders to go into battle, orders for anything else whatever. Things seem to be reaching a crisis of some sort. Whatever it is, having now rejoined his regiment "in the front," your correspondent will be in for it. Yours truly,

DUNN BROWNE

In politics Samuel Fiske was a staunch Republican, and he was greatly alarmed by Democratic gains in the fall elections across the North. Writing to his brother, he asked, "Is it true then that the North is going to divide & finally back down & recognize the accursed Confederacy?" In this letter Fiske was right to assume the Republican's slant on the results was the same as his. The paper editorialized that the recent elections must signal a renewed and vigorous prosecution of the war by the administration: "If it shall fail to do this . . . a disgraceful compromise and a hollow and hated peace will be the result—a peace that will stink in the nostrils of all Christendom."

About the State Elections

Near Fredericksburg, Va.
Nov. 21 [1862]

Dear Republican: So it seems that the newly-resurrected Democratic party is sweeping over the North with one of its old-fashioned victories, and nobody remains faithful but the good old states of Vermont and Massachusetts, that are absolutely immovable, like the everlasting hills. Well, the philosopher who can't account for all existing facts, no matter how stubborn or unexpected, and reconcile them with his theory and principles, isn't fit, for instance, to edit the Republican, or to be a line officer in the army (he might answer for a brigadier-general perhaps, or to edit some of those second-rate papers that they publish in New-York City). I haven't read your explanation of the phenomenon alluded to above; but I doubt not it is the same with mine, which is this: The victory of the Democratic party doesn't mean that the North is opposed to the war, or sympathizes with the rebellion. But it does mean that the nation is disgusted with the mode in which the war has been carried on; with the corruption and mismanagement, the utter shiftlessness and imbecility, of those who have had it in charge; the reckless waste of its resources of men and money, poured out with free devotion unparalleled in the history of the world. It does mean that the country at large is not patient, or rather has at last come to the extremity of its most wonderful patience, under the repeated demands made upon its treasures of life and wealth so coolly by a military administration that has promised, but not performed; that has played with the wrathful thunderbolts of a nation's righteous vengeance, yes, sold them for old iron, to put pence in their own miserable individual pockets. The nation has been in earnest, while these leaders have made trifling boys' play of the momentous men's work before them; and this is the nation's rebuke to them. The people do not blame the government and the generals for carrying on the war, but for not carrying it on. They don't wish the war to cease by compromising with the rebels, but by speedily crushing them. It has the means now in the field for bringing about this result, in spite of all the previous waste; and let any administration use wisely and energetically the means to that end, no matter how many defeats it may have sustained at the polls, it will triumph in the hearts of the people, and be sustained even by its enemies.

But I will go no farther on this point. If this tremendous rain now deluging us does not prevent the advance of our army, we mean to be in Richmond yet speedily. But God is over all. The health and spirits of the army are better, now that we are in motion; and we hope for a big series of crushing victories to finish our fall campaign.

DUNN BROWNE

Taking over from McClellan, Ambrose Burnside marched the Army of the Potomac swiftly to the Rappahannock opposite Fred-

ericksburg, reaching there before Lee had all his forces assembled to contest the Federal advance. Then Burnside waited, day after day, for his pontoon trains to arrive so that he might bridge the river. The brigade containing the 14th Connecticut, dispatched to guard the army's supply depot at Belle Plain on the Potomac, was commanded by Colonel Oliver H. Palmer.

Travel and Travail

Belle Plain, near Aquia Creek
Nov. 23, 1862

Dear Republican: Writing my last to you, I was in the midst of some wise (or otherwise) political observations, and was brought up rather suddenly by the order, circulated through our camp, to strike tents at once, pack knapsacks, and be ready to march at a moment's notice. The little ink-horn is screwed up straightway; your letter sealed, and dropped into the regimental mailbag, for which the boy on horseback happened to be that moment waiting; and, in about fifteen minutes' time, our whole brigade was in line, with weapons, clothing, provisions, houses, and all a soldier's *impedimenta* upon our backs, and the leading columns beginning to file off upon their line of march. We supposed we might be going over the river into Fredericksburg, as we know our batteries through the day had been shelling those of the enemy that defended the crossing; and we somewhat expected a fight too, not knowing how we might be received on the other side: but when we reached Falmouth, the little village opposite the city, Gen. French, our division commander, halted and addressed us, saying that our brigade had been detached from his command, much to his own regret, and were about to march right away from the enemy, back to Belle Plain, near Aquia Creek, to protect the landing of stores for the grand army on its march towards Richmond. So, with some complimentary words, he bade us adieu; and we took up our march for Belle Plain, or supposed we were doing so.

It was already dark; and we marched on slowly till towards nine o'clock, and pitched our camp for the night. We started betimes the next morning, for it looked like rain, and marched on, and up this hill and down that one, and wondered if we were almost there (for it is only a march of seven or eight miles); and the rain did come, and the mud gathered, and the roads became by-roads and cross-roads, and finally went out altogether; and our brigade, with its long train of wagons, came to a dead halt, and countermarched, and tried new courses, and tangled itself up so completely that at two p.m. we were probably nearer Fredericksburg than when we encamped the night before. But after inquiring the way at various log-houses, and crossing and recrossing a stream two or three times to the wetting of our feet, we got into the true road along towards night; and by *boosting* the wagons by men's shoulders up all the hills (on account of the tired horses refusing to draw them) we managed at last, an hour after dark, to drag through to our destination, and laid our tired bodies down on the muddy ground, putting up some tents, and getting what shelter we could. We found one or two other regiments, that had started the morning after we did from the same place, arrived two hours before us, and with their fires built, and tents well put up, quite snugly prepared for the night. Some evil-disposed, fault-finding persons attributed our long and toilsome march to bad guidance and mismanagement; but I account for it entirely on the ground of the reluctance of our brigade to march away from the enemy. You see, it took twenty-four hours and upwards to get us less than ten miles on the back track. Wouldn't we be a first-rate brigade to cover a retreat?

That same was the worst night we have yet been called to experience. The men have only "shelter tents," so called; that is, two little pieces of sheeting about six feet square, to button together and pin to the ground over a horizontal stick about two feet high, to protect them from the weather; and the mud and water, even in the larger officers' tents, varied from an inch to three or four inches deep. There was little sleeping in our camp, and a great deal of coughing, sad to hear; and, I am sorry to add, a still greater amount of cursing. And two days more have not been much better as to weather—a drizzling rain persisted in its disagreeable attentions. Our colonel sends off his teams to bring us wood (and I fear, from the character of some of it, that the country for some miles around will need to be newly fenced), and we make ourselves as comfortable as may be; and men can get used to almost anything. We don't take cold now at what would have nearly killed us six months ago. The weather is clearing up to-day, and, I trust, may be such for a month to come as to favor the great march to Richmond. Let us hope that the gallant Burnside may make a successful accomplishment of the oft-defeated undertaking. We greatly fear that our detention here may keep us from sharing the hardships and perils and glories of the remainder of the campaign. But the Aquia Creek and Fredericksburg Railroad will, in a few days, be open, we hear, and our depot here, in consequence, be broken up. So we may yet be in time.

Having obtained a turkey to-day, we are going to make sure of a Thanksgiving dinner any way, if it does come a few days too soon.

Here's wishing you personally, dear Republican, a happy Thanksgiving, and the same to all the dear ones at home; and to our country a joyful thanksgiving over successes gained, and a wicked rebellion broken.

DUNN BROWNE

Thanksgiving Day, long a tradition in New England, would be proclaimed a national holiday in 1863 by President Lincoln. The Scriptural phrase parson Fiske adapts here is from I Peter 5:8: ". . . the devil, as a roaring lion, walketh about, seeking whom he may devour."

Dunn Browne's Thanksgiving in Camp

Camp at Belle Plain, Va.
November 29 [1862]

Dear Republican: I wished you a happy Thanksgiving in my last epistle, and doubt not you wished us here the same with equal heartiness. I am going to tell you how happy a Thanksgiving we did have in that part of old Connecticut comprised within the limits of the camp of the 14th. We held with great reason that Gov. [William] Buckingham's proclamation extended so far into Virginia at least as this, and rejoiced in thinking, with the good governor, that we have still some things to be thankful for, and in attempting to observe his recommendation to the best of our ability under existing circumstances. The line officers, in general assembly convened on Wednesday eve, resolved with great enthusiasm, to add tent to tent to obtain a sufficiently spacious dining room, to purchase three pounds of candles (regardless of expense) to light it up, to borrow a score or two of cracker boxes of the commissary department to pile up for tables, and inviting in the field and staff, to close up the exercises of the day with a dinner and social entertainment on a scale of magnificence not to be surpassed (it being stipulated in a postscript to each invitation, that every guest should bring his own knife, fork, cup, spoon and plate with him). A committee of four captains was appointed to procure the needful supplies of fish, flesh and fowl. And as there has been nothing in the shape of money in the old 14th for some weeks, save a few specimens of secesh shinplasters, they were instructed to "run their face" at the commissary's for a large amount of coffee, salt, soap, &c. to barter away with the inhabitants of the surrounding country, on the same principle upon which trade is carried on with other barbarous tribes. Armed and equipped in this engaging style and attended by a guard of faithful men to see that they came to no detriment, our valorous commanders were to sally forth at early dawn, take shipping and proceed to the other side of Potomac Creek (on which our camp lies) on a voyage of discovery, or to apply, in slightly varied circumstances, the Scripture phrase, to "go up and down, seeking what *we* might devour."

Having thus satisfactorily arranged this indispensable matter, we proceeded, arising betimes the next morning, to carry out the other needful preparations. Evergreens were brought to adorn the tents withal; a beautiful arch was erected in front of the colonel's tent with the flags crossed in the back-ground; the tents were put together according to the program for our dining hall; the tables were arranged and adorned; crackers had holes whittled in them for candlesticks, and other ingenious devices were resorted to supply every possible requirement of the occasion. The music was selected and rehearsed; our fine regimental band furbished up their instruments and prepared to discourse to us in sweetest harmonies, the old big drum bottling up his heaviest thunders, the bugles lubricating their silver throats in readiness to pour forth their wild, enchanting strains, and the solemn trombones lengthening if possible their tremendous gullets, and straining wider open if possible their gaping mouths. The speakers (for who ever heard of an American celebration or assembly or occasion of any kind without an abundance of speech-making?) turned over in their minds what they should say; and so went on harmoniously and busily and pleasantly the whole array of varied preparations, physical, mental and spiritual. Our thoughts reverted to the far off home scenes; our wishes, desires, affections, prayers were hovering over the New England fire-sides left behind. The only interest we could get up in our rude preparations arose from their association with the keeping of the day at home. Deceiving ourselves as pleasantly as might be then in our mock preparations, the forenoon passed away; one, two, three o'clock came and we looked anxiously for the return of our supply committee, who had promised to be back by 10 or 11 a.m. at the latest. The hour for the public exercises arrived and they were postponed, for we wished their participation. One or two of the expected speakers indeed were of their number. As the day waned we began to fear lest they had been captured by some prowling band of rebels, lest seeking a mouthful for us they had become themselves a mouthful for a squad of Stuart's cavalry.

Finally the services could be no longer postponed, and as the brightness of the beautiful day began to decline, the companies filed in under the conduct of their orderlies to the open space in front of our colonel's tent, and our public exercises of prayer and praise and patriotism took place. We thanked the Lord, I trust, with some true devotion and sincerity, for the privilege we have enjoyed of laying our individual sacrifices upon the alter of our country, of passing through privations, hardships and perils in her defense. We praised Him for his goodness to ourselves and our families. We prayed Him to bless and keep us and ours through the weeks to come, and to carry our cause triumphantly through this present crisis of our destiny. We encouraged each other's hearts in the speeches of our surgeon, our chaplain and others. We had a right good and pleasant hour of it with our sweet music and friendly talk and thoughts of home and friends, our [Lieut.] Col. [Sanford H.] Perkins presiding, and then separated, to get what sort of a Thanksgiving dinner we might, mostly alas, for soldiers and officers, of the inevitable "hard tack and salt junk," washed down with the bean coffee. Our officers' banquet was a garlanded hall and empty tables. We of course voted to extend Thanksgiving over until Friday night and sought information of our estrayed officers. Received tidings just at night of their being aground in a big barge on the other side of the inlet. Couldn't send them any help that night, and so went to bed rejoicing that they were not captured and resolved to have a good laugh at and with the poor fellows whenever they did come, over their Thanksgiving spent in cold and wet, making frantic efforts to push a heavy old barge off a sand bar.

And a good laugh we did have, and not bad dinner into the bargain, by waiting a day for it. Our committee brought us in a fair supply of poultry and four good-sized quarters of beef, enough for ourselves and to present a soup to a good part of the regiment. And such roasting, boiling, stuffing, baking and stewing under difficult circumstances, with few condiments, spices and sauces to do *with*, and scarcely any pans and dishes to do *in*, perhaps you may have seen in your varied experience, Republican, but I never did before. However, Yankee ingenuity and a sutler's big tin oven, that we took almost forcible possession of, carried us triumphantly through. Our banquet was a success. Turkeys, chickens, partridges and roast beef disappeared like ghosts at break of day, even though we had no bread save hard crackers and no spices of any kind (not even pepper, save Cayenne), nor sauces and ketchups for a relish. The songs and speeches needed no spices to make them relish. No small amount of fun was produced by the recital of the sufferings, adventures, achievements and perils of the committee in their sea and land excursion. Stories were told, our regimental affairs talked over, war prospects discussed, home friends remembered, wives and sweethearts toasted, &c., &c., till Friday had changed to Saturday, when we separated very well satisfied with our two days' Thanksgiving celebration, and relieved in conscience as to any failure of compliance with the recommendation of our worthy governor.

And now, having given you this long narrative, you will not expect me to enter upon any other topic. We are all wondering here, as you are there doubtless, what can be the meaning of this sudden and long stoppage of the great movement upon the enemy at this critical last moment, as it were, of the year too. A

whole fall campaign with a million of men wasted, as it looks
now. If I ever go to another war without going as commander-in-
chief with unlimited powers, then my name is not

DUNN BROWNE

*The sector of the Fredericksburg battleground that Fiske describes
below was the assault of Sumner's Right Grand Division against
Marye's Heights back of the town. Suffering from typhoid and dysentery, Fiske could reach only as far as the head of one of the
pontoon bridges across the Rappahannock on the day of the battle. "The fight was a most foolish, desperate, valiant & useless
affair," he summed up for his brother, and his rationale, recorded
here, that even a horror like this was all part of God's plan seems
strained. His brigade lost 291 men at Fredericksburg, 120 of them
from the 14th Connecticut. The rumor that Richmond and Fort
Darling defending it were taken was, again, nothing but a rumor.*

Dunn Browne on the Battle Field

Fredericksburg
December 15 [1862]

Oh, Republican! My heart is sick and sad. Blood and wounds
and death are before my eyes; of those who are my friends, comrades, brothers; of those who have marched into the very mouth
of destruction as coolly and cheerfully as to any ordinary duty.
Another tremendous, terrible, murderous butchery of brave men
has made Saturday, the 13th of December, a memorable day in
the annals of this war.

On Friday, Fredericksburg was taken with comparatively little
trouble and loss. On Saturday, the grand army corps of Sumner
marched up against the heights back of the city, where the
enemy lay behind strong fortifications, all bristling with cannon
and protected by rifle pits; while our men must cross a wide
space of clear, open ground, and then a canal whose every crossing was swept by artillery so perfectly trained beforehand that
every discharge mowed down whole ranks of men. Into this grand

semi-circle of death our divisions marched with rapid and unflinching step. French's division (to which we belong) behaved
splendidly, and the others no less so if we may judge by the
losses. Of whole companies and regiments not a man flinched.
The grape and canister tore through their ranks, the fearful vol-
leys of musketry from invisible foes decimated their numbers
every few moments; the conflict was hopeless; they could inflict
scarcely any damage upon the foe; our artillery couldn't cover
them, for they would do more damage to friend than to enemy;
yet our gallant fellows pressed on, determined to scale those
breastworks and take the position of the rebels. But there were
none left to do that work. A little handful of a great division
approached, and even in a few instances began to climb the
works, but only to leave their mangled bodies on the bloody field;
a few torn and blackened remnants of the fine regiments sternly
retired to the city. The wounded were mainly brought off, though
hundreds were killed in the benevolent task. The city is filled
with the pieces of brave men who went whole into the conflict.
Every basement and floor is covered with pools of blood. Limbs
in many houses lie in heaps, and surgeons are exhausted with
their trying labors.

But I will not sicken you with a recital of the horrors before
us. Why our noble fellows were pushed on into such a hopeless
and desperate undertaking I am not military man enough to say.
Or why the grand division of Hooker were marching and countermarching all through the day on the other side of the river, and
didn't cross over till just at night to help in the bloody business,
if it must be undertaken, I do not know either. Indeed I don't
know anything hardly save that I am sick at such a destruction of
noble human lives, necessary or unnecessary, useful or useless.

Personally, dear Republican, I was not much in the fight except to be under the shell fire a considerable part of the day in
my anxiety to reach my regiment, and failing that to get as near
as possible, as a spectator of the terrible scene. Sick for two
weeks of a fever and diarrhoea, I heard the heavy firing of Thursday from a hospital ten miles distant, got permission from the
surgeon in charge to mount a U.S. wagon laden with medical
stores and start for the regiment. But the fearful roads of corduroy under a foot or two of mud, and the feeble state of the teams
living for weeks on half forage, hindered us, and prevented your

correspondent from reaching his post till the day after the battle. And doubtless the sight of the poor remnants of his regiment—one hundred men only reported for duty—and of his brigade, not enough to make half a regiment—and then not having been in the scene where the change was effected, have come over his feelings more powerfully than would otherwise have been the case, and given a sad tinge to what he ever wishes to write cheerfully. For God is over all, and even this thing is right, and shall come out in a result of good, sometime. God grant we may see it!

December 17: Night before last, quietly and without disturbance from the enemy, we evacuated Fredericksburg, and marched back to our respective old camps on this side the Rappahannock. In the darkness and through the deep mud the tired soldiers plodded wearily on their way, and then on their arrival were obliged to lie down on the ground and make the best of a rainy winter's night, before they could proceed to arrange themselves any comfortable quarters. Let us hope that the shattered divisions that bore the brunt of the fatal fight behind Fredericksburg may be left to a little rest before meeting any more of the horrors of a winter's campaign in this terrible country. Oh for a month of that beautiful weather that we wasted in the autumn. We hear rumors of the capture of Fort Darling and of Richmond, but do not credit it. If it only could be so, and that our desperate attack at Fredericksburg could have the excuse of being a part of the preconcerted plan to occupy the attention of the enemy and keep his forces here, it would much relieve many sore and discouraged hearts.

We brought off all our wounded from the city, and have left little that is valuable on the other side, save our unburied heroes on the field of battle. The pontoon bridges too are saved and ready to throw across again, and our heavy artillery command the passage of the river at any time, I suppose.

DUNN BROWNE

Union prospects were on a downward slide when Fiske composed this letter, which appears to be aimed primarily at bracing morale on the home front. As he notes, a catalog of disaster filled the newspapers—defeat at Fredericksburg, failure at Vicksburg, renewed fighting in Missouri, in Texas Galveston retaken, sinkings by the cruiser Alabama, *the* Monitor *lost in a storm. His remarks on ungentlemanly war stemmed from Jefferson Davis's message to the Confederate Congress condemning actions against Southern civilians by Federal generals Benjamin Butler and Robert Milroy. Lieutenant Fiske's critique of the tactics at Fredericksburg, where he was an onlooker, probably would not have been accepted by survivors of the assaults on Marye's Heights. The "absurd rumors" he mentions in regard to Colonel Clark of the 21st Massachusetts perhaps refers to that officer's decision to pull back his regiment at Fredericksburg when it exhausted its ammunition.*

The Spirit of the Nation

Camp near Falmouth, Virginia
January 17 [1863]

Dear Republican: You and the other papers keep in the standing advertisement that "All is quiet along the Rappahannock," and we intend you to keep it in "till forbid." But for all that we are going to do something pretty soon. We have hushed up some little quarrels among our generals and cabinet ministers at Washington, formed our plans again, let the enemy know what they are (though for military reasons we haven't promulgated them North yet), and just as soon as they have finished the preparations to meet us, we are going to pitch in. If, however, Davis and his compeers are really going to execute the threats of his recent proclamation, as touching the hanging of Butler and Union officers, &c., and carry on the war henceforth in the ungentlemanly and discourteous style there shadowed forth, we shall be forced, much against our inclinations, to change our tactics also. We positively won't let Lee know a single thing we are going to do, no, not one week beforehand. We will attack him in some unexpected way; we won't put a single supply train in his way to cut off; nor furnish him with any more of our big guns and ammunition. We will go into him, in short, utterly regardless of his feelings, and when we have whipped him once, we won't stop as we did at Antietam for him to get up and brush the dirt off his clothes, and get ready for another round, but we'll hit him when he is down and go in and finish him.

This is a time, Republican, that is trying the spirit of the nation; a time of disappointment, discouragement and reverses on all hands. Checked here, at the great center of operations; checked in our grand sweep down the Mississippi; taken again in the rear in Missouri; surprised in Texas; our navy insulted by one bold piratical craft that defies our 500 vessels; our little Monitor lost, and none of our other iron-clads accomplishing anything— our prospects have never looked so gloomy since the war began. The country is indignant, grieved, disappointed at the waste of its resources, and the general mismanagement of the contest, and is almost desperate as to the prospect of ever getting its armies properly cared for in the camp or used in the field. And now, in such circumstances, the question is, shall we lie down in despair and give up the cause for which we took up arms, or shall our spirit rise with the danger, and meet the discouragement and conquer all the obstacles that we have met? How can there be but one answer to this question in the hearts of a nation that has called itself the foremost nation on the globe? How dare we think of but one answer, after all our boastings and proclamations at the beginning of the contest? We are discouraged, wearied, indignant, disgusted; we have found war no boys' play, no easy game of glory and rewards, but a serious, terrible, heart-breaking, soul-sickening reality; but we are not yet fallen so low as to prefer a dishonorable peace. God forbid I should believe that the people, whom I left so confident and assured of triumph, should be so reduced in spirit in five short months! God forbid you should believe that the army, which then came forth in such proud and gallant array, can be broken down to such a craven preference! We grumble, indeed, dear Republican, as soldiers will, and as these soldiers have good reason to grumble. I have done my share of it (I am ashamed to think a little more than my share), but I grumble henceforth no more. And all we grumbling soldiers, now we find that the people of the North are usurping our (supposedly exclusive) privilege, or rather following our bad example, are going to shut our mouths and relieve ourselves in hard blows at the enemy, instead of hard words at our friends. I believe this is coming to be the spirit of our army, what are left of us. Our leaders may make blunders, and put us in wrong and difficult positions, but an array of brave and determined men can change even a blunder into a glorious stroke of policy, and make a mistake into a victory.

I am obliged to acknowledge to you, oh Republican, that notwithstanding our brave bulletins and our dreadful losses, there has been after all, even in our grandest battles, but little real fighting. It takes an army of recruits a good while to learn that it is less dangerous to push right on to an enemy's battery than to get up within range, and lie down, and be shot all to pieces by it. Charge right home on the works of your foe, you won't lose half so many men as in lying the same time within range; and when you have reached him, face to face and hand to hand, the attacking party has all the advantage. The defenses you feared and in which he trusted are overcome—a hundred to one, he runs, and you with a cheer tear down the rebel rag and run up the glorious stars and stripes! Let us hope we have learned this most important truth. Why, even at Fredericksburg, under all the disadvantages of our attack, the main cause of our overwhelming loss, as any man with half an eye could see, was that our lines, when they had passed through that long gauntlet of fire and reached almost the very foot of the enemy's works, lay down and began to return the enemy's fire and remained till their forces had almost melted away in the focus of that arc of musketry and cannonading. Their work, difficult and well-neigh impossible as it was, was well-neigh accomplished. A few rods more of rapid advance would have put our flag into the enemy's works, and taken our men out of the thickest of the firing, saved them the cruel necessity of retreating over the same long road of slaughter, and in fact changed Burnside's "fatal blunder" into a glorious victory and a masterly piece of strategy! So endeth your correspondent's first lesson in military criticism.

I have varied my invalid life to-day by a splendid gallop on horseback some four or five miles over to the camp of the 21st Massachusetts, to pay my respects to my old friend and classmate, the gallant and dashing Col. [William S.] Clark—your familiar acquaintance, and, as we hear whispered in military circles, not unlikely to become soon, notwithstanding his comparative youth, a brigadier. His regiment, reduced in a dozen hard battles (four campaigns, as they may be truly called, in a single year—viz: under Burnside in North Carolina, under Pope through Virginia, under McClellan in Maryland, now under Burnside again on the Rappahannock) to scarcely more than a single company, is still in good heart and courage, and bound to sustain the well-earned reputation of the "fighting twenty-first." I throw in here this rather personal incident, because I know you are interested in the welfare of the gallant regiment referred to, and partly to discountenance, so far as my little word may, some absurd rumors, that have been circulated in quarters where my friend is not so well known as he ought to be, derogatory to his character as an officer and a gentleman. You know him too well, however, to need any testimony of the sort.

But I am making up for my long silence by a wearisome prolixity, so that, whereas you may have regretted not hearing from me, you now will still more regret the hearing from yours truly,

DUNN BROWNE

Most veterans of the Army of the Potomac regarded the Mud March (as it came to be known), on January 20–22, 1863, as the nadir of their military experience. Rather than make another headlong rush at the enemy at Fredericksburg, Burnside attempted a flanking movement by means of an upstream crossing of the Rappahannock. The result was as Fiske graphically describes it, and the consequence was the end of the winter campaign and a new general, "Fighting Joe" Hooker, in Burnside's place.

The Mud Campaign

Camp near Falmouth, Va.
Friday, January 23 [1863]

Dear Republican: The army has tried to move and been prevented by reasons over which man has no control. The order came to advance again across the Rappahannock and meet the enemy. Tuesday morning camps were broken up, tents struck, knapsacks packed, and soon long lines of troops were in motion

over hill and dale all around us. The roads for miles were choked
with supply wagons, ammunition trains and rumbling batteries.
All was noise, confusion and utmost activity. Trumpets sounded,
drums beat, whips cracked, mules squealed and teamsters
cursed. In short all things showed that a vast army was on the
move. Excitement took the place of the quiet that has reigned
in our midst for a month. Hearts beat high with hope and patriotic ardor, and spirits sank in dismay at the thought of approaching danger, wounds and death. Some left couches of sickness,
roused to new strength at the call to arms. Some who had been
perfectly well paled into sudden sickness at the same prospect,
and came sneaking round the surgeons' tents, and crawling into
hospitals.

For ourselves, under orders to be ready for instant march, our
regiment waited through the livelong day, with three days'
cooked rations in their haversacks and 60 rounds of ball cartridge disposed about their persons, blankets, shelter tents &c.
rolled up and guns at hand to march in a moment, all constitut-
ing a fair mule's load, and what is in military phrase facetiously
termed "light marching order"; waited all day, watching the
troops that rolled like a river unceasingly by us and wondered
when we should be emptied into the stream; but waited, most
fortunately for us, in vain. For the clouds gathered all day thicker
and darker, and night ushered in a storm of wind and pouring
rain, harder for that moving army to encounter than a hundred
thousand enemies; a driving rain that drenched and chilled the
poor shelterless men and horses, and that poached the ground
into mud deeper than the New England mind can conceive of
and stickier than—well I am at a loss for a similitude. Pitch, for
cohesive attraction, is but as sand compared with it. So the artillery and the wagons stuck fast on Wednesday, the pontoons
couldn't go on wheels, and though the rain continued in floods
there wasn't quite enough to carry them by water, and so the
river rose and couldn't be crossed, and so everything got mixed
up and all our fine arrangements spoiled, and we experienced the
uncertainty that attends human events and especially a winter
campaign in Virginia. And so our noble Burnside goes up to report his disappointment at Washington, and the army comes
dragging back in the deep mud and drizzling rain to its old quarters. All yesterday and to-day the bedraggled and tired regiments

are passing us, and all the roads and streams are full of dead horses and mules (I presume 50 are in sight from the top of the hill back of my tent) and pieces of wagons, and the way obstructed with caissons and pieces of artillery and pontoons and all sorts of vehicles fast in the mud.

We must wait till the earth is dried up a little from the effects of this storm and then try it again, running the same risks. And I suppose poor Burnside must take all the blame of failures now, whereas I am disposed to look back to the man who kept us two months in inactivity after the battle of Antietam, in the most beautiful and precious time of the whole year, to find the shoulders on which to lay the blame. However, finding fault now isn't going to help the past. Something must be done even now, as you and the whole North tell us. Only you must consider what a winter's campaign in these regions really means when you make up your judgment of us and our doings. It means to the soldiers wet feet every day of the march, the cold ground to lie upon, and insufficient food for them to eat. It means coughs, colds, consumption, rheumatism, and fevers; a row of unmarked graves all along the track of the army, and desolation and mourning to thousands of pleasant homes. It means the pain of seeing in every company brave fellows sinking right down to death before your eyes, with no possibility of helping them or even of doing much to soothe their last hours. It means, if battle comes, the wounded left to freeze in the severity of the nights, and to mingle their blood with the deep mud on which they lie. It means every possible form of human suffering, privation and hardship. Make all allowances for us, then, and pray for our strength, endurance and success, and drop a tear over the brave fellows who are sacrificed, not merely to the demon of battle, but to the more dreaded severities of the winter season. But the mail closes, and I must close. Yours truly,

DUNN BROWNE

4

DUNN BROWNE VISITS DIXIE

The following Dunn Browne tirade in the Springfield Republican
*ended a month's silence, and was, again, directed at demoraliza-
tion on the home front. The activities that winter of the peace Democrats—the so-called Copperheads—inspired numerous Union
soldiers to send "addresses" and letters like this one to their
hometown papers. On February 18, in convention in Hartford,
Connecticut Democrats had nominated Thomas H. Seymour for
governor on a platform terming the effort to restore the Union by
force of arms a "monstrous fallacy" and calling for a negotiated
peace—what the* Republican *condemned as "a peace on any
terms." Fiske was reminded of the Hartford Convention that had
opposed the War of 1812. His mention of "our western Egypt"
referred to an area of southern Illinois, known as "Egypt," where
Confederate sentiment was strong. In the spring election the administration party would be victorious in Connecticut, with Seymour soundly defeated for the governorship.*

On the Connecticut Copperheads

Camp near Falmouth, Va.
February 25 [1863]

Oh Republican! Give me a Hartford Times or some other appropriate receptacle, for I am about to vomit. I am sick, nause-
ated, poisoned; have taken something that, most emphatically,
doesn't agree with me; have swallowed the vile and traitorous
resolutions of the recent Democratic convention at Hartford,
and have read in connection some of the speeches on the same
occasion, filled with ribaldry and profanity just about in keeping
with the whole spirit of the meeting. And I am ashamed and
confounded, disgusted and grieved, to see what proportions trea-

son has attained even in dear old New England. I knew that such
things were talked in the darker sections of our western Egypt. I
wouldn't have been surprised to read of proceedings a little like
those at Hartford as having taken place in some very ignorant
district in southern Indiana. But in Connecticut, faugh! I can't
begin to express my feelings, and yet I am obliged to confess that
I am one of her citizens. If the dear old state doesn't spew out of
her mouth this ill-savoring Tom Seymour Democracy at the coming April election, we of the army will march North instead of
South to get at the heart of the rebellion.

Talk about demoralization of the army! Well, we have fallen
pretty low. We haven't the same strain of lofty patriotism in our
talk as when we first came out. We have been knocked round and
starved and frozen till we have some of us forgotten the distinction between a good government and its sometimes corrupt
agents, and in our personal indignation we lost sight, for the
moment, of our correct principles. We have said many things
that were not complimentary to our lawful civil and military leaders; yes, we have said many things that we shall be ashamed of,
if we ever get home; but I do still fully believe and hope that if
any man should talk such foul stuff as that of this modern Hartford convention in any of our camps, we should have principle
and decency enough left to roll him in one of our Virginia gutters
and drum him out of camp. Thank God we are not so demoralized yet as to suffer downright, earnest treason to be talked in
our presence.

But enough of such a disgusting subject. Let us roll some
more pleasantly flavored morsel under our tongue to get that
taste out of our mouth. Spring is coming, our time of hope, of
fresh life and vigor, our time of accustomed triumph. The winter
is almost over. Let us hope that the "winter of our discontent,"
of our discouragement, reverses and distress, shall pass away
with it, and that when the mud dries up, and the grass grows
green, we may also "dry up" our murmuring, and our laurels
grow green. I look for a great series of spring victories like those
of last year—of grand, crushing, final victories—victories that
shall shut off all question of foreign intervention, make such a
performance as this Hartford convention a thing for even Connecticut Seymour Democrats to be ashamed of, and take away
every shadow of hope from their fellow traitors at the South. I

say I am *looking* for such victories. I shall continue to *look* for them very attentively and anxiously. Oh how happy we shall all be if we only find them. Yours, as ever,

DUNN BROWNE

The Army of the Potomac had settled into winter quarters after Fredericksburg, and returned to them after the Mud March, and there waited out the particularly harsh weather of that season. Fiske's thoughts in this period were again directed at the home front, as demonstrated in this tale—a more or less secular sermon, in parable form. His reference to Confederate cavalry raiders "seeking what sleeping brigadiers they may devour" is a tart comment on the capture, on March 9, in his bed at Fairfax Court House, of Brigadier General Edwin H. Stoughton. Although Fiske datelines his letter from camp at Falmouth, to give authenticity to his reporting from the army, he was in fact home on furlough on March 13, as revealed in the letter following this one.

Mules and Mud in Virginia

Camp near Falmouth, Va.
March 13, 1863

Dear Republican: Speaking of mules, did I tell you a little anecdote illustrative of the suicidal spirit that sometimes takes possession of these dulcet-voiced animals who lull me to rest by their nightly melodies here on the sweet plains of old Virginia? The other morning as I was taking the air a little before breakfast (in other words, lugging a big log of firewood a couple of miles through the mud to camp on my shoulder), stopping a few moments to admire the beautiful scenery before me (as well as to rest my back a bit), I noticed quite a commotion in the water of a little stream that flows through the valley below where I was standing. Three men were up to their middle in the brook, pulling and lifting at some large object which I took to be a stump or log of wood which they were trying to rescue from the flood for the fire. But soon up drove another man with a span of mules and a long log-chain attached, which he quickly passed in to his comrades and they dexterously fastened round a projecting part of the object in their hands. Crack goes the whip, and out comes (with a strong pull) not the log I had expected to see, but the dead body of a mule. Well, thought I to myself, it is a little queer here in the army to see so much pains taken to keep the soldiers on the stream below us from having mule and water to drink, but let us be thankful for one instance of comparative civilization and decency. But lo, the fellows, having waited a moment for the water to drip from their pantaloons, began to belabor the carcass with clubs and whips and kicks, and after some minutes of this process, as if brought to life by the cruel abuse, up springs the deceased mule and trots off to his tying post as lively as ever. In investigating the matter, I learned that that mule, becoming disgusted with life in Virginia, or else being at heart a secesh mule, and wishing to deprive Uncle Sam of his valuable services, had deliberately availed himself of the pretext of going to water to lie down and attempt suicide by strangulation; and if the teamsters hadn't plunged in and held up his head and actually hauled the creature out of the water, by the chain round his neck, the deed would have been accomplished. If anybody is disposed to doubt the above story, tell them your correspondent was there and saw the whole thing with his own eyes. Still, as he wouldn't have believed it without seeing it, he will give everybody else the same privilege, always provided they don't impugn his veracity in any degree.

Could we make an improvement of the subject by likening the southern confederacy in any measure to that mule seeking self-destruction, and conclude that our only way is actually to hitch on and "snake" the creature out by a rope round its neck? Isn't the trouble with our Union team something like this, that one hitches on to this leg, and another to that one, and another to the slippery tail or ear, and thus act ineffectually or against each other, instead of tackling right round the neck of the beast with one long pull, strong pull, and pull altogether? Certainly if mules and southern confederacy were none of them in existence we should all sleep better nights these times. For the cold "spell of weather" brings us an unusual amount of music from the complaining animals shivering in the midnight winds, and the raids of the rebels make us frequent and untimely alarms. Some say that three brigades of cavalry are prowling around this side of the river, roaming up and down like raging lions, seeking what sleeping brigadiers they may devour. Others that 15,000 infantry have crossed over a few miles above us and are watching for an exposed flank on which to attack us.

But in either case it strikes me that our foes are mighty invisible. If we should cross over to their side, somebody would probably see us in the course of a few days and be inquiring what we were after. The weather is pretty good if it wasn't so bitter cold, and the mud begins to dry up, so that the "tops of the mountains appear" occasionally and we can have faith to believe that there is firm ground somewhere underneath even our most desperate mire holes. Robins and blue-birds are about; spring is coming, and with it movement, life, energy, success let us hope, to our armies. Yours truly,

DUNN BROWNE

Joe Hooker swept the Army of the Potomac with a wave of martial reforms, not the least of which was a new policy for furloughs. "Never enjoyed ten days so much in my life," the furloughed Fiske assured his brother. Among his pleasures was his first look at his six-month-old son. At a stopover at his church in Madison, Connecticut, he was greeted by his congregation with "handshakings somewhat after the manner of McClellan & other popular idols." Here he blesses the women of New England—the women of the North—he believed were standing solidly in support of their men at the front.

Dunn Browne on Furlough, and Sees Women

Camp near Falmouth, Va.
March 17 [1863]

Dear Republican: Your correspondent feels refreshed. He has taken something that agrees with him. A delightful trip back to home and friends—an invigorating breath of New England air— ten days of relief from the monotony of camp life—not ten short days of respite whose pleasure was clouded by the thought of a speedy return to stern warfare—but ten long and most happy days, full of enjoyment, full of greetings and hearty welcomes, of the blessings of aged parents and brothers and sisters, of tender wifely love and the sweet caresses of children—days whose remembrance will lighten up this whole coming spring campaign with all its weary marches and night watches and scenes of blood, yea even soften the bitterness of wounds and of death if one be called thereto.

Only once in the seven months up to this return to civilized life had I undressed and slept in a bed. I had some doubts as to how I should bear the trial now—some expectation that I might have to take a sheet and pin it down over some crotched sticks in the door-yard for a tent, in order to get a comfortable rest. But no, I find I can yet easily submit to the effeminacy of houses and beds and good meals and Christian habits of life. I was quite struck, during my short sojourn in your country, Republican, with the size of the rooms, the height and grandeur of your houses, the convenience of tables to eat from as compared with low boxes which you can't put your legs under, and chairs with backs to sit upon as compared with camp stools or the damp ground. There are very many things indeed in your mode of life which an impartial observer must acknowledge to be more agreeable than some of our soldierly ways. But to leave the minor differences unspoken of—the grand advantage you have over us is—women.

Having scarcely a glimpse of a petticoat for a series of months, and when seen, nearly always with a black face and thick lips above it, I confess to the most affectionate and loving emotions toward the sex during my recent vacation, even when merely thrown accidentally into their society in a rail-car. And not the young and pretty ones merely. Indeed, the multitudes of rosy, plump-faced, ringletted young creatures that I saw here and there on the journey seemed, somehow, too much chatterboxes and gigglers and (may I say it?) thoughtless of anything save their own pretty selves, for these serious times of ours. Those that I heard making the most noise and disturbing most the quiet of a car and steamer, were not drunken soldiers (of whom we had occasionally a few on board), but giggling young misses with piles of books under their arms.

No, those that most attracted my interest and attention (except perhaps the little children, whom I always love) were the older faces on which lines of thought appear, where character has had time to express itself—the wives, the matrons, the grandmothers—the quiet, thoughtful, sometimes sad and lonely face, whose eye lighted up with a ray of recognition as it observed a soldier's dress, as though a husband or a brother or a son were in the far away army; the lady in mourning who sat in a corner seat, whose eyes filled with such a tide of emotion at sight of a uniform, that I was on the point of asking her in what battle her husband was killed—the gray-headed old lady, of seventy years perhaps, who sat by my side and asked if I knew her two grandsons in the Army of the Potomac, and talked with such hearty enthusiasm in their praise—the young mother with a three-year-old boy coming down on the boat to Aquia Creek, and on with us in a rough baggage-car, to make happy the hut of her officer husband by a short visit to him in his winter quarters—the many, many noble women whom I heard utter such patriotic sentiments, who seemed so anxious to encourage the hearts of the soldiers, and whose very great sacrifices in the country's cause I am acquainted with—these were the beautiful faces to my eyes— these are the ones who are miniatured on our hearts, when we go into perils and stand night watches and make weary marches. God bless the women of New England—the women of our whole North. I don't believe there are many copperheads among them. I was right glad to go home—all ready to come back. I made you a bow as I passed your door, so to speak, riding up the dear old Connecticut valley. Will try to drop in upon you next time. Yours truly,

DUNN BROWNE

There is every likelihood that Samuel Fiske was the instigator behind the regimental resolutions reproduced here—indeed, that he drafted them. Certainly as Dunn Browne he had railed against the Seymour peace Democrats of Connecticut with arguments like these. The resolutions were apparently inspired by letters from disaffected soldiers that had appeared in what Fiske lists as the state's leading Copperhead newspapers. The Springfield Republi-

can, *printing this at the first opportunity in its April 4 issue, en-
sured the 14th regiment's stand a wide circulation two days
before the Connecticut elections.*

The Connecticut Volunteers vs. the Copperheads

Camp near Falmouth, Va.
March 24 [1863]

Whereas, We have heard the statement made and seen it published, that a majority of the 14th regiment Connecticut volunteers would like to see the election of Thomas H. Seymour as
governor, and would endorse the platform of the recent (so
called) Democratic convention at Hartford: and whereas, we fear
lest some complaints which we, officers and men, have in time
past made, and considered that the treatment we received from
government agents justified us in making, may have been mis-
construed, as evidence that we have changed our views since
coming out, and do not now heartily support the government in
crushing out high-handed rebellion—therefore

Resolved, That the 14th regiment Connecticut volunteers rejoices in the privilege it has enjoyed of doing and of suffering for
the Constitution and government, the laws and the Union, and
counts all the losses it has sustained as so many sacrifices made
in the most noble of earthly causes, the cause of rational liberty
and human rights, not for one nation only but for the race—the
cause of republican government, of democracy against aristoc-
racy, of freedom against slavery.

Resolved, That so far from having repented the sentiments of
patriotism and devotion which animated us in coming into the
field last August, we feel that the blood of our slain brothers, our
best and dearest, cries unto us out of the ground, even the
bloody battle grounds of Antietam and Fredericksburg, to go forward with the more firmness and energy in our righteous cause,
and carry our torn banners deeper into the ranks of our country's
foes.

Resolved, That complaining of nothing but irresolution, mismanagement and lack of energy in putting down the rebellion,
we go in most emphatically for the earnest, thorough and rapid

prosecution of the war, the condign punishment of those in high or low stations through whose corruption or personal rivalries or concealed treason our resources have been wasted and our armies defeated; and the speedy conclusion of the war in the only honorable way which we are as yet able to see to that end, i.e., the submission of our enemies, and the restoration of the authority of the government through the length and breadth of our land.

Resolved, That we utterly despise and abhor as the meanest of all treason, the effort that is being made in many parts of the North to take advantage of the reverses and consequent temporary discouragement of our people, to bring about a dishonorable peace, which would give up in substance the whole issue we have been fighting for, acknowledge ourselves to have been in the wrong from the beginning, and make the blood of our brave and beloved brothers slain in this conflict virtually blood spilled by our own murderous hands; that we hold these home traitors to be worse than the armed traitors we meet in the field, a disgrace to our people, a "fire in the rear" of our patriot army that ought not to be tolerated, and rely on our friends at home, all true and loyal men, all *real* democrats, without distinction of party, to rise in their might and put down these enemies with the ballot, while we try the bullet upon the comparatively more open and honorable enemies to the southward.

The above resolutions were adopted by the 14th regiment of Connecticut volunteers, on dress parade, Tuesday night, March 24th, with almost perfect unanimity, only one officer in the whole field, staff and line, dissenting, and five or six enlisted men; and two or three of these last said they should have voted yes, only they couldn't hear the whole paper very distinctly at the end of the line, and were not going to vote for anything that they did not thoroughly understand. A copy, attested by the commander and the adjutant of the regiment, is to be sent for publication in the Connecticut papers.

Similar and even stronger resolutions have been sent on to Connecticut from other regiments in the field, and whatever lying letters may be published in the Register, or Times, or Sentinel and Witness ("Sentinel and Wickedness," the boys here call it) as to the conversion of the soldiers to Seymourism, and their universal or very general dissatisfaction with the war, you may rely on the army as altogether patriotic and earnest for crushing out the rebellion. Their dissatisfaction has been with the management of the war and not with the war. They now wish it ended, but ended in the only right way. They long to go home, but to go home with honor. They will give a great deal for peace. They will not give their country, their principles, their conscientious convictions of duty for it. They dislike to waste their lives. They are still ready to pour out their blood like water, if it may be made to avail in their country's defense and the overthrow of her enemies.

I say this, firmly believing it to be true, of the main body of our troops. There is an occasional tired and discontented man who would go home at any price—an occasional one who would sacrifice his principles to his bodily ease and safety; and if I had such principles I would sacrifice them, the first chance I could get. In short, there is an occasional Tom Seymour Democrat in the army, but the proportion of them to the whole army is not greater than that of Judas Iscarot to the other disciples. Yours truly,

DUNN BROWNE

Any number of Union soldiers (and, for that matter, Confederate soldiers) wrote home in these months to describe their winter huts along the Rappahannock in ironic or satirical terms, and Samuel Fiske's effort here is one of the best; certainly it is one of the most literate. The W. S. Tyler he mentions had been Fiske's professor at Amherst, and one of his fellow travelers on his prewar tour of the Old World.

Winter Quarters from an Architectural Point of View

Camp near Falmouth, Va.
March 30 [1863]

Dear Republican: I wish you would visit the army of the Rappahannock. You might not learn much about the war, because that hasn't been in our line of business for some months past; but there are a good many things you would learn, I doubt not, that would add to your stock of experience not a little, and be of great use to you in all your future career. For instance, if you didn't confess to getting some new notions on the subject of architecture, I would be willing to pay your expenses out and back myself. Now as doubtless you wish Mrs. Republican and the little Republicans to be housed in the most appropriate and tasteful way, and cheapest withal (the newspaper business can't be very profitable, I take it, with the present high prices of the raw material), really hadn't you better think of it?

Why, I have a house myself I would like to show you, with a brown mud front, water in every part of it (at this present writing) and all the modern (army) improvements, including a real door on hinges, with a latch to it, a chimney that never smokes (unless the wind is very strong from the northeast), fire-place warranted stone-backed, and garnished with actual crane-hooks, our patent army transparent water-proof roofing, and everything about the whole building so convenient that I may say I can put my hand upon it, sitting here by the fire as I am with my feet upon the mantel (not marble, that proves too cold for comfort) in true Yankee style. The parlor, sitting-room, dining-room and library are so arranged as to be easily thrown together into one apartment. The sleeping rooms are well ventilated, and to be brief, the whole forms a snug tenement for a family of suitable size, such as is rarely to be found, and I might add (if you won't charge this as an advertisement) could be rented on easy terms, with a limited amount of furniture, as the owner is thinking of moving to Richmond.

There is a good deal of variety in the style of army architecture. My own building is a severe classic, without ornament, rather low and heavy, inclining to the Doric, or perhaps even to the Egyptian order. But we have specimens of the airiest, most fantastic Gothic, of the tasteful Corinthian capitals, of fluted Ionic columns, of Moorish arches and arabesque ornaments, of the Chinese pagoda roofing, of the "a la catacomb" excavations. One of my neighbor's is nearly on the model, on a somewhat smaller scale, to be sure, of the Athenian Parthenon (yet I presume the idea of imitating the proportions of that ancient structure never entered his mind). Some model after a heathen temple, some after a Yankee woodshed, some after an Indian wig-

wam, and some after a woodchuck's hole. But the Hotentot style
of architecture, on the whole, it must be confessed, prevails over
every other; and for every kind of structure that can rise out of
mother earth, that can be created from Virginia mud with some
ribs and framework of logs, let me commend you to the whole
region round about. I couldn't do full justice to the subject, however, in a dozen letters, so I may as well stop in one place as
another. Why, we oldest inhabitants here are finding every day
something new to wonder at, some still more extraordinary odd-
ity of structure that has risen out of the ground.

If I had paid a more faithful attention, in my early college days,
to my good friend Prof. Tyler's Saturday morning recitations in
that delightful work, the Manual of Classical Literature, I might
have done better justice to the subject I have here attempted.
Supposing at that time that I should always carry about with me
a copy of that scholar's *vade mecum* (little idea had my verdant
mind then of the amount of baggage a U.S. officer would be allowed to carry, or indeed of the career military that was in the
far future before me), I unfortunately neglected to commit it all
to memory. Still, if I had the whole architectural portion thereof
perfectly in mind, I couldn't have described all the orders and
styles of which we have specimens. I am taking notes and making
drawings and elevations, however, to accompany some sugges-
tions I mean to make to the professor, with reference to a new
edition of that immortal work. If he objects to my *materiel* as
being too modern to embody into a work on classical antiquities,
I shall show him that a large part of what I describe already exists
only as ruins, and that the whole certainly has a greater appearance of age than many of the fresh and ever beautiful ruins we
looked on together in Italy, Greece and Egypt.

Ah, what a contrast between those days of wandering amidst
the beauty, glory and decay of the old world, wandering in peace,
for health and pleasure and education—and these marches of
war and scenes of camp! Between "tent life in the Holy Land"
and tent life on Virginia soil in rebel times! And yet there is a
sort of similarity between them too; and I sometime forget all
our warlike accompaniments and paraphernalia, and enjoy the
wild out-of-door freedom of camp life, the strange scenes and
companionships one meets, and the new experiences of men and
of life he passes through. There is a great deal of poetry in war

and in camp, after all—though somewhat smothered in mud here at present. Yours truly,

Dunn Browne

On the date this letter was written, the Army of the Potomac was under marching orders—eight days' rations, sixty rounds of ammunition—but so tight was General Hooker's security that no one, including Samuel Fiske, had any idea where they were headed. A rainstorm canceled the operation, and the spring campaign would commence only on April 27. Fiske was impatient, writing his brother, "Over 130,000 men for duty in our grand army! Doesn't it seem as if something might be accomplished by us?" Since it was never officially acknowledged that the army had taken up winter quarters, Fiske entertains his readers here with allusions to Doubting Thomas and to the "courtship" of Huldah, goddess of marriage.

Farewell to the Rappahannock Camp

Camp near Falmouth, Va.
April 15 [1863]

Dear Republican: We have not been in winter quarters—oh no, not the slightest; but it must be confessed we have made a rather long encampment here on the banks of the Rappahannock. Zekiel didn't "sit up" with Huldah last Sunday night. He only made her a call. To be sure it was half past one when he went away. It was early in December when we bivouacked among these forest-covered hills and ravines. It is late in April now that we are gathering up our traps to leave. The forests have disappeared. The whole country is intersected with roads leading from one city of ten or five thousand inhabitants to another. Every knoll and gully and projecting rock is familiar to our eyes. The winter has passed over us and gone. We have had our houses and dwelt in them, our daily routine of duties and performed them, our pleasures and enjoyed them, our dreams and reveries, our hopes and our sorrows, our letters and our newspapers, our Sabbath services, our hospitals and all their touching scenes; we have had our graveyards and been buried in them. So that, perhaps, after all, it is very much as if we had been in winter quarters. If it isn't Thomas it is his twin brother.

There is nothing very attractive about this locality. It is bare, bleak and desolate, muddy, dusty and in ruins, all the beauty trampled out long ago under the ruthless tread of a great army. And there are no visions of glory to endear it to our memory, no successes gained, no wreaths and laurels to crown it in our recollections; and yet it is somehow a little hard to pull up our stakes and tear down our walls for departure after all. We have something of a home feeling for our poor little mud-built cities. Our streets are not Broadways, but a part of our life has grown round these little log huts and chimneys of plastered sticks. A home is a home if it is in a Hottentot kraal. It is with a sort of shrinking and momentary reluctance that we push out from the little eddy where we have lain so snugly for a time, and commit ourselves again to the raging current of war. But it must be. The stream of events have gotten hold of us and we are whirled along. Nay, rather, we are intending under Providence to constitute a part of the moving power ourselves, to do something towards shaping the course of things for the months to come. May God make this army of the Potomac, or Rappahannock, a sort of lesser providence to shape for good the destiny of this nation in these critical weeks that are now upon us!

I shall not tell you, Dear Republican, where we are going to-morrow or the next day or the day after, because I would not wish your enterprising sheet to set forth prematurely any plans that should give aid and comfort to the enemy, and also because—I don't know. But should we enter Richmond in triumph before the 4th of July, I pledge you my word to give you an early and authentic account of the festivities of the Independence day, and a condensed report of the speeches from the state house steps. As present, I am, at some considerable distance from the rebel capital, yours truly,

DUNN BROWNE

After the mid-April false start of what would come to be known as the Chancellorsville campaign, the Potomac army settled back

into its winter quarters to wait for the rain to stop. Fiske had grown particularly knowledgeable about the running of an army in this spring of 1863 after he was promoted captain and appointed acting assistant inspector general "of a brigade next to us"—Samuel S. Carroll's brigade of French's division of the Second Corps. When he took over the command, Joe Hooker expanded the corps of inspector generals in order to give teeth to the various reforms in army administration that he instituted, and thus Captain Fiske gained a step up the ladder of command. When the campaign opened forty-eight hours after this letter was written, he would be serving in Carroll's brigade rather than with his company in the 14th Connecticut.

On Rain and Camp Life

Camp near Falmouth, Va.
April 25, 1863

My dear Republican: We have been having showers constantly for the last two months, and now it has turned into a settled rain. Of all the wet seasons that ever threatened to drown out and wash away this dirty continent of ours, this is the climax. There is no "oldest inhabitant" in these regions to inquire of, else I would get his testimony to add to my own. But if you don't believe me, come out here and take the testimony that comes down from the skies in a continual dropping from morning till night and from night till morning. I suppose Noah may have experienced harder rain, after he drew in the gang-plank of his "Great Eastern," and with his menagerie "all aboard" quietly awaiting the commencement of his voyage to the new world, but I don't believe he heard it patter so many nights over his head in the old ark-attic as I have now heard it pattering on the canvas roof of my log shanty this spring. If this army could only move in an ark over against the rebels, and on to Richmond, it wouldn't make so much difference; but, we being restricted to legs, it would seem, to our human judgment, desirable that the rainy season might come to an end. At least there is nothing for it now for us but to wait till the shower is over and the puddles dried up.

Meantime, while we are waiting, what are we doing with ourselves? When a great army is doing nothing, how is it employed? Well, it is said, you know, that idlers always have the hardest kind of a life to live. However it may be in other things, certainly soldiers have to be pretty busy even doing nothing. An army lying still is always on the move. Its ordinary functions of respiration and nutrition keep in motion a good many very active agencies. It eats and drinks through the toils of a host of busy commissaries and teamsters, and details of men by night and by day. It doesn't put on its clothes but by the labor of many hands and the thoughts of many brains. To keep its pot a-boiling requires the rumbling of many fuel wagons, and tires the limbs of thousands of braying mules. It doesn't sleep at night, but with its eyes wide open, and every officer and soldier has to take his turn as eye for his regiment or camp about once in three or four days. It keeps its long arms stretched out in all directions, feeling for danger and avoiding surprise, and all in turn must take their share of this active duty; each serving his turn as a finger, so to speak.

As so with guard and picket, inspections, parades and reviews, with all the little and great necessary and unnecessary matters of camp life, rubbing up guns and distributing rations, writing letters and attending courts martial, bringing wood and water and plastering houses, reading newspapers and pitching quoits, we manage to fill up pretty easily all the waking hours of the twenty-four. A little time to read or study, a little time to chat, a little time to meditate, a little time to devote to the dear ones at home, and (it must be confessed) a good deal of time to sleeping and eating and lounging, and our day gets by from "reveille" to "tattoo," and through the night watches to morning roll-call again; a dull, monotonous, stupid, indifferent, make-shift of a life, soon to be broken in upon by the excitement of a great and eventful campaign.

If I write you nothing, Dear Republican, it is because I have nothing to write you.

DUNN BROWNE

Here is Captain Samuel Fiske as on-the-spot war correspondent on Day Six of the Chancellorsville campaign—the day of Stone-

wall Jackson's celebrated flank attack on the Army of the Poto-
mac. Carroll's brigade of the Second Corps, to which Fiske was
attached, saw no action on May 2, and Fiske carefully prefaces
reports of what he did not witness with "they say." Indeed, rumor
sped along the Union lines that day, such as the supposed repulse
of a morning assault by Jackson or the false claim that Confeder-
ate communications had been cut by Federal cavalry. But Fiske's
eight p.m. bulletin was entirely accurate when he recorded the
devastating impact of Jackson's rout of the Eleventh Corps on the
Federal flank.

A Day at Chancellorsville

Chancellorsville battle-field
May 2, 1863

Dear Republican: This has been a most beautiful night; bright moonlight. We slept very little, lying upon our arms all night; our brigade in line of battle, and expecting to go into action at any moment, from about noon to midnight. We were not called in, however. The action yesterday was very severe, but indecisive: we were advancing quite rapidly in the morning, and, I suspect, without much thought of the enemy's making a stand, when they opened on us; and some of our troops thrown out as skirmishers did not behave very well. They drove back one or two of our divisions for a time, and, at one o'clock, things looked uncomfortable; but fresh troops went up on the double-quick, and we drove them back with heavy loss on both sides. We don't know much how things lie this morning, but hope that we shall gain a great victory to-day. We rose at three o'clock, fed and saddled our horses, had some coffee and hard-bread, and have been waiting for orders to march ever since. It is now about seven o'clock. The night was so cold, I could not sleep. The day was very hot, the night very cold. We lay on some fence pickets laid on the ground. The eastern sky at sunrise was red like blood. The sun is just at this moment breaking out; but, on the whole, the prospect is for rain before night. Moreover, yesterday was quite fine; and such a thing as two fine days in succession would be indeed an absurd thing to expect in this region.

"They say" that we have a line of battle in half-moon shape, convex towards the enemy, and a splendid position; and that the bridges in the rear of the enemy are destroyed, so that they can't retreat without immense loss, and so must now fight decisively. Our army is in grand spirits. Gen. Hooker is riding along the lines, and the men are cheering him madly.

Gen. Stonewall Jackson charged down upon our front this morning (they say) in deep, heavy columns along the plank-road: our batteries opened on him, big and little guns, and plowed him through and through, so that his troops retreated a mile and a half in double-quick time.

Eleven a.m.—Nothing done yet in the way of fighting since seven o'clock. The day is pleasant: we have marched out a mile to a new position in the line of battle, thrown out skirmishers, and are now digging a sort of rifle-pit to protect a weak spot in our line.

Three p.m.—Still nothing done! The cannon are roaring around us, but not much musketry save skirmishing. We are in an open field of perhaps a hundred acres, lying with stacked arms, waiting an attempt of the enemy to flank us on the left. It would seem, however, that he has abandoned the attempt, or some change of strategy is adopted, for we lie perfectly idle. Our long line of rifle-pits, three feet wide and two and a half deep, is completed the whole length of one side of the field, the dirt thrown up so as to make a four or five foot barrier. Very likely we may have no use for it, however.

Six p.m—Hard fighting again, terrific musketry and cannonade from the enemy; our guns ceasing a while for the 12th corps to storm the enemy's hasty entrenchments. Our boys are moving on nobly, and, we think, have already carried the works, as the musketry grows less terrific and more distant. Glorious old Hooker sits quietly on his horse, and directs the movements far in the front. Sometimes the storm of shot and shell, even before this last charge, during the artillery duel that has been kept up all day, was so thick around him, that his aides and orderlies could scarcely be induced to come and take his orders. The army is full of his praise. We hope for a great and decisive victory, and only fear that the enemy will find some way to slip out of our grasp. Just at this moment, things are perfectly still; and I hardly think we can have much more fighting to-night.

Eight p.m.—We have met a serious reverse. Our 11th corps, and the 12th perhaps, have most shamefully run; and we are in danger of a defeat, which the Lord forbid! We shall have a hard time, and nobody knows who will live through it. I don't know as I want to, if we are now shamefully defeated. Oh! some of our soldiers haven't their hearts in this thing, and haven't principle enough, I fear, to be worthy to fight in our noble cause. The rebels are desperate, and in earnest, by comparison at least. Still I hope we shall make a victory of this.

DUNN BROWNE

In its issue of May 16, 1863, under the heading "Death of Captain Samuel Fiske," the Springfield Republican *announced that Captain Fiske of the 14th Connecticut, "better known to the readers of The Republican as the genial correspondent Dunn Browne, was shot from his horse in the Sunday battle at Chancellorsville, and his body has not been recovered." An obituary followed, closing with an expression of deep sorrow "at the loss of the fast friend, the genial gentleman, the faithful pastor, and the brave officer." The next issue, May 23, however, carried a notice at the head of its editorial page that Captain Fiske "turns up alive and well, not a hair of his head harmed. . . . Good for 'Dunn Browne'! He will have the rare treat of reading his own obituary, and The Republican the good fortune of printing more of his pleasant correspondence." True to its word, the paper on May 30 ran the following four letters from what its editor praised as "among the first of army correspondents."*

Dunn Browne in Dixie: How He Happened to Go There

Libby Prison, Richmond, Va.
May 9 [1863]

Dear Republican: There is nothing so likely to secure an observer from prejudice and false views and representations of things as to take a fair look at both sides before giving his final opinion upon any question. Your correspondent accordingly, having already made a survey of the great rebellion from the northern side, has now crossed the frontier and is making observations, with his usual philosophic imperturbability, upon the southern aspect of the secesh monster. His opportunity for this unbiased and impartial view of things came to him in this wise.

He was acting on the staff of a general of brigade last Sabbath morning in the thick of the battle about Chancellorsville. Things were in a decidedly mixed condition. The splendid semi-circular line of battle of Gen. Hooker had been broken the night before (Saturday, May 2d) by the disgraceful failure of the 11th and 12th army corps to maintain their entrenched position, although attacked by a greatly inferior force of the enemy. Our brigade, the 1st in French's division, in the early Sabbath morning was ordered to leave its position, in rifle-pits pretty well over to the left of our line, and cross over the plank-road towards the right to recover the ground, a portion of it, lost the night before. Our boys charged in splendid style through a thicket of tangled wood for half a mile or more, driving the enemy before them like chaff, slaying many, taking some prisoners and fairly running over some and leaving them in their rear. Indeed, they charged with too much impetuosity and advanced so far that they were not properly supported on the flanks and were exposed to an enfilading fire of artillery as well as musketry. To halt our line and form it anew a little further to the rear in the woods, I was sent forward by the general, together with a fine young friend, one of his aides, both on foot, as our horses were left behind as utterly impracticable in that thicket of undergrowth. We had separated, he to the right and I to the left, delivered our orders to the colonels and assisted in executing it in the midst of a fire, the most diabolical that my eyes have yet witnessed, from front and rear (our own artillery from behind the wood occasionally dropped a shell among us) and both flanks, from at least 64 different points of the compass, I should say, and then I hastened to retrace my steps to report progress to the general.

I was hindered some little time in picking up prisoners (whom I didn't like to leave with arms in their hands in the rear of our line). I would disarm and put them in squads of 3 or 4 in the charge of some one of our slightly wounded men, first seeing that his gun was loaded and capped, and then on again till I had picked up some 20 or more of the "butternuts." Had a couple of the fellows on my hands and none of my own men in sight and was hurrying them forward by the persuasion of a cocked revolver, expecting every moment to come upon our general, when all at once pressing through a terribly dense portion of the undergrowth, I found myself face to face, at not twelve feet distance, with at least a whole regiment of the brownest and most ill-looking vagabonds that I ever set eyes on, every one of them with a gun in his hand, who were that moment rising up from behind a long line of rifle-pits they had taken from us the night before.

Here was a fix for an amiable and well disposed correspondent of yours, who had traveled some and ought to have known better, to get himself into. Here was a big mouthful to swallow for a belligerent patriot, intent on squelching the rebellion, who had just gotten his blood up, hadn't been fighting more than an hour, and was bound to distinguish himself before night. Here was a capital chance for a man, who had just gotten his hand in at the business of capturing prisoners, to put a thousand or fifteen hundred more in his bag—if they would only let him. The undersigned is compelled to acknowledge that in this one instance he found the situation too much for him. He had drawn a mighty big elephant in a lottery and didn't know what to do with him. One of the impudent wretches he had captured a few minutes before turned round with a grin and says, "Cap'en, I reckon things is different from the way they was, and you'll hev to 'low you're our prisoner now." A very sensible remark of the young man, and timely, though he hadn't a shirt to his back and only a part of a pair of pantaloons. Things *was* different from the way they were, with a vengeance. I gracefully lowered my pistol to an officer who stepped out from the ranks and presented it to him, apologizing for so doing by the remark that, "doubtless it would be more disagreeable to a whole regiment to surrender to one man, than to one man to surrender to a whole regiment." The hard-hearted fellows didn't seem to care at all for my misfortune, and only laughed when I told them my story. I was courteously treated and sent at once to the rear, minus my pistol and trusty sword (the loss of which I the more regretted, as it was not the purchase of money but the gift of a friend), and so hath ended ingloriously, for the present, my military service.

The transition from the fierce excitement of battle to the

quiet stillness of my walk of near a mile through the woods with my guard, was so great that I could hardly realize it. It seemed the flitting of a vision before my mind's eye. The roar of the cannonade and rattle of the musketry sounded far away to me, and I was like a boy rambling with a friend in the forest of a summer morning. Not for long though could the horrid sights and sounds of battle be put away from one's thoughts. We soon came upon other portions of the bloody field and had to pick our steps among mangled corpses of friend and foe, past men without limbs and limbs without men, now seeing a group of surgeons and assistants operating on the wounded under a tree, and now passing a group of ambulance men carrying on a stretcher some groaning sufferer. Occasionally a wounded horse struggling in his death-agony would kick at us, and occasionally a wounded secesh would mutter a curse as he saw the "d—d Yankee" pass. And in a little time we were far in the rear, and I was turned over to the care of the provost marshal, into a crowd of 1,700 captured "Yankees" about to be marched in the broiling sun, without a mouthful to eat, save the few who had their haversacks and rations with them, to Spottsylvania Court House, about 10 miles distant. Never did that nice black horse I drew a few weeks ago from provident Uncle Sam seem a more desirable underpinning to my weary fleshly tabernacle than now that I could only remember him left in the edge of that fatal forest, with my blankets and provisions on his back.

Yours, forlornly and in bonds, but yet a "prisoner of hope,"

DUNN BROWNE

Samuel Fiske's heaping of blame on the Eleventh Corps—mostly composed of Germans, derided in the army as "Dutchmen"—for the Chancellorsville defeat accurately reflected the verdict of the vast majority of soldiers in the Army of the Potomac. However, while his description of the Eleventh's rout is true enough, the fact of the matter is that the poor Dutchmen, ill positioned to begin with, were struck by an overwhelming force of Jackson's troops on May 2. And Fiske was misinformed in including the Twelfth Corps in his indictment. The fighting at Chancellorsville on May 3 (the day Fiske was captured), on both sides, was as desperate as

any in the war. Therefore the intended irony of his second para-
graph, on what was to be learned about the truth of a battle from
men taken prisoner in it, may possibly have been too subtle for
readers back home; perhaps they actually believed "there hasn't
been much of a fight up there on the bank of the Rappahannock."

Prison Reflections on the Chancellorsville Fight

Libby Prison, Richmond, Va.
May 11 [1863]

Dear Republican: Richmond is jubilant over the great victory that the South has gained, the tremendous thrashing the chivalry has given "the best army on the planet," though to be sure their joy is fringed with mourning to-day over the funeral ceremonies of their hero, Jackson. Doubtless a great many reasons are given for our most disgraceful and disastrous defeat. There is only one real reason, and that the simplest possible. Our army didn't fight as well as that of our enemies. We had every possible advantage. Our numbers more than doubled their's till Longstreet's reinforcements came up, which didn't then bring their forces up to 100,000 to oppose our 130,000. Indeed, it would now seem that Longstreet didn't come up at all. We had the advantage of position, and no inconsiderable amount of entrenchment. Gen. Hooker's plan was admirably arranged and excellently carried out, until the fighting took place. He exposed himself in the hottest places of danger, and set an electrifying example of heroism to the whole army. The terrible loss of life among our generals shows that on the whole they were not found wanting at their posts of duty. We had men enough, well enough equipped, and well enough posted, to have devoured the ragged, imperfectly armed and equipped host of our enemies from off the face of the earth. Their artillery horses are poor, starved frames of beasts, tied on to their carriages and caissons with odds and ends of rope and strips of rawhide. Their supply and ammunition trains look like a congregation of all the crippled California emigrant trains that ever escaped off the desert out of the clutches of the rampaging Comanche Indians. The men are ill-dressed, ill-equipped and ill-provided, a set of ragamuffins that a man is ashamed to be seen among, even when he is a prisoner and can't help it. And yet they have beaten us fairly, beaten us all to pieces, beaten us so easily that we are objects of contempt even to their commonest private soldiers, with no shirts to hang out of the holes in their pantaloons, and cartridge boxes tied round their waists with strands of ropes.

I say they beat us easily, for there hasn't been much of a fight up here on the bank of the Rappahannock after all, the newspapers to the contrary notwithstanding. There was an awful noise, for I heard it. There was a tremendous amount of powder exploded, for I saw the smoke of it ascend up to heaven. There was a vast amount of running done "faced by the rear rank," but I cannot learn that there was in any part of the field very much real fighting. I have seen men from every part of the ground fought over, men from almost every division of the army, and have inquired diligently after every vestige of conflict, and not one of them all had *seen* a great deal of spirited fighting, though a good many had *heard* a vast amount of it. The particular brigade or regiment or company of each man was captured because the enemy appeared in vast numbers on their flank or in their rear. They didn't fight much because they were so unfortunately situated or surrounded that there wasn't much use in resisting. I never heard of so much cross firing and enfilading fire, and fire in the rear, in all the history of battles with which I am acquainted. Do you point to the big lists of the killed and wounded, 15,000 or 20,000 on our side, as evidence of the desperateness of the encounter? I tell you that when men get up and run out of their rifle-pits and breastworks like a flock of sheep, instead of staying in and defending them, not only they deserve to be shot, but as an actual matter of fact they do get hit and killed about four-fold what would be hurt if they did their soldierly duty like men.

Am I saying things that oughtn't to be spoken of out of school? That had better be smoothed over and explained away? I'm not certain about that. I think people ought to understand somewhere about where the truth lies, and I do not think soldiers ought to be eulogized and told that men never fought more gallantly on the face of the earth and the victory would have been theirs if their officers hadn't mismanaged, when as a matter of fact their officers gallantly did their duty and were left to be killed or captured on the field because their men turned tail and ran away from them. Mind, I don't mean to say that this was very generally the case in the late battle. But I do mean to say that according to my best information and belief the great 11th corps of our army, attacked by an inferior force of the enemy, gave way with only a shadow of resistance and ran out of their entrenchments like a parcel of frightened deer, thus making a great gap in our grand line of battle and disconcerting all our good arrangements, and opening the way for the disasters that followed. And from all I can learn the 12th corps didn't do much better, and though a very large portion of the army did their duty very fairly, I have yet to learn of any considerable body of troops that displayed that real gallantry and determination to win which only can restore a losing battle and atone for the disgraceful flight of the cowards and panic-stricken. I know of whole regiments and brigades, long and heavy lines of battle, that gave way before lines of the enemy so thin and straggling as hardly to be considered more than skirmishers. I saw regiment after regiment and brigade after brigade of those corps I have mentioned come pouring back through our reserves till they covered acres and acres of ground, enough to have made a stand against all the rebels in Virginia, and only breaking our lines and telling such cock and bull stories of being cut to pieces in front and surrounded and attacked in the rear as carried evidence of their absurdity on the very face of them, till I could have cried for shame and grief to be obliged to acknowledge myself as belonging to the same army.

Still in spite of all I have said, it is by no means the truth that our men are a parcel of cowards and poltroons. They are as brave as the average of people—quite as brave as our enemies are. But we don't fight in such a common-sense way as they do. Shall I tell you how one of our lines of battle engages? They go in fine style, steadily, in a good line and without any flinching, halt at what is held to be a desirable point, and at the command commence firing, standing, kneeling or lying down, as may be ordered. Then, as in all their previous training they have been told to load and fire as rapidly as possible, three or four times a minute, they go into the business with all fury, every man vying with his neighbor as to the number of cartridges he can ram into his piece and spit out of it. The smoke arises in a minute or two so you can see nothing where to aim. The noise is deafening and confusing to the last degree. The impression gets around of a tremendous conflict going on. The trees in the vicinity suffer sorely and the clouds a good deal. By-and-by the guns get heated and won't go off and the cartridges begin to give out. The men have become tired with their furious exertions and the excitement and din of their own firing, and without knowing anything about the effect produced upon the enemy, very likely having scarcely had one glimpse of the enemy at all, begin to think they have fought about enough and it is nearly time to retire.

Meanwhile the enemy, lying quietly a hundred or two hundred yards in front, crouching on the ground or behind trees, answer our fire very leisurely, as they get a chance for a good aim, about one shot to our 300, hitting about as many as we do, and waiting for the wild tornado of ammunition to pass over their heads, and when our burst of fighting is pretty much over they have only commenced. They probably rise and advance upon us with one of their unearthly yells as they see our fire slacken. Our boys, finding that the enemy has survived such an avalanche of fire as we have rolled in upon him, conclude he must be invincible, and being pretty much out of ammunition, retire. Now, if I had charge of a regiment or brigade, I'd put every man in the guardhouse who could be proved to have fired more than twenty rounds in any one battle; I wouldn't let them carry more than their cartridge box full (40 rounds), and have them understand that that was meant to last them pretty much through a campaign, and in every possible way would endeavor to banish the Chinese style of fighting with a big noise and smoke, and imitate rather the backwoods style of our opponents.

Whenever we choose to defeat the armies of the rebels, we can do so, and we don't need 500,000 more men to do it with either. There are men enough in Hooker's army now to march straight through to Richmond. Too many men are only an encumbrance. There isn't the general living who has shown his ability to manage properly, certainly, more than 100,000 men. All we have to do is to make up our minds not to run before an equal number of the enemy, to keep cool and save our ammunition to shoot something besides trees with, and when the butternuts find we don't run away, they will. Meanwhile, till I am able to return and effect in our army this change in their method of fighting, I have the honor to assure you that these brown-coated fellows are not so bad as they might be, only they don't furnish us any sugar to put in our coffee, nor yet any coffee to put sugar in. Yours affably,

DUNN BROWNE

At this stage of the war, captured Federal officers were confined in Libby Prison, a large building in Richmond that had housed Libby & Son Ship Chandlers & Grocers, until they came up for exchange. The delay in transporting them from the battlefield that Fiske describes was caused by Federal cavalry raiders damaging the railroad. Captured enlisted men, it may be noted, had to march the fifty miles to Richmond, where they were held in the notorious, comfortless Belle Isle prison compound.

How the Rebels Treat Their Prisoners

Libby Prison, Richmond, Va.
May 13 [1863]

Dear Republican: I have been among Italian brigands, and Greek pirates, and Bedouin Arabs, but for making a clean thing of the robbing business, commend me to the confederate states of America, so styled. They descend to the minutiae of the profession in a way that should be instructive to all novices in the art. Nothing is too small to escape their microscopic rapacity. No article of apparel is sacred from their omnivorous clutches; no crumb of provision but their acute olfactories will smell it out. They ransacked our haversacks, and confiscated the little rations of sugar we happened to have therein as contraband of war. They stripped the canteens from the shoulders of the thirsty soldiers, and are sending them off on a long march to suffer no small inconvenience from this privation. They are taking away all our blankets, without which these cold nights will be almost insupportable till we can obtain a new supply. They picked our pockets of the few stray envelopes and sheets and half sheets of writing paper we chanced to possess. And this, be it understood, not as a precaution to prevent our writing in prison. There is no regulation to prevent that, no prohibition of our sending out and purchasing all the paper we wished. But it is just a specimen of the scale on which they conduct business.

And in another way, the official proceedings of this chivalrous confederacy are just about as small. A system of petty annoyances and oppression on the smallest possible scale has been uniformly observed in reference to the Union prisoners in their hands. When they wished to remove the hundred or so federal officers by rail from Guiney's station to Richmond, they ordered us to prepare to move at 3 p.m., kept us standing in ranks in a pouring rain for several hours, then marched us half a mile to the cars, and kept us waiting there, the rain still pouring furiously upon us, till half past 10 p.m., when they marched us back to our flooded camps again, with orders to be in readiness at a moment's notice, two or three hours hence, or any time during the night. Losing all our rest that night, and wandering about forlorn and dripping, we heard nothing more of moving till the next p.m., about 4 o'clock, when we were put through the same process of waiting, and the second time kicked our heels about the station in the deep mud till 7 or 8 p.m., when we were ordered back to camp again, but afterward did get aboard and spent the night in the box cars (awfully dirty), although we did not move till noon the third day. All this, of course, as a mere annoyance to us, and to make a display of their power, as nothing could be easier than to know when there was a train for us. And of a piece with this is the order given to the sentinels here to prevent us from looking out of the windows of the Libby, on pain of being fired upon. In the same style is pretty much the whole of the confederate behavior to us-ward. To be consistent to the end, they woke us about half past 11 last night, and told us we should be paroled and marched for City Point at 3 a.m., so no more sleep for that night. It is now 1 o'clock p.m., and we have not started yet, and shall have to march all night to-night to reach our destination.

Our prison has proven a very comfortable one. A hundred of us officers have occupied a room in the fourth story, 120 feet by 50 feet, a very clean, airy, commodious apartment. Our ration has been a half loaf of good bread, and perhaps one-half a pound of bacon per man, a pretty short allowance, but enough to sustain life, and then we have been able to purchase occasionally a little sugar ($1.50 per pound), a few eggs ($2.50 per dozen) or potatoes ($18 a bushel). I suspect we must have created a panic in the market of these latter two articles, as they have risen since we came here from $1.50 a dozen and $12 a bushel respectively. Of the city we have not seen a great deal, as you may well suppose, none of us having been out of this room in the week of our stay. We have seen quite as much as we wish to, however, of the capital of secessia, until we can enter it in quite another style. Yours very affectionately,

DUNN BROWNE

P.S. When about 100 of us had passed out of the room, the door was suddenly slammed in our faces that were toward the last, and "no more go to-day" uttered in our surprised ears. We couldn't even send a letter or any word to our friends by our comrades who were the fortunate ones. I (and my letters to you) remain behind. Yours disconsolately,

DUNN BROWNE

Captain Fiske's view here of a failing Confederacy was not a concoction he designed to raise the morale of his newspaper readers. A few days after he was paroled, he wrote his family that he had "come back more than ever convinced of our inevitable ultimate success & the desperate straits to which the enemy are reduced." City Point, on the James River southeast of Richmond, was the exchange point for prisoners of war. The fellow-prisoners Fiske mentions were Colonel Abel Streight, captured with his cavalry raiders by Nathan Bedford Forrest, and Captain George Brown, whose gunboat Indianola *had been taken on the Mississippi in February. William H. Ludlow was the Union officer in charge of prisoner exchange.*

The Secession Bubble, and Homeward Bound

Libby Prison, Richmond, Va.
May 16 [1863]

Dear Republican: It is a great thing to live in a great metropolis, even if you have to look at it through a barred window, "play

checkers with your nose through a grating," as the boys call it.
(There are no actual bars, however, on the windows of our apartment.) It is worth something to see the wealth of the nation
wafted on the white wings of commerce and laid at the confederate feet. (Two wood smacks and five canal boats, as well as one
schooner partially laden with lumber, and one little thing that
smoked after something like a steamer, have arrived during the
week of our stay.) It is worth something to hear the busy hum of
industry around us. (A circular saw is running several hours a
day within a few rods of us, and a planing mill semi-occasionally.
Three negro mule drivers are flourishing their wood teams about
the wharf, with a vast amount of excitement and bustle, and a
suspender factory is running on full time across the street.) And
it really is a great sight, without any joking, to see the airs these
rebels put on, and contrast the grandeur of their talk with the
evident ruin and wretchedness of everything around. One cannot
be within their lines for ever so short a time, even in such circumstances as ours, without an irresistible feeling that the se-
cession bubble is on the point of bursting. I know we have talked
this way so long that it may seem ridiculous, but I do believe
now more than ever, that we have ample power to put down this
rebellion utterly and permanently. It is only from our blunders
that we have failed to do it long ago. We cannot much longer
help it, even with all our mismanagement, for our enemies are
almost exhausted. The bear has nothing but his own paws to
suck and they are getting to be mighty poor nourishment. The
whole talk and actions, bluster, swagger and rant of the high and
mighty confederacy seem like the acting of a tragedy. You can't
make yourself believe that it is earnest. You can't find the substance of it under the shadow. It is the most astonishing thing
in the world to me how the thing has maintained itself so long
as it has. If the Lord hadn't some great plan to work out in reference to the settlement of the question of slavery on this continent, he would have let the bubble be pricked long ago. He won't
interpose his shield for the protection of this airy structure of
iniquity much longer, we may be sure. And without that special
interposition which the Lord does use to shield crimes till they
are fully ripe, it must drop.

City Point, May 22d

Moralizing over the rebellion I fell asleep, and so left my letter unfinished. I now add a word to tell you that I am released, and on my way home, that is, into our lines. Indeed the dear old flag now waves over us. About 150 officers and 400 or 500 privates have just come on board the steamer State of Maine, paroled, not, I suppose, exchanged. We have had Col. Streight and his officers (who were captured by Col. Forrest near Rome, Ga.) and Capt. Brown and 30 officers of the Indianola with us in the Libby for a week past. We are right sorry to leave them behind, especially as Capt. B. and his naval officers have already had a painful confinement of three months in Vicksburg and Jackson. We understand that enough rebel officers were brought up yesterday to entitle us to the discharge of all our officers in the Libby, and that it is by some breach of faith that a part of us are left behind. I hope that Major Ludlow will succeed in getting our friends to-day or to-morrow. Dear Republican, if the letters I have written you of late, and which I believe have been detained, have grown too old to interest your readers, pitch them into your waste paper basket and oblige your readers and yours truly,

DUNN BROWNE

5

GETTYSBURG

Although City Point, near Richmond, was the actual exchange site for prisoners of both sides, they remained on parole, on their honor not to return to the fighting, until the paperwork was completed and they were officially exchanged one-for-one. Fiske writes here from Annapolis, Maryland, the camp for newly released Union parolees. In 1861 the Naval Academy had been moved from Annapolis to a more secure location at Newport, Rhode Island, and, as Fiske notes, the vacated buildings used for a military hospital. As to his own experience, he could not resist comparing it to the Prodigal Son's journey into a far country. Captain Isaac Bronson, eulogized here, had commanded the 14th Connecticut in the fighting at Chancellorsville. For Samuel Fiske, sadly, as it proved, reading one's own obituary would be a once-in-a-lifetime experience.

Dunn Browne Reads His Own Obituary

Annapolis
May 28, 1863

Dear Republican: Did you ever happen to read your own obituary notice in a newspaper? Probably not, and long may you be spared not to do so. "Serus in coelum redeas." But and if at last the thing should happen to you, may you be there yourself alive and well to read it as I read mine yesterday. It is queer kind of reading though for a man. You read it rather hesitatingly as if you might be intruding on words that were not meant for your ears. You run over it rather curiously, as wondering what sort of news item your exit will make. You read it somewhat sadly and pityingly as sympathizing with the thrill of sorrow that will pass through some loving hearts as the eye glances over the column.

You read it with some sort of joy as exulting in the consciousness that you are nevertheless alive, on better authority than that of any newspaper in existence. You read it on the whole pretty seriously, and hang around it many thoughts and fancies, many questions and meditations of that unknown existence in which the printer's type has temporarily placed you. You read it I hope with some feeling of devout gratitude to Him whose sparing hand hath made the notice for the present untrue, and given you opportunity to furnish material for a better one by and by.

Grieve not then, oh veracious Republican, that your notice in this one instance was lacking in truth. That is a very common failing in obituary items. Rejoice with our readers over this your returning (very) prodigal correspondent, who was dead and is alive again, who was lost in the wilderness about Chancellorsville, wasted his living among the harpies and Jews of secessia, was fain to eat the husks of the Libby prison, and is very glad to be found again back in a region where fatted calves are not yet among the things that were.

There could scarcely be a more appropriate place for a man to read his obituary notices in, for Annapolis is about the deadest old village it was ever my fortune to be buried in. Very pretty indeed, but quaint, grotesque, every house minding its own business and paying no attention at all to the direction of the streets or the situation and architecture of any of its neighbor dwellings. The state house, an interesting and venerable pile, in whose cozy little Senate chamber, with its old-fashioned open fire-place, Gen. Washington resigned his commission, is the hub, out from which all the streets of the little city radiate like spokes of a wheel, and from the dome of which is one of the sweetest views my eyes ever rested upon. The buildings of the naval academy are now occupied for hospital purposes. And pretty much all the other houses in the town (a great proportion of which, indeed, are boarding houses and hotels) are occupied by our Union officers and soldiers who are staying here, paroled, awaiting exchange. The shops are kept almost without exception by Germans and Jews, and all of them have just the same things exposed for sale, dry goods and hardware, groceries and provisions, ready-made clothing, boots, shoes, confectionery, stationery, jewelry, hats and caps, millinery, gunpowder, hoop skirts, soap and candles, paints and oils, drugs and medicines, children's toys, harnesses and trunks, cooking-stoves, tinware, grindstones, &c., &c., all in a mess together. The "paroled" camp is about two miles from the state house, and a tolerably comfortable place. But new barracks are immediately to be erected, clean, comfortable and airy, for the more perfect accommodation of those who may be called hereafter to experience a residence therein. May they be few and far between.

But I must give some feeble expression of my sorrow—and that of the whole circle of his brother officers and soldiers—in the tidings we have just received of the death of Capt. I. R. Bronson of the 14th, sorely wounded in the fight near Chancellorsville on Sabbath morning, May 3. He was one of the most earnest, honest, and fearless patriots whose life has been sacrificed in this great cause. In camp, which is far too often made an excuse for relaxing the principles of morality and religion that are a restraint at home, he led a pure and Christian life. Where profanity and obscenity are, I am forced to say, almost the rule, and decent language the exception, no impure or irreverent words came from his lips, nor, unrebuked, from those of his men. Of a courage that never left him satisfied to be away from his post when action and danger were before us, of an earnest patriotism that left none of us in doubt what were *his* motives in coming to the field, of an enduring fortitude that shrunk from no extremities of hardship and privation that came upon us, of a generous and cheerful spirit that was an example to us all, he was a soldier worthy of our cause, a patriot without a blemish, a Christian that did not dishonor the name, a comrade of whose loss I can scarcely trust myself to speak. Since the death of the lamented [Samuel] Willard, of my own town and home, slain at Antietam, no stroke has come home to me, personally, so deeply. Noble Christian soldiers, both! A tear to their memory, and a lesson to each of us from their lives. Yours truly,

Dunn Browne

This dispatch demonstrates that inside the soft glove he habitually wore Samuel Fiske had a hard fist with which to pummel a detractor. His letters he defends here are those of May 9 and 11, which had appeared in the Republican *on May 30. It may be*

hoped that the armchair editor of the Portland Press *slunk away from this encounter with his tail between his legs. Fiske's comment about "all our boasting" refers to General Hooker's ill-advised address to his troops, issued in the midst of the Chancellorsville campaign: "Our enemy must either ingloriously fly or come out from behind his defenses and give us battle on our own ground." The phrase about pridefully belonging to the Army of the Potomac is from another notable address to the army, this one issued by General McClellan on the eve of the Peninsula campaign.*

Dunn Browne Defends Himself

Annapolis
[June 1863]

Dear Republican: Your unfortunate correspondent finds himself restored to life only to be killed over again, it seems. Escaping from his enemies, he has fallen among his friends. Delivered from the Richmond Dispatch (which was only recently favoring his hempen suspension), he is crushed under the Portland Press. That valuable down-East organ, taking umbrage at the humble sketches and opinions of the undersigned touching the late Chancellorsville f(l)ight, has just seized its biggest pen and, with one flourish, blotted him out.

Your correspondent hasn't had the fortune to see the article, in the above-mentioned Press, whereby he has come to his end (the victim very often doesn't see the bullet that kills him); but, from the accounts of a friend who did read it, the deed is accomplished. The obituary-notice recently published may as well stand for true, and there's no use in any more talking. There should be nothing more said by your (late) correspondent, save for one thing—the attack which the Press article is said to have contained upon the *modesty* of Mr. Dunn Browne. Now, as this is the one quality that has always especially distinguished that individual; which has been, so to speak, the crowning-grace of his character (as all his friends can testify to have often heard from his own lips)—such a charge is enough to wake even a dead man long enough to add a protesting codicil to his "last speech and confession."

The prisoner is at the bar, your honor and gentlemen of the jury, that is to say, of course, most Rhadamanthine editor and most impartial readers, is accused of boasting of his own achievements, vaunting of the number of prisoners that he took, &c., while disparaging the valor of our brave army, and calling that a defeat which was, in fact, a—a—a return to this side of the Rappahannock, as an easier place to supply the soldiers with rations and such like. The prisoner humbly confesses that he did mention his picking up a few scattered butternuts, one or two at a time, whom his brigade, in their furious charge that Sabbath morning, had knocked down and run over, or who had crept into their rear from the flank; but he respectfully submits that his object in mentioning the circumstance was not particularly to sound his own praises, but to give a more vivid coloring to the relation of his own capture a few minutes later, by the striking contrast and the surprising disappointment of the captor all at once becoming captive. He is free to acknowledge that a very strong motive for his exertions in capturing said rebels was his fear lest the brown-coated rascals, if left behind, would fire at him when he got out of pistol-range; and, on the whole, he considers that there was more of the ludicrous than of the heroic in his personal adventures on that day, although he claims to have done his duty in a quiet, common-sense way during the hour that it was his lot to be in the fight.

As to the remarks of your correspondent in reference to the issue of the battle and the conduct of our soldiers, and his comparison between their style of fighting and that of our enemies, he can only say that he used the very best of his judgment and observation, and information derived from a large number of officers and men from every part of the recent field of battle, as well as what experience he has been able to pick up in something like a year's service; all which together may or may not be so good a basis of an opinion as the Portland Press may have at its disposal. Your correspondent expressly disavowed any disparagement of the courage of our soldiers, taken as a whole; but he did beg leave to be excused from singing paeans of praise to the valor and conduct of an army which had been driven back from a position of its own choosing, after time for considerable entrenchment, by a vastly inferior force, worse equipped, and infinitely inferior in all the arms, supplies, and munitions of war. He did and does feel chagrined, after all our boasting that if the enemy would only come out of his entrenchments and give us a fair field, we would ask nothing better, and would make short work of him, that now, at last, when we had a field with the advantages nearly all on our side, we have made a grand failure and an inglorious retreat. He does feel, and thousands feel with him, that worse than capture, wounds, and imprisonment, worse than the jibes of our enemies, or the weariness of marches, or any of the hardships and privations that have been our lot, is the disgrace of our army recrossing the Rappahannock; and we do hope and pray for a speedy opportunity of wiping out that shame, and making it still possible to tell our children in future years with pride, "We also belonged to the Army of the Potomac." As things are up to this time, your humble servant would take no special pains to impress that fact upon the minds of the little Brownes that shall come after him.

The Press has its privilege of making just as much better a story out of our doings as it possibly can (God knows the astonishing disappointment of one heart; the reluctance, for a time the absolute refusal, to accept as truth the news which it did hear, and finally was forced to believe). Your correspondent gives his account of what he sees, hears, and does in the great campaign with as deep a consciousness of the imperfection of his narrative as the editor of the Press or any other man can have. A battle of 200,000 men is such a tremendous thing; such a mixed and confused thing; such an exciting, tumultuous, smoking, and thundering thing; such a haphazard, harum-scarum, accidental matter; such a lying and cheating, self-glorifying, and everybody-else-condemning humbug of a subject—that it is very difficult to get at the rights of it at all. Your correspondent can only give the impressions of one soldier, who is acting his own small part somewhere under the smoky cloud. He is glad to believe that they have a certain value, after making all due allowances for their necessarily fragmentary character, because they are genuine, such as they are—daguerreotypes, and not fancy sketches. He doesn't see much, but what he does see he believes. He scarcely expected that his sketches would be noticed so far away as the metropolis of the down-East state. But if he can afford any amusement to the editor of the Press; if his broken fragments can be shaken up in said editor's kaleidoscope in such forms as to please the readers—why, so much the better, in these times, when there's so little to amuse anybody.

Doubtless, dear Republican, this is as much space as you can afford to the shade of a defunct correspondent. Trusting that you will not suffer the Press to abuse his ashes, he remains yours faithfully,

DUNN BROWNE

Captain Fiske seems to have returned to duty, after his parole was lifted, in something of an ill humor. He had expected the 1863 spring campaign to bring victory; instead it came a cropper at Chancellorsville. He had hoped the new broom wielded by General Hooker would bring permanent reform to the army. On the evidence of this letter and the one following, he was deeply disappointed. The proposition here that it was intemperance among "the higher officers of the army" that set the tone for the whole is a thinly veiled reference to the widely believed allegation that Joe Hooker was intemperance personified. This was not true, but the perception remained. These letters were written on the march northward in pursuit of Lee's invading army.

Intemperance in the Army

Gainesville, Va.
June 21st [1863]

Dear Republican: There is one great advantage which the confederate army has over us, and I do not know but it is sufficient of itself to account for our frequent ill success in contending with "our erring brethren." Whisky is sixty dollars a pint in Richmond, while in our camps it can be obtained of our commissaries at ninety cents a gallon. Accordingly there are five hundred thirty-three (and a fraction) chances of any given soldier or officer in our ranks being found drunk, when his tour of duty comes, to one for a rebel officer or soldier. And I am sorry to say that there seems to be no want of disposition to avail ourselves of these odds in our favor. The rebels will drink all the whisky they can get, no doubt, but the month's pay of a general wouldn't more than enable him to treat his staff once round, and the month's pay of a private would scarcely purchase him a smell at an empty rum bottle. So they are sober in drink for the same good reason that they are temperate in eating, say in Vicksburg at this present time.

Really, dear Republican, though I have been long enough in the army not to be very easily overcome in my feelings, I am shocked at the progress of intemperance in our army, more particularly among our officers. It is not often indeed that the men can obtain any quantity of intoxicating beverages, and the punishment of those who supply them in violation of orders is frequently at least enforced. But there is not the same restraint upon the officers, unfortunately. And very many young men who have been hitherto models of sobriety have, since coming to war, lost their good principles and are falling victims to this evil habit. It is getting to be held a duty of hospitality to offer something to drink to every brother officer who calls upon you. The public feeling of regiments is getting demoralized on this subject. Scarcely are there any of the general officers of this army who do not use freely wines and liquors of all sorts; very many whose mess expenses for "fluids" greatly exceed those for solids. Not only are officers frequently in a state of intoxication when on duty, but such offenses against military discipline are getting to be held in light esteem. Those who prefer such charges against men are held to be officious meddlers. Even when convicted by courts-martial the sentences are very light. Men are repeatedly returned to duty who are known to be without any control over their appetites and liable at any, no matter how trying, emergency to be found utterly unfit for duty. Men complain, and with good reason, that the very officers who put them under guard and punish them in various ways for drunkenness and noise in camp, themselves offend much more grievously and outrageously with comparative impunity. I have seen a drunken officer lecture and swear at his men an hour at a time on their heinous offences in the rum drinking line. But I doubt the efficacy of his lecture, although to be sure, his words were accompanied by a moral and a warning patent to their eyes.

However, I almost feel that it is useless to say anything about this matter, for I am sure I scarcely know of anything feasible to do to check the progress of the evil. Until the higher officers of the army begin to change their habits and set a different example to their subordinates it will be difficult to effect a reformation. As a king is so is his court, and every general is a sort of king, and the satellites revolving around him reflect his habits and opinions in the main. If the general swears, you may expect his staff and subordinate officers to swear also, and his orderlies and servants to fill their mouths with profanity and the whole atmosphere about him to be blue with cursing and oaths. If the general drinks, his military family will adopt his habits in this particular also; and down to the very servant who blacks his boots, toddies and whiskies are the fashion. Still, doubtless much may be effected by the earnest efforts of those who do see and deprecate this increasing evil, to produce a voluntary temperance in our army which shall approximate in some degree the enforced abstemiousness which is doing so much for the rebels. Yours truly,

DUNN BROWNE

Since the Dunn Browne letters were invariably published a week or two after they were written (this one, for example, appeared in the Republican *on July 4, which also carried in its pages first reports of "a great conflict in Pennsylvania"), Captain Fiske made no attempt to report current news. In this case, he realized that to his readers the crossing of the Potomac by the Army of the Potomac in pursuit of Lee was old news. He was still on the staff of Colonel Samuel Carroll's brigade, in the division now commanded by Alexander Hays, in the Second Corps under Winfield Scott Hancock.*

Common Sense

Frederick City, Md.
June 23 [1863]

Dear Republican: I think I may have previously somewhere remarked (anyone in doubt can easily ascertain by looking over your files for a year past) that common sense is a good thing to have in a family, or elsewhere, as for instance in military operations. Our corps and other commanders must have a large accumulated stock on hand, for surely they waste precious little of the article in any of their movements. They manage most ingeniously to get the greatest possible amount of exercise out of their men in any given operation. They spare no pains to insure to Uncle Sam the maximum worth of his money in labor, toil and weariness from the $18-a-month-paid volunteer. They make every mile the soldier marches fully equivalent to three, such is the perfection of military organization, such is the tax on the luxury of being under orders. Shall I give you an instance, one of the many that came under my own personal observation, "a part of which I was"? Then I will speak of the way our division got over a river.

Problem: A division and its trains to cross the Potomac. Means: A double pontoon bridge. Time needful for doing it: Just about one hour. Way in which the thing was, militarily, accomplished: Said division was encamped after a day's march near Edward's Ferry on the southern side. At 9 p.m. orders came to strike tents, pull up stakes and move. We accordingly moved—about half a mile, and halted till nearly midnight, then crossed over and stood in the muddy road two or three hours waiting for orders to encamp. Finally receiving orders, turned off into a large field of wheat just ready to cut and bivouacked, at 4 a.m. At 6:30 a.m. received orders to evacuate the wheat field (which was already destroyed and Uncle Sam will have to pay for) and encamp in a grass field a little distance away (which Uncle Sam will also have to pay for). Then a little later came the order to move on the day's march. So here was the hour's work accomplished in the course of the night, by making three removes of camp and at the trifling expense of a night's rest to the troops between two days' marches, and with the ultimate result of getting the same exhausted troops to Frederick City a day later than they were ordered and expected.

But this isn't the worst of it. Such things vex and dishearten the men and greatly damage the efficiency of the army. For the impression gets abroad that the commanders don't care for the comfort of the troops. They don't know where the fault lies, and blame all their officers from the lowest to the highest. There is nothing more to be desired, toward the efficiency of an army, than a cordial understanding between the soldiers and officers—a feeling on the part of the men that their comfort is cared for, that all are engaged in the same cause and with the same motives and ready to endure the same privations. But the mail boy is leaving, and accordingly I will put an end to this disquisition. Yours affectionately,

DUNN BROWNE

This report, one of Samuel Fiske's most thoughtful, offers glimpses of parson Fiske in the pulpit, paraphrasing Proverbs ("a little more sleep . . ."), invoking Jehovah. By this writing, the Second Corps had marched from Falmouth, opposite Fredericksburg, to near the Pennsylvania border. The village of Gettysburg lay some eighteen miles to the north. In regard to his picture of the "neglect and barbarity" to be seen on the Second Bull Run battlefield, it may be pointed out that the field there had been in Union hands for the past eight months.

Toward Gettysburg

Uniontown, Md.
June 30 [1863]

Dear Republican: There is a deal of romance about this business of war. We lay us down at night under heaven's glorious canopy, not knowing if at any moment the call to arms may not disturb our slumbers. We wake at reveille, cook and eat our scanty breakfast, thankful if we have any to dispose of in that way. At the bugle-call we strike tents, put on our harness and packs, and start off, not knowing our direction, the object of our march, or its extent; taking everything on trust, and enjoying as much as possible the varied experience of each passing hour; and ready for a picnic or a fray, a bivouac, a skirmish, a picket, a reconnaissance, or a movement in retreat. There is no life in which there is more room for the exercise of faith than in this same soldierly life of ours—faith in our own good right arms, and in the joint strength and confidence of military discipline; faith in the experience and watchfulness of our tried commanders (happy if they be not tried and found wanting); faith in the ultimate success of our country's good and holy cause; faith in the overruling care and protection of Almighty Jehovah, who holdeth the movements of armies and nations, as also the smallest concerns of private individuals, in His hand.

Our marches for the last few days have been through the most lovely country, across the state of Maryland to the east of Frederick City. There is not a finer cultivated scenery in the whole world, it seems to me; and it was almost like going to Paradise from—another place; the getting-out of abominable, barren, ravaged Old Virginia into fertile, smiling Maryland. It is a cruel thing to roll the terrible wave of war over such a scene of peace, plenty, and fruitfulness; but it may be that here on our own soil, and in these last sacrifices and efforts, the great struggle for the salvation of our country and our Union may successfully terminate. Poor Old Virginia is so bare and desolate as to be only fit for a battle-ground; but it seems that we must take our turn too, in the Northern states, of invasion, and learn something of the practical meaning of war in our own peaceful communities. I sincerely hope that the scare up in Pennsylvania isn't going to drive all the people's wits away, and prevent them from making a brave defense of homes, altars, and hearths. When I read in a paper to-day of the "chief burgess" of York pushing out eight or ten miles into the country to find somebody to surrender the city to, I own to have entertained some doubts as to the worthiness and valor of that representative of the dignity of the city. It would be well for the citizens of Pennsylvania to remember that Lee's soldiers are only men, after all, and that their number is not absolutely limitless, and that they have not really the power of being in a great many places at the same time.

Also, that, if they wish to enable the proper military authorities to defend them understandingly, it will be just as well to see to the accuracy of the information they carry, and not magnify a half-dozen cavalrymen into a huge invading army. It is the very best time in the world now for everybody to keep cool, and use a little common sense. When there isn't any danger near, it doesn't matter much about that. The simple truth is, that the enemy cannot by any possibility, leaving many of his men behind to keep his long line of communications open, carry into Pennsylvania anything like the number of forces we can bring to meet him; and it is only the circumstance of our being frightened to death at the audacity of his movement that can save him from repenting most ruefully the audacity of his crossing the Potomac northward. We of the unfortunate "grand army," to be sure, haven't much reason to make large promises; but we are going to put ourselves again in the way of the butternuts, and have great hopes of retrieving, on our own ground, our ill fortune in the last two engagements, and, by another and still more successful Antietam conflict, deserve well of our country.

Our troops are making tremendous marches some of these days just past; and, if the enemy is anywhere, we shall be likely to find him and feel of him pretty soon. For sixteen days we have been on the move, and endure the fatigues of the march well. There is much less straggling, and much less pillaging, than in any march of the troops that I have yet accompanied. Our men are now veterans, and acquainted with the ways and resources of campaigning. There are very few sick among us. The efficient strength, in proportion to our numbers, is vastly greater than when we were green volunteers. So the Potomac Army, reduced greatly in numbers as it has been by the expiration of the term of service of so many regiments, is still a very numerous and formidable army. An innocent "Dunker" (if you know that religious denomination), at whose house we staid last night, thought that he had seen pretty much all the people of the world when a corps or two of our forces had passed his house.

We passed, in our march up the Potomac, the field of the two Bull Run battles; and I was much shocked to find such great numbers of the bodies of Union soldiers lying still unburied. Their skeletons, with the tattered and decaying uniforms still hanging upon them, lie in many parts of last year's battle field, in long ranks, just as they fell; and in one place, under a tree, was a whole circle of the remains of wounded soldiers, who had been evidently left to die under the shade of which they had crawled, some of them with bandages round their skeleton limbs, one with a battered canteen clasped in his skeleton hand, and some with evidence, as our boys fancied, of having starved to death. On one old broken cart lies what is left of eight Union soldiers, left to decay as they were laid to be borne off the field, and the vehicle struck, probably, by a cannon ball. In many instances the bodies which were partially or hastily buried are now much uncovered; and a grinning skull meets our gaze as you pass, or a fleshless arm stretches out its ghastly welcome.

Still it is wonderful to notice how quickly and how kindly Nature covers up the traces of murderous conflict on her face. The scars are mostly healed, verdure reigns, and beauty smiles over the bloody field; and save in a lonely chimney here and there, and the ghastly sights I have above referred to, which result from human neglect and barbarity, and are not to be charged at all to Nature, you would not suspect your feet were pressing the sod that one year and two years ago was reddened in human gore.

Enough of moralizing for the present, and "a little more sleep and a little more slumber" for the heavy eyelids of one who was in the saddle fifteen hours out of the last twenty-four, and expects to be as many more in the next twenty-four. No news except that which can be gathered from the date of this epistle. Yours truly,

DUNN BROWNE

For on-the-spot perceptive reporting of the progress of the Gettysburg struggle, sent off to the Republican *without revision and correction, no account surpasses this dispatch by Captain Samuel Fiske. His vantage point was at the center of the Union line on Cemetery Ridge, and his brigade was unengaged except for skirmishing and reinforcing the right on Cemetery Hill late on July 2, leaving Fiske free to observe and record. Of the Union generals he mentions, George Gordon Meade had replaced Hooker in command of the army four days before the battle; and John F. Reynolds, leading the First Corps, was killed in the first day's fighting. Darius Couch, put in charge of the Pennsylvania militia, was not advancing on the enemy's rear as Fiske thought. Privately Fiske was a good deal less generous describing the Eleventh Corps than he is here. "The stupid cowardly Germans," he wrote his family on July 5, ". . . break & run at almost the first fire. . . ." As he closed his letter, the Confederates were massing for Pickett's Charge.*

At Gettysburg

Battle field near Gettysburg, Pa.
July 2, 12 noon [1863]

Dear Republican: I am sitting here under a noble oak, in a splendid central position, all ready to describe a battle to you, but somehow it hangs fire. We have been waiting ever since 5 o'clock this morning, expecting every moment to go in, but all is yet quiet, save the sharp skirmishing in our front. I am in a dilemma; for now that I have leisure to describe, there is no battle going on to task my descriptive powers, and on the other hand, as soon as the battle commences to give me a theme, then I must take my share in it and shall have no leisure to write.

We are drawn up in a nice position on the elevated ground on one side of a valley and meadow. The enemy occupying (we suppose) a somewhat similar position on the other side of said valley, say a half a mile distant, we send a line of skirmishers down into the meadow among the grass and wheat fields. The enemy push out a rather stronger line from their position and crowd our boys back. We put in a few more companies and force them to a retrograde movement, and so the line wavers to and fro. A very pretty sight to see, but having things connected with it that are not at all pretty, as for instance, just this moment passing, not five rods distant, a captain borne on a stretcher with a minie ball through his face, and just back yonder a corporal from our brigade with a bad hole through his hand. A few minutes ago away to our left our line of skirmishers drove the enemy so far and so furiously that I thought the business was growing into the magnitude of a battle, but the firing is dying away again now, and I think I see our line retiring once more, looking in the distance like little black dots in the wheat field. We seem to be a little in doubt whether the enemy is seeking to entice us into the valley to take us at a disadvantage, or whether he is just withdrawing himself entirely and keeping up the firing in a small way to cover his retreat.

I incline to the latter opinion, and am much afraid we shall lose all our pains in the recent 20 or 30 miles a day marching. Much afraid that by the time we have lain here three or four days waiting for Lee to come and attack us we shall learn that he is three days' march ahead of us on the way to Old Virginia, with the jolly little pickings and stealings he has gleaned up in fat Pennsylvania, and just crossing the Potomac with 50,000 head of cattle and horses and the reputation of having again eluded and bamboozled the grand army of the Potomac. But as Gen. Meade has not asked me to give him my views upon the present aspect of things, nor even requested me to take a brigade across to yonder grove and see what is in it, perhaps it will be as well to wait the issue of events quietly. Very likely the butternuts will burst out upon us about sundown, after the old Jackson style, with the heaviest kind of an attack, which will give all of us as much battle as we can wish for, no matter what our aspirations for military glory, and give me no opportunity to finish this epistle for some days if ever. So I will just tell you the little I heard of the sharp fight of yesterday and then lie down to sleep under this grand old oak till something else happens.

We met the body of Gen. Reynolds as we were marching up last night, and were told that he fought the whole force of the enemy with one of his divisions for two hours, exposing himself most gallantly and soon falling, shot through the head. The rest of his corps coming up maintained the fight, but with great loss, and were forced to retire before overwhelming numbers, until the arrival of three more of our corps, which put a new face upon affairs. In the little time that remained before night we regained a portion of the lost ground and captured a considerable number of prisoners, variously estimated at from 1,200 to 2,000. And last night and this morning the rest of us came up and we are now, as I told you above, all in position and as ready as we can be, I suppose, for an engagement.

The enemy, as your correspondent has reason to know, in his complete and quite undesired opportunity recently enjoyed for learning their views, are arrogant and think they can easily conquer us with anything like equal numbers. We hope that in this faith he will remain, and give us final and decisive battle here, and not put us under the necessity of more long marches and maneuvering, and a longer suspense as to the result.

Friday, July 3, 7 a.m.

Sure enough, the enemy has shown us that he had no disposition to run away. At 4 p.m. yesterday a tremendous cannonade

was opened on us, and responded to with double fury by our batteries, and a strong rush was made on the left of our semi-circular position by the rebels, and at nearly the same time (indeed I
don't know but before) on our extreme right, while a spirited
skirmishing was kept up all along the line, as well as the most
terrible artillery fire that I have yet heard. It was as if the lid of
the infernal pit had been removed, and its horrid contents spilled
over the upper world. The tremendous uproar of hundreds of
cannon, the screeches and hisses of shells tearing through the
air and bursting over our heads, and burying themselves in the
earth at our feet, the sharp crack of musketry and whirring of
bullets, the sulphurous canopy of smoke that soon darkened the
air and made all things dim around us, the rapid movements of
troops flying hither and thither to take up new positions, consti-
tuted altogether such a scene of excitement and confusion and
grandeur and horror, as nothing but the simile of hell broke
loose is at all adequate to describe. The murderous conflict continued until half past ten last night, and ceased then with the
result of a repulse of the enemy from every point of our position,
although at one or two vital points the issue was several times
doubtful.

It has been up to this time a right noble and well fought battle,
the enemy attacking fiercely and our forces bravely meeting the
shock, no flinching, no cowardice anywhere, so far as I have
heard. I heard one say, indeed, that the 3d corps, or a part of it
gave way once on our left, and had to be replaced by the gallant
5th, and it occurred to the brigade with which I am connected
to move from the center towards our right just in the nick of
time to save a couple of batteries that were being fiercely
charged by Early's division, and a vitally important position that
had just been abandoned by a portion of our 11th corps. But
even these fellows that gave way had fought well and held their
ground some hours, and the 11th as a corps have done tolerably
well, I understand. So I trust in God the Army of the Potomac is
going to redeem its reputation in this battle, and yet deserve
nobly of a rescued and grateful country.

10 o'clock a.m.

A most obstinate and fiercely contested battle has been going
on since 4 o'clock this a.m. on our extreme right. Six hours of as

hot work as the history of battles can tell, and the business still going on as briskly as ever. We cannot see yet that either side has a decided advantage. Two divisions of the 12th corps have just held Ewell's corps at bay for seven hours, and now (for I have been hindered by several errands and it is now 12 a.m.) have driven him back with heavy loss, and a great many demoralized stragglers we can see in the distance. At this moment we hear distant guns and take it to be Couch's advance. So between us I think the rebs will rue the day they came into Pennsylvania, and get back over the Potomac in a good deal worse shape than after Antietam. I can give you no estimate of the losses, &c. Our brigade captured a stand of colors, 3 field officers and about 50 privates last night. The fighting is not done yet by a good deal, we expect; but we hope for the best and for a glorious Fourth tomorrow. Hastily,

DUNN BROWNE

This account of Pickett's Charge, on the afternoon of July 3, ran prominently with the letter above in the Springfield Republican *on July 11 under the heading, "Dunn Browne Sees and Describes the Gettysburg Battles." The same issue carried accounts of Vicksburg's surrender on July 4. Port Hudson would fall four days later, opening the Mississippi, affirming at least that part of Fiske's formula for closing the war. Of the regiments that Fiske praises here, the 14th Connecticut suffered 66 casualties at Gettysburg, and the 8th Ohio 102.*

Field of Glory

Near Gettysburg, Pa., on the field of glory,
the evening before the 4th of July, 1863.

Dear Republican: I have at last had the desired opportunity of seeing a battle in which there was real fighting—hard, persistent, desperate fighting—fighting worthy of a noble cause and the confidence of a gallant people and of the glorious anniversary that is upon us. Whatever the ultimate issue of this series of battles (and I am sure I cannot see how it can be anything but the total destruction of Lee's army), the dear old brave, unfortunate Army of the Potomac has redeemed its reputation and covered itself with glory in this day's work.

After a lull in the fury of the contest for a couple of hours or so succeeding the obstinate engagement on our right in the morning, the cannonade recommenced with unexampled fury a little after noon; such a cannonade as I believe no battle of this war has yet begun to compare with, and after raging about an hour, and doing fearful havoc, especially upon our batteries, hundreds of whose horses were killed, also pieces dismounted, caissons exploded, and in several instances whole batteries silenced, the enemy advanced for a desperate attack upon our left and center, evidently hoping that our batteries were so knocked to pieces that they could not retard their advance. But our reserve batteries had replaced all the disabled ones, our line of infantry (mostly behind a low stone fence) just lay low, kept cool and poured death into the ranks of the advancing foe, while grape and canister from a hundred huge brass mouths swept them down as hail does the mowing grain, till human courage could not longer stand against such a tempest of lead and iron; their steady lines wavered, rallied, quailed again and began to break and flee. This was our time. With a tremendous shout catching from regiment to regiment along our line, our boys sprang up, over the fence and down the slope upon the wavering enemy with a rush that nothing could withstand. The enemy fled, throwing away everything. We captured thousands of prisoners, among them two generals, scores of colors and arms of all descriptions without number—and returned to our old position, for their long line of batteries, most formidable and well served, covered their retreating columns and checked our pursuit, which was not organized and regular, but a sort of spontaneous impulse of our boys when the enemy began to waver.

So has the enemy been decisively repulsed in every attack he has made upon us, and I think will scarcely try that performance again. Ours is now to attack him, to follow up our success with unflinching energy, give him not a moment's rest, and use him up entirely before he reaches the Potomac, or else chase him through Virginia to Richmond and close up the rebellion at its great center, while Grant and Banks gather in Vicksburg and

Port Hudson, and our iron clads knock to pieces the defenses of Charleston.

All our regiments have done nobly. Be it my glad privilege to speak first of the ones in which I am most interested, though my position was temporarily elsewhere on the field. The 14th Connecticut (under the command of Maj. [Theodore] Ellis), in the field now less than a year, and reduced from a thousand strong to about two hundred effective men, by the losses of marching and sickness and participation in the three great battles of Antietam, Fredericksburg, and Chancellorsville, can claim at least an equal share with any regiment in the field of the glorious third of July at Gettysburg. Its position was in the center of the enemy's advance, and nowhere did the heaps of rebel dead lie thicker than in its front. Three regimental battle flags are trophies of our boys' prowess; prisoners to just about the number of a man apiece, one colonel, one lieutenant-colonel, a good many other officers, and something like a hundred privates. Hurrah for the gallant old 14th. She is getting some pay for Fredericksburg and Chancellorsville. In the brigade to which I am attached for the present, the 8th Ohio had an especial share of glory in this last conflict. Three battle flags are also this regiment's trophies, and from their advanced position in support of the line of skirmishers, the prisoners they took were probably ten times the number of their own men. One private came in a few minutes after the battle with a captain, three lieutenants, and thirty privates. But time presses and I yield to the pressure. Yours truly,

DUNN BROWNE

P.S. July 4, 6 a.m. The pickets of our brigade have just entered the town of Gettysburg and report their column just out of the town and in full retreat. The prisoners are coming in rapidly. Two squads of about a hundred apiece have just now passed me. Oh for a glorious 4th of July celebration, not in speeches, fire-crackers and the noise of unshotted cannon, but in earnest, energetic action in pursuing these defeated enemies, in the stern speech of shotted cannon and musketry, thinning the ranks of our haughty invaders, and pushing their columns, torn and bleeding, back to utter rout and destruction. Our rations are out. For a day or two past we have had little to live upon. I haven't tasted coffee for now the third day, but I understand there are crackers and pork up this morning to give our boys a scanty supply, and I trust we shall immediately push forward, and do the hurrahing and the feasting by and by. Excuse, dear Republican, the haste and un-connectedness and illegibility of this communication, and be-lieve me, as ever, yours,

DUNN BROWNE

Second P.S. Hurrah for the Union and down with the rebels.

Clearly intended for a Connecticut audience, this letter was sent to a local paper there, probably one serving Madison, the home of Fiske's congregation. His admiration for Colonel Samuel Car-roll—who commanded at the brigade level for two years before finally being advanced to brigadier general's rank, which he gained only in May 1864—was heartfelt. Privately Fiske wrote his family at this time that Carroll "behaves coolly and magnificently under fire & in all movements of troops is the ablest soldier I have seen." The fight of Carroll's brigade that he details took place on Cemetery Hill late on July 2. Fiske's accounting of Pickett's Charge is notable for his frank appreciation of its gallantry.

Gettysburg Reviewed

Battle field near Gettysburg
July 4, 1863

I presume you may have half a dozen accounts of the campaign in Pennsylvania before this, but, as my opinion of the battle of Chancellorsville was called in question by some of my friends, I wish to say through your columns that, in my humble opinion, the battle of Gettysburg yesterday and the day before was not at all like that of Chancellorsville, but has been a clean, well-conducted, hard-fought, and every way glorious fight, in which the Army of the Potomac has redeemed its reputation, and de-serves well of the country; or if my opinion was wrong, and we

did fight well at Chancellorsville, this has been a battle in which
the said army has eclipsed its former glories, and given the country reason to be glad and grateful to God for this our national
anniversary.

The arrangements of the action were admirable, the execution
almost perfect, and the conduct of the troops most creditable. I,
of course, can speak more particularly of our own glorious old
fighting division, the third of the second corps, which has again
crowned itself with glory. The 14th Connecticut, in whose welfare nearly every portion of the state is interested, had a splendid
opportunity, being in the very center of the line attacked on the
afternoon of the 3d instant; and never was an opportunity better
improved. Although my own regiment, I can speak with comparative impartiality of its doings, because my duty on detached service at present called me away to another part of the field. I had
occasion to view the whole length of our lines, to ride over every
part of the field; and in no part of the whole line was there evidence of harder fighting or a more gallant charge. Five regimental battle-flags are the trophies of its valor, as well as about a
prisoner for each man engaged. It was a grand sight to see in
this portion of the battle the charge made by the rebels, and the
way it was met. The most terrific cannonade of the war commenced at about one o'clock, and continued, perhaps, about
three-quarters of an hour, followed by the impetuous attack of
their infantry upon our left and center.

In three magnificent lines of battle, preceded by a line of skirmishers, the rebels charged across the valley and up the slope,
at the crest of which our single line of troops lay behind a stone
fence ready to receive them. In most gallant style they came on.
I don't believe troops ever made a firmer or more persistent
charge under such a murderous fire. But it was too much for
human valor to accomplish. It was just a reversal of the work at
Fredericksburg. Here the attack was on the outside of the circle;
and at Fredericksburg our attack was on the inner, and they
could concentrate their fire upon us.

Our batteries mowed down their ranks with grape and canister, and our continual and terrible musketry fire cut them all to
pieces. Their lines wavered, re-formed, closed up as the men fell,
rallied many times, and pressed forward, but finally were compelled to fall back. I understand that a few of them reached the

top of the hill, and almost gained possession of one of our batteries, an officer mounting one of our pieces, and waving his sword as he fell; when our boys sprang up, and charged down the hill with a tremendous shout, and a rush that could not be resisted. Soon began to come in troops of prisoners; and the contest was over, and the enemy repulsed along the whole line.

This was only one part of the battle. A contest still more obstinate if possible, at least much longer continued, took place on our extreme right, on the morning of the 3d. From four a.m. till ten, two divisions of the 12th corps resisted and finally repulsed the attack of Gen. Ewell's corps (formerly Jackson's); and on the 2d also, from four p.m. till nearly eleven, the battle raged on the right and on the left with the greatest ferocity. It was in this fight of Thursday night that Gen. Carroll's brigade, of the third division of the second corps (to whose staff I am at present attached), came to the support of two batteries of the 11th corps in the very nick of time, when their infantry supports were on the verge of yielding, and the rebels were already among the guns, and the artillerists defending themselves with their sponge-staffs. We killed fifty rebels inside of our line of stone fence, and retook the position lost in the dark (about eight p.m.), and, amidst a perfect tempest of shell and bullets, saved the batteries, and held the position; which if the enemy had occupied, and turned the guns upon us, would have lost us our whole position, probably, and turned the fate of the day.

Our general (he is only a colonel commanding, although a graduate of West Point, and acting brigadier for more than a year), in the darkness and confusion, on unknown ground, and amidst a terrible fire, moved with perfect coolness, made his voice heard above the whole uproar, disposed his men with as much skill as if on familiar ground and in open day, and showed himself, as he always does, a thorough soldier, and an unsurpassed commander of men. It would have done your heart good to hear the artillerists cheer when they heard that it was Carroll's brigade that was coming to their rescue. The brave fellows, with tears in their eyes at the thought that they must lose their beloved guns, shouted to each other, "It's Carroll's brigade! There'll be no more running. We're safe!" Yet men have been promoted over his head time and again, who have neither experience nor brains nor coolness nor courage. His name has been sent in for a generalship two or three times, but not confirmed, for want of political influence in his favor. I say these things in bare justice to a most accomplished soldier and skillful leader, in a time when the country greatly needs such to serve her in high places, and not from any reasons arising from my personal connection with him, which is only an accidental and temporary one. He has no Connecticut regiment under him; but his adjutant-general is one of our Connecticut boys, and a credit to his native state for his gallantry and two years' valuable service in the war. His name, mentioned honorably in several official reports, is John G. Reid, captain, son of Rev. A. Reid of Salisbury, Conn. He had his horse shot under him in the Thursday-night engagement—the familiar gray stallion that the boys like to see moving along their lines (but whose heels it wasn't always safe to approach), as cool under fire as his rider.

But I must close my rambling and inadequate sketch of these eventful days by saying that we are having a happy and glorious Independence Day, and look forward with great confidence and hope to the utter rout and ruin of Lee's army.

I can not tell you of the particular doings of other Connecticut regiments, but know that all have acted an honorable part, and deserve well of the country.

Our loss in generals has been very great. Gens. Reynolds, Weed, and Zook, killed; Sickles, Hancock, Gibbon, Paul, Vincent, Barlow, and others, wounded.

Three brave boys in the Madison company, of the 14th regiment, have given their lives toward obtaining this glorious success—Moses G. Clement, Willie Marsh, and Aaron Clark: the two first, in the final charge down the hill upon the enemy; the last, in the original position on the crest of the hill—all brave soldiers, and a loss to the community and circles of mourning friends.

Samuel W. Fiske,
14th Conn. Volunteers

Samuel Fiske (writing, to be sure, as Dunn Browne) was one of the first to raise in print the controversy—the lasting controversy—over Meade's decision not to counterattack at Gettysburg on July 4. Fiske's particular contribution to the debate was his contention that the troops were "eager, anxious, panting" to fight that day. His private view matched his public one. He wrote his sister this same day, "I am greatly pained to be obliged to think & say that we have lost another golden opportunity, the best in the war, by not following up our success yesterday & utterly crushing the defeated enemy."

Dunn Browne Critical Again

Battle field near Gettysburg
6 a.m. July 5 [1863]

My Dear Republican: I sent you yesterday a couple of letters, giving a partial account of our glorious contests and victories of July 2d and 3d. Yesterday I expected to enjoy as the most glorious anniversary of its national independence the country ever saw. But it proved to be the most anxious and finally miserable day I ever spent, for we did absolutely nothing!—lay there through the whole day utterly inactive—and now I have scarcely a doubt the enemy has taken himself away from us. Gen. Meade has shown such skill and ability hitherto, that we are all inclined to trust him to the uttermost; but how can it be that he has not lost the most glorious opportunity of the whole war? We had repulsed the enemy most decisively and tremendously along our whole line. The men universally were eager, anxious, panting to be led on to complete the triumph and utterly crush the defeated and despairing enemy. This spirit in the troops I know, for I had occasion to be along every part of our line during the day, and one could not mistake the whole import of their words, looks, gestures. They were like hounds on the leash, panting to be let loose. And then it was Independence day! Good Heavens! We could not be defeated that day. I would stake my life a thousand times over on the issue. It was the surest thing that any leader ever held in his hands. I wouldn't have so insulted our gallant army and the inspiration of the blessed 4th of July as to have been in doubt for a moment of the victory, no matter how obstinate a defense the sullen foe might have made. And the whole army would have gone forward with a sublime confidence that all rebeldom in arms could not have resisted.

I know Gen. Meade and not I is the one who has disposed the troops and guided them to victory, and whose opinion is worth a thousand times more than mine, and that he is almost certainly right, and I wrong; but if that were a dead certainty (yesterday being the 4th of July) I wouldn't give up my opinion. He may be all right and the result show it gloriously, but I can't be wrong in thinking as I do. Even if he doesn't let a remnant of the army of Lee get back across the Potomac, I shall still contend that the work of annihilation were better done yesterday. However yesterday has gone by (like the day after Antietam, only a hundred times more so) and we have only to-day in our hands. I don't see how Lee is going to extricate himself from his position without tremendous loss, and how we can well help pretty nearly or quite annihilating him if we follow vigorously but cautiously, under Meade's able superintendence, his retreating columns, pressing constantly upon him and harassing him with cavalry.

Perhaps, indeed, he hasn't yet retreated at all. On our left they (our troops) were digging rifle pits and constructing defenses yesterday, as if still expecting an attack, but the indications are all the other way. The pickets of our brigade, and a part of the 11th corps, advanced before light yesterday morning as far as the village, and took a good many stragglers, and brought in a great number of our own wounded left behind by the enemy, whom they reported departing by the Cashtown road as they entered. Lee's skirmishers to be sure kept up a lively firing all along our left, but he would of course do that to cover the signs of his departure, and now this morning we learn that his artillery has been moving all night, and I suppose there is scarcely a shadow of doubt the old fox is gone. I see no indications of our moving yet. Your disappointed, but still hopeful

DUNN BROWNE

In trying to put Gettysburg in perspective, Captain Fiske draws here on his experience observing the Crimean War in 1856 during his Grand Tour, observations that he had shared with readers of the Springfield Republican *at the time. It is clear that his praise*

*of the Army of the Potomac's soldiery as superior to Europe's did
not include the "Dutchmen" of the Eleventh Corps. Ever-hopeful,
Fiske anticipated that Meade would pursue Lee to a showdown.*

Reflections and Speculations

Five miles from Gettysburg, Pa.
July 6 [1863]

Dear Republican: In an account of one of our recent engagements in a newspaper that strayed into our camp, I noticed that
the musketry firing was stated to have been the most terrific
that the writer ever saw, and then, a few sentences after, that
the contest described was the first battle in which he had ever
been concerned. It occurred to me that, considering the last
mentioned fact, the first statement was not very strange. Now
there is doubtless a tendency to make out every battle described
a very grand affair, and if all the "probably most desperate and
bloody engagement of this war" were gathered together and
counted up, their number would be dozens or scores; and we
have had no small number of "battles that have no parallel in
history."

Now, I always make a little allowance for descriptions of this
kind, and discount somewhat on the strength of the American
characteristic of hyperbole. And having seen the broken bits of
iron-mongery that were scattered in and about Sebastopol, over
a circle of many miles in diameter, consisting in part of 10 or
12-inch solid shot and fragments of 36-inch shell, I should
scarcely dare to speak of even a very lively explosion of field
pieces as the most "terrific cannonade the world ever heard."
Still, in all moderation, this last affair of ours with Lee at Gettysburg can be spoken of as a big thing. And the cannonading,
about 75 pieces on each side, throwing say at least 200 shot or
shell per minute, and continuing for an hour or two at a time in
full blast, though hardly to be compared to the bombardment of
Sebastopol, or even some of the engagements in which naval and
siege guns have been brought to bear in our own war, yet was
sufficiently exciting and awful for all practical purposes; and one

who was in the midst of it would hardly wish for another hundred a minute for the sake of adding to the grandeur of the scene.

It was touching to see the little birds all out of their wits with fright, flying wildly about amidst the tornado of terrible missiles, and uttering strange notes of distress. It was touching to see innocent cows and calves feeding in the fields torn to pieces by the shells. It was still more touching to see the artillery horses standing quietly in their places, veteran warriors, cool and unconcerned in the most terrific fire, and falling in death without flinching any more than their brave human companions. Several batteries had from 30 to 40 horses each killed in one day's engagement. It was a nobler sight to see the sublime bravery of our gallant artillerists, serving their guns with the utmost precision and coolness, right in the focus of the most terrific storm of shells and musketry, knowing they were the mark aimed at by an equally brave and skillful enemy, and clinging to their beloved pieces to the bitter end. We found the boys of some of the batteries we rushed in to save when a part of the 11th corps gave way on Thursday night, just standing among their guns, beating over the head with their rammers alike the enemy who were rushing in to capture their pieces and the cowardly Dutchmen who were running away from their defense. All honor to the gallant battery boys who so well sustained the honor of the flag in those soul-trying times. It was a sight of horror to behold the position our batteries held when the fight was over. The bodies and limbs of mangled men and horses, broken wheels and carriages, dismounted guns and exploded caissons, timbers dashed to pieces, the branches and even trunks of fallen trees cut down by the shot, and the ploughed-up earth, and shot and shells scattered over the ground, all made a picture for a painter, but one hardly desirable to be looked upon in its actual reality.

It has been a great battle; probably not much inferior in magnitude and carnage to Waterloo itself, though of course not to be compared with it in the vitality and decisiveness of its issue. We probably have other battles to fight before the enemy is utterly routed and driven back across the Potomac. It has been a plain, open, visible battle, in which we could understand what was doing and what was attempted, know the object and witness the success of every movement. All wasn't confusion and chance, but almost every man engaged could see what was expected of him and know how to calculate his resources. We boast of the American soldier as superior to the pure military machine of the European despot for the very reason that his education is superior and his feeling of personal independence and manliness stronger. If we wish to make the most of this superiority, then we must fight the American soldier intelligently, let him know what he is expected to accomplish, and give him some knowledge of the general plan and object of the battle he is fighting. Here is just where our leaders have so often failed. They have treated the soldier as a machine, and so a machine he has become. Treat our brave boys as men. They are and will be men.

We lost the opportunity of the 4th, the most glorious opportunity a general or an army ever had, but we are being moved now with great skill and judgment to the execution of another plan which promises great and victorious result, if one may be allowed to guess from the direction we are taking, and we wait with hope and good courage for the issue of our next battle. In great haste, yours truly,

DUNN BROWNE

As Fiske acknowledged in his letter of July 2, it had long been his ambition to fully describe a battle. At Antietam he was in the action and had no vantage point. At Fredericksburg he was ill and only saw the fighting from afar. At Chancellorsville, in the Wilderness of Virginia, very little was to be seen but forest. But Gettysburg was a highly visible spectacle, and Captain Fiske was posted at the center of it all. Here once again he describes the progression of the action, in effect lecturing newspaper correspondents whose accounts he found so lacking. At this writing, the Federal army was approaching the Potomac in pursuit of the Rebels. The reports that D. H. Hill had, and Beauregard might, reinforce Lee were without substance.

A Plain and Simple Affair

Jones's Cross-Roads, Md.
July 11 [1863]

Dear Republican: It's queer that scarcely anybody can give a correct account of a battle. No, it isn't queer, either; for no man can see more than a small part of a great battle at once, and each one wishes to make his share as conspicuous as possible, and praise his own corps or division to the utmost; and things are so confused at best that it would be more strange that a man should, than that he shouldn't, give an accurate account of the whole matter. But the late battle of Gettysburg was such a comparatively plain and simple and easily comprehended affair, that I should suppose the main purport of it might be rightly put. But I have seen all sorts of incorrect statements of it in the papers every day since the battle; such as "We have attacked the enemy in his own chosen position, and swept him from the field." "After a most obstinate and bloody contest, the enemy gave way, and left us the possession of nearly the whole ground."

Now, the simple state of the facts is just this—that we repulsed the attacks of the enemy, repulsed them tremendously and effectually; and in this was our victory. It was Fredericksburg over again, with the opponents in reversed positions. The first day (Wednesday, July 1), we were advancing, indeed, and may be said to have attacked the enemy; but his numbers were overwhelming, and we were driven back a mile or two, quite through the village, and this side of it, to a strong position, whose front was Cemetery Hill; and the contested ground and our wounded, and a large number of prisoners, were left in possession of the enemy. And the battles of Thursday and Friday were, with some small exceptions and diversions, attacks of the enemy on our own ground, a strong, elevated position, sometimes at one point and sometimes at another, but always without success. Our position was almost in the form of a horseshoe, so that we could reinforce any attacked point with the greatest celerity. The enemy, to move from his right to his left, must march a circuit of six or eight miles. When he had been all day, or all night, massing his forces to the right or to the left for an attack, we could, in a few minutes, bring our troops across the neck of the horseshoe to help one another, and repulse him. Then our whole line was on the crest of a hill (or range of them), and behind strong stone fences, except around to our left, where the ground sloped down to nearly a level; but we had three batteries on a hill, which swept the whole front of our lines with an enfilading fire or flank fire. So we were in as strong a position almost as we could have; and in the battles of the 2d and 3d, when the rebels came up the hill to storm our position, we drove them down the hill again with tremendous loss, and held our own position, while they retired to theirs. Our boys sallied out a little way to pick up and bring in the prisoners and the wounded; but we retained our position, and the rebels retained their original position. There was no advance of our lines in any part of the field, that I am aware of.

If, early on the 4th, we had advanced on the broken and dispirited enemy, and attacked him with the same valor with which he had attacked us, which was what our boys were expecting and longing for, I doubt not we should have utterly routed and ruined Lee's whole army; but it may prove that what we have done is for the best: we are all disposed to place the utmost confidence in the skill and prudence of our leader. D. H. Hill, and his troops from North Carolina, are said to have joined Lee: so, if we defeat and destroy the rebels here on the Potomac now, it will be a bigger defeat and destruction than if it had been Lee alone on the 4th. This is a point to be considered, no doubt. Perhaps, if we wait a little while longer, Beauregard's army may be up also, still further to increase the magnitude of our victory. Yours truly,

DUNN BROWNE

Fiske's indictment of the Eleventh Corps, heavily German in make-up, is an accurate enough reflection of the attitude of the army as a whole. Gettysburg proved to be its last service with the Army of the Potomac. That fall the Eleventh and Twelfth corps went west, under Joe Hooker's command, to join the Army of the Cumberland. On this date, as Fiske indicates, Meade had his army arrayed against Lee's forces at the Potomac, in the vicinity of Williamsport; and, that very night, Fiske's worst fears were realized.

The Germans

Jones's Cross-Roads, Md.
July 13 [1863]

Dear Republican: Our boys came back out of Pennsylvania with no very exalted opinion of the German inhabitants of that portion of the state we visited, or of the German regiments in our army of defenders. The people seem to be utterly apathetic as to our great national struggle, and careless of everything but their own property. If each old farmer's hen-roost and cabbage-patch could only be safe, little would he care for the fate of the country, or the success of our army. The German regiments, mostly in the 11th corps, had an excellent opportunity to redeem their soldierly reputation, lost, or at least greatly injured, at Chancellorsville. I am sorry to know that this was only partially accomplished. Many of the regiments in the corps behaved splendidly. (I saw the 17th Connecticut and 33d Massachusetts standing their ground most manfully in a trying position, the other regiments around them running like sheep); but very many just broke and ran shamefully: their officers could not control them in the least, and acknowledged, in my hearing—officers not low in rank, either—that they could not get their men into position behind their stone fence, even after the firing had ceased. I saw some of these regiments when we were under the tremendous shelling of Friday, with the enemy's guns on both sides of us, as a shell came from one direction, spring over the fence to the opposite side, and then hop back again to their original position as a shot came from an opposite battery; and then, too, groups of half a dozen at a time starting up to run to the rear, till one part of the line was left nearly defenseless, while not an enemy was yet in sight in our front.

Still, the Germans, mixed in with our Yankee regiments, make some of our very best soldiers; I never want better or braver men than many of those I have had in my own commands. One German sergeant in a regiment of our brigade, in the late battle, took two of the enemy's colors with his own hand. But, as it is, the reputation of the 11th corps is at a low ebb with their brother-soldiers in the Potomac army; and very undeservedly, too, to the many brave regiments which had always done their duty but have suffered from the ill conduct and want of support of those by their side.

Did I tell you what a sad scene of desolation and desecration the beautiful cemetery at Gettysburg presented after the terrific cannonade of the 3d? what, with its broken and upturned monuments, and shattered railings and ornamental work? what, with its mangled carcasses of horses and men, broken gun-carriages and caissons, and solid shot and bursted shell over all the ground? If I did not tell you, on second thought I will not; for a sight that I am trying to forget out of my own mind entirely I will not seek to impress upon other people's minds.

I have not said a word about the thing you are most interested of all to hear—that is, what we are now doing here on the banks of the Potomac—because I don't want to commit myself, and don't exactly know what are our plans. I judge we have the enemy pretty effectually surrounded so far as this side of the river is concerned. I *hope* we are sending a force up the other side to cut him off, and destroy his trains in Virginia, and then we can afford to wait, and let him attack us, storm, or surrender, whichever pleasant alternative he may choose. But, not being sure that we are getting a force up between him and Richmond, I fear we may wake up some fine morning, when the Potomac subsides a little, to find ourselves closely investing *the place where he was!* It is still raining, and the river is high, Providence favoring us beyond what we had any reason to hope in that respect. We are in good spirits, and full of hope. Wait!

DUNN BROWNE

General Meade had scheduled a movement against Lee's bridge-head north of the Potomac for July 14—against the advice of his corps commanders—but Lee anticipated him and on the night of July 13 crossed his army safely into Virginia on a makeshift bridge. Fiske's mention of the Federals twice crossing and re-crossing "a great river" refers to the Rappahannock, during the Fredericksburg and Chancellorsville campaigns. Predictably, Fiske was appalled at the escape. So was the President. When he learned that Meade had let Lee slip away, Mr. Lincoln bowed his head on his desk and wept in frustration.

An Open Door

Williamsport, Md.
July 14 [1863]

Dear Republican: There is a beautiful door up here, open, and with the appearance of having been passed through lately; a very fine road, with tracks in it, leading away from us; a fine fox-hole, but no fox in it. We made a very skillful and cautious approach, and found, after a few days, that we had irresistibly invested—the place where Lee was. We have made a sure thing of it, and risked not a single mistake, and captured the situation. The Army of the Potomac (Rebel) reached the river, defeated, dispirited, straggling, hungry, and dirty. The Army of the Potomac (Union) arrived in the same vicinity, tired, equally muddy and straggling, perhaps, but flushed with victory and anxious to ruin Lee and finish the war. Providence, to favor us, had sent, and continued to send, heavy rains to make the Potomac unfordable.

First day: Discovered the situation of the enemy; dispatched our vigilant and indomitable cavalry to watch them; heard from the inhabitants that the enemy were getting their trains over the river. Providence still rains upon us and our foes and the Potomac. Second day: We approach within ten miles of the whole circuit of the enemy's outer lines, encamp, and send home word that we are about to "bag" their whole force. Rains still. We throw out, cautiously, strong pickets. Third day: We proceed to contract our lines to within, say, four miles of the enemy; make reconnaissances in force, and come upon the enemy's lines, with some skirmishing; immediately retire a mile and a half, and throw up entrenchments all night. It was in a defensive battle that we conquered at Gettysburg. We accordingly get ready for the enemy's attack now; hear, from various sources, that Lee is crossing the river with trains and artillery; send home another dispatch that we are sure to capture or annihilate the whole force of the enemy. It still continues raining, to retard as much as possible the enemy's bridging and crossing operations. Fourth day: Advance our forces from one-fourth to one-half a mile, and throw up another line of entrenchments; hear that the enemy has crossed over a large part of his forces, and is only holding his lines with a strong rear guard to protect the passage. We immediately telegraph to our friends that Lee cannot possibly escape, and we are sure to destroy or capture his whole force. Cavalry retires to the rear, and we sleep on our arms or in the rifle-pits, awaiting a momentary attack. Rains incessantly. Fifth day: At daybreak we give the word to advance along our whole line. We "move upon the enemy's works." Works are ours. Enemy, sitting on the other side of the river, performing various gyrations with his fingers, thumb on his nose. We contemplate ruefully the nondescript bridge he has contrived out of confiscated timber and canal-boats, which it was "impossible" he could build, or cross upon if built. Rain still continues more violently than ever as a judgment upon us for not improving it as a blessing a few days before.

Nevertheless, although the laugh is rather against us for letting the enemy get away from us so leisurely, it must be allowed that it is no easy thing to keep an army of 50,000 men, occupying a very strong position as Lee did, from crossing a river. Our army crossed a great river twice, in the face of the enemy, without much loss; and twice in retreat, after a defeat, entirely unmolested and unharmed: Whereas we have damaged these fellows considerably in the last of their crossing, capturing prisoners, variously stated at from two to four thousand. Yours truly,

DUNN BROWNE

6

MARKING TIME

At this writing, the Army of the Potomac was crossing the Potomac in continued pursuit of Lee. On July 13 rioting had broken out in New York City to protest the implementation of the military draft. Elements of the Potomac army were sent from Gettysburg to help put down the rioters. Apparently Fiske had seen newspaper reports of blank cartridges being fired at the New York mobs.

In Good Spirits

Harper's Ferry
July 15 [1863]

Dear Republican: Twenty-five miles' march to-day, and after our month's continuous hard work too. So, you see, we are still hard after the enemy, if he did give us the slip yesterday. We mean he shall do some of the "tallest" kind of marching if he succeeds in reaching Richmond at the end of his race; and he won't get there with all his 50,000 men either. They straggle amazingly, and, we think, pretty willingly, as they journey back to beloved Dixie; and the stragglers count for us the way we are journeying now. Our army is in good spirits, as you may well suppose, but *very tired* and knocked up, having done an amount of labor in the past five weeks that must be shared and seen to be appreciated.

I believe the country does, in some measure, appreciate, and is grateful for it. This army "deserves well of the Republic" for the work of these few weeks especially. Let the country have it in remembrance. The empty sham of the rebellion is collapsing fast and finally. Let Northern copperheads beware! We are reading the accounts of such scenes of blood and violence as are taking place in the city of New York to-day with an indignation that scarcely finds words to express itself; and we see who are responsible for these outrages. We are coming home soon, and we shall not fire *blank cartridges* at riotous "friends" who resist the laws, and fill our streets and houses with blood. Yours truly,

DUNN BROWNE

Although Fiske was still temporarily attached to Carroll's brigade, he had continued to monitor events in his regiment (14th Connecticut) and brigade. The exploit of Captain James P. Postles that he relates here, which it is obvious he witnessed himself, took place around the Bliss barn in front of the center of the Union lines at Gettysburg on July 2. Postles was mentioned in the report of his brigade commander, Colonel Thomas A. Smyth, as a "really meritorious officer." Another of those earning Fiske's admiration, Lieutenant John S. Sullivan of the ambulance corps, was praised by the division commander, Brigadier General Alexander Hays, for the "courage and the fearless manner" in which he brought off the wounded under fire.

Pleasant Scenes and Noble Deeds

Bivouac six miles up Loudoun Valley
from Harper's Ferry, July 20 [1863]

CHARGE ON A BLACKBERRY FIELD

Dear Republican: You ought to have seen our corps move into the huge blackberry field, or rather succession of them, last evening after their hot midday march. The habit of military discipline prevailing kept the men in the ranks till they were regularly dismissed, though every tread crushed out the blood of scores, and Uncle Sam's stiff brogans were soaked in (dewberry) gore. But when the orders "Stack arms!" "Rest!" had been given, in an instant, in a nothing of time, in the hundredth part of the "twinkling of a bedpost," the whole battle array was melted away; the glittering lines of stacked arms were all that was left upright in the field, the backs only were visible of a half dozen thousand tired soldiers, who are not wont to turn their backs on the enemy; and as the manna which came from heaven to the Israelites in the wilderness, when the dew rose in the morning, so disappeared this gracious provision of heaven's bounty for our weary boys, and they rose (not very soon) refreshed from their luscious banquet. There were enough and to spare. Fields and hills all around us are black with them—more millions of tiny blackamoors than our army of abolitionists can put out of the way in a week. But we are doing our best; heaped bowls and plates of blackberries for tea and for breakfast; a few black-berries as we went to bed, a few on waking this morning to take the cobwebs out of our mouth and throat (how much better than fiery whisky for that purpose), and now a few more to start on just as we are leaving. It has been a blackberrying on the grandest scale I have attended for a long time.

We are rather leisurely moving up the valley this time, it seems to me, but perhaps as fast as is wise, considering our march-worn men and used-up mules and horses. I have no news for your never-satisfied newspaper maw. You are getting so much and such glorious news from all over the country in these times, that the little items I might give you would most likely be overlooked if sent.

Exploit Of A Hero

To show you that all the gallant and chivalric exploits are not confined to the history of ancient battles, to the knight-errant and feudal times, I am going to tell you of one little incident of the late battle which I know you will thank me for relating, and for the truth of which you may put me down as authority.

There was a huge barn right in the track of that desperate charge of the enemy on the 3d, whose blackened brick walls are doubtless remembered by every visitor of the battle field as one of its most prominent objects. It is the same barn which a part of the 12th New Jersey charged and carried in gallant style on the evening of the 2d, capturing therein 97 prisoners, and at another time two companies of the 14th Connecticut, also with a similar result but not so many prisoners. Indeed it was on the debatable ground between the two armies, and the scene of many a sharp conflict between the advancing and receding pickets, where not a few noble fellows breathed out their lives during the three bloody days. The incident I speak of occurred on the afternoon of the 2d.

The skirmishers were firing very briskly and those of the enemy, heavily reinforced, were pressing our line back. Eight or ten of our boys were holding the barn, but the enemy's line had come up even with it and more, and it was evident that our little party must fall back and let the butternuts gain the advantageous position for harassing us. The colonel in command of the 2d brigade, 3d division, 2d army corps, called for an officer to volunteer to go down to the line and order our boys to fire the barn before retiring. Quick as thought my hero put spurs to his steed (most men would have crawled down on foot to a front where bullets were buzzing as they were there at that time) and dashed down the slope with at least fifty skirmishers practicing on him as a target. Right up to the barn he charged (which I have told you was flush with and even a little beyond the enemy's line of skirmishers), coolly delivered his message, and then turned and rode back to our lines, exposed to a redoubled fire. As the surprise of the rebels at his coming was over, and knowing that he must return the same way, they had time to prepare and to take deliberate aim from all sides. Miraculously not one of the hundred bullets that whistled near him touched either rider or horse. On reaching our lines (though by no means out of range of the balls), he reined his horse round, waved his hat in the air and made a graceful bow to the unseen marksmen, who, I really don't believe were sorry to see him escape unharmed. To make the thing complete, our noble Gen. Hancock and several other generals were at that time passing that part of the lines, saw the gallant deed done, and the general lifted his hat in honor of the brave soldier who at that moment rode up. I have told you the story and now I tell you the name of the hero—Capt. Postles of the 1st Delaware, acting inspector general of the 2d brigade of our division. Many more brave deeds may he live to perform and escape as fortunately.

I heard a practical man say that it was a foolish thing to do; that the captain might as well have effected his object by going down cautiously on foot, &c., &c. Away with such practical notions. The example of such a dashing deed as this and scores of other similar ones I might mention, is of a worth inestimable in an army. It is by such a high spirit of courage, such a scorn of danger, that the tone of an army is to be kept up. I tell you, soldiers in a trying hour will follow such a man as that wherever it is necessary to go, and it is positively necessary sometimes to go into very dangerous places indeed to gain battles.

OTHER BRAVE MEN AND DEEDS

And it is not the combatants alone that improve opportunities for displaying courage. You have seen many incidents narrated of surgeons and of chaplains' coolness and bravery. Be it for me to speak of those qualities in the ambulance corps. Where men are killed and wounded, there must go the officers of the ambulance brigade, and the stretcher carried to bring the poor fellows off the field. And many a time did I see the stretcher carriers fired upon and wounded while bearing away the wounded, even in some instances the wounded rebels. But they did not desist from their humane work, and many a time did I watch anxiously (fearing every moment to see him fall) our ambulance Lieutenant Sullivan (of the 14th Indiana; you see we of the states are mixed up together, brothers in the good cause) as he coolly rode all over the field, sometimes in the thickest of the firing, and away to the front even of our pickets, on his errand of mercy, not satisfied to leave a single suffering man uncared for on the bloody field, and having his black horse at last shot under him, besides many hairbreadth escapes. All honor to such noble fellows wherever they are. I will call names in such case. I am proud to be the feeble chronicler of such incidents; proud to have opportunity to mingle with them as comrades, to grasp their hands in true fraternal friendship, and ever to count them in after life as those who have been tried and not found wanting in times of need. There are rare and precious flowers growing out of the blood-drenched soil of war. I know you will thank me for sending you occasionally a bouquet of them. Yours truly,

DUNN BROWNE

The Army of the Potomac was now back in northern Virginia, moving slowly east of the Blue Ridge while Lee moved in parallel up the Shenandoah Valley. There was no longer any sense of urgency in the Federal camp, as Fiske makes clear in this report of

his first foray into the realm of independent command. "We are rather out of the game now for a few weeks," he told his brother. "We had trumps in our hand but didn't play 'em, & now the cards have got shuffled. . . ."

D. B.'s First Campaign

Bivouac near Bloomfield, Va.
July 21 [1863]

Dear Republican: Modesty leads me to speak of the leading personage in the subjoined military bulletin in the third person, and using only his initials.

REASONS FOR ASSIGNING D. B. A SEPARATE COMMAND

Foray of the enemy on our flank. Rebel lieutenant passes gap in Loudoun Heights, descends in force upon a party of our teamsters who were strayed away (contrary to orders) seizing hay near said gap, captures three of our mule drivers and seven mules, disperses rest, fifty in number (men and mules taken together). Accounts differ as to whether said lieutenant was armed with a pistol or unarmed; also as to the truth or falsity of his (the rebel lieutenant's) statement that he had a party of armed followers in the woods, some of the teamsters asserting that they distinctly saw three or four armed rebels through the trees.

D. B. IS ASSIGNED A SEPARATE COMMAND

In this trying emergency, the general in command of division naturally looks around for an active and efficient officer to take charge of a detachment, rush to the scene of action, investigate the circumstances, repel the enemy or punish him, and recover the prisoners and property if possible. Equally naturally his choice falls upon D. B. "Captain, take a couple of lieutenants and twenty men, go over and attend to this business. Don't go far up the mountain into the woods, for the gap is doubtless held by a force of the enemy's cavalry, and you must not run risks. You can't catch those mounted fellows or the mules, it isn't likely, with your infantry; but we never have any cavalry on hand when they are wanted, and the thing ought to be looked into by somebody." The officer addressed accordingly orders his gallant steed, borrows a revolver (with three chambers loaded), details his forces, and prepares for an instant movement.

ADVANCE MOVEMENT

Having reviewed his troops, made them a spirited address and ordered them to load, D. B. turns his face towards the scene of operations (2 miles distant), advancing in good order, throwing out his cavalry (which consisted of one man from the Q.M. department mounted on a broken-down plug and armed with a carbine) to the front for reconnoitering purposes, riding himself at the head of the column, closely followed by the 2d lieutenant and two of the remaining teamsters to act as guides, and the 1st lieutenant bringing up the rear.

MASTERLY STRATEGIC OPERATIONS

As we approach the point of danger, a detachment of two privates is ordered to take possession of a house on the left and hold it till our return, guarding against surprise from that direction, while our whole right wing (nine men) was deployed to skirmish through a piece of woods on the opposite side, where suspicious movements (of a small dog) had been reported. The main body, reinforced by an additional unarmed teamster, advanced with the utmost steadiness, but with caution, and took possession of the house and barn where the capture had taken place, the owner thereof sitting calmly on his porch as if nothing had happened. Parties are dispatched to search the three houses in the neighborhood and gather together the masculine inhabitants, others to bring in all the horses that could be found, with a view to their confiscation if their owners should be proved secesh. The skirmishers on the right having been called in and a sergeant and three men left as a guard, the commander-in-chief with his two corps commanders and whole available force, consisting of fourteen non-commissioned officers and privates, spreading out his line to a great distance to avoid being flanked by the enemy, proceeds to skirmish up the mountain about three-quarters of a mile, nearly to the crest of the gap. Traces of the missing mules are discovered leading over the gap. But ordering a halt at this stage of operations and calling a council of war of his inferior officers, D. B. decides that his orders and the smallness of his force (although their zeal to press forward is very great) will not allow him to make a farther advance, and with that prudence which united with fiery valor and untiring energy constitutes the perfect military chieftain, orders a retrograde movement to our base of operations, the house and barn aforesaid.

Successful Retreat And Grand Summary Of The Campaign

The horses collected from the vicinity being examined and found to consist of three or four aged mares with colts, two lame work horses, one wall-eyed brute with a swelling on his near hind foot as big as a peck measure, and two or three yearling colts, it was unanimously decided that the owners were good Union men and we should be scarcely justified in any measures of confiscation. We accordingly returned in the same order we came, taking with us the owner of the house and barn where the fracas first occurred (on whose person we found a pass from the rebel lieutenant above referred to) as our single prisoner. The casualties of our command in this expedition were one deserter, who stole a saddle and decamped while we were making our advance up the gap; one man wounded (not dangerously) by falling upon the lock of his musket going over a brook; and one shoe lost from the near fore foot of the hard-trotting horse ridden by the commander-in-chief. All the party, officers and men (including the cavalry), were honorably mentioned in the dispatches; the conduct of the chieftain was approved by the general ordering it; the prisoner was turned over to the provost marshal and after a day's detention discharged—and D. B. returned to his usual round of subordinate duties.

Thus endeth his first separate military campaign.

DUNN BROWNE

Although fringed with irony and cynicism, Captain Fiske's "pressing invitation" to the Union's new conscripts was a sincere appeal to the home front to help finish the job. And Fiske genuinely believed that just then the Confederacy, following Get-

tysburg and Vicksburg and after what he had seen as a prisoner in Richmond, was on its last legs. Those he condemns in the first sentence were New York's Democratic governor Horatio Seymour and his cousin, the Connecticut Copperhead Thomas H. Seymour, and New Yorker Fernando Wood, a particularly notorious Copperhead. The $300 he mentions was the commutation fee for exemption from the draft call. Dunn Browne would soon have a good deal more to say about conscripts and the draft.

Dunn Browne Speaks of and to the Conscripts

Warrenton Junction
July 27, 1863

The Draft And The Drafted

Dear Republican: I see the draft is going forward on the whole perhaps as well as was to be expected throughout the North, seeing you couldn't quite muster up courage and decision enough to hang a couple of Seymours and Fernando Wood as an appropriate preliminary measure. If they had been properly suspended at the outset, say on a brilliantly illuminated gallows, to form a grand closing piece at the fireworks 4th of July night, the draft needn't have been suspended a single day in New York or elsewhere.

Not that I am in favor of a draft myself at this later period of the war. It would have been the most fair and righteous way to have obtained our soldiers in the first place, would have been submitted to quietly, and would have saved the vast sums lavished in extravagant and unequal bounties and the injustice done to those who didn't receive any. But now I foresee many difficulties and much friction in the carrying out of the plan. The difficulty of getting the men into the field will be very great and the loss by desertion large. There will be much ill feeling bred between the old soldiers of the various regiments and the new ones brought in to fill up their ranks. The cry of "conscripts" will be the greeting of the new men from the mischief-makers in our ranks. The old soldiers will want all the promotions, and the new will be and will think themselves entitled to their share. And in many respects it will need the greatest care and prudence on the part of the officers and all concerned to prevent collisions and keep matters smooth and pleasant.

I say this not as a foreboder of evil, but as referring to a practical matter that may, if foreseen, be in a great measure guarded against. There is no good reason why these new recruits should not come joyfully and gratefully to the service of their country in this final and doubtless brief struggle to end the war and establish the authority of the government. Nor any reason why they should not be fraternally welcomed. The hardest of the work is undoubtedly done, even though the contest should yet be considerably prolonged. The power of the rebel lion is broken; its resources nearly exhausted; the success of our armies certain and not far off. The hardships to be endured now are not so great as they have been. The unnecessary annoyances and privations caused by the blunders of green commanders are of course lessened, with the experience acquired. There is the opportunity of doing valuable service to one's country and of getting the glory of finished up the war, of being in at the death of the rebellion. It is the ones that complete the job that get the credit.

A PRESSING INVITATION

Come on then, my brave friends who have hitherto been kept at home by the pressure of other important avocations. Come and spend a few months in getting an experience that will be of the greatest value to you for the whole remainder of your life. Come, editors and professors, merchants, armorers, clergymen, mechanics, farmers, legislators, office holders, lawyers, clerks, and everybody. Save your $300 and wreathe your brow with military laurels; wear Uncle Sam's brilliant uniform, eat his bounteous rations and put his beautiful greenbacks in your pocket. Come out and fall into the ranks with us and get familiar with your facings and your wheelings and your "shoulder arms" and your "charge bayonets." If you do your duty right manfully we'll make you corporals—we'll raise you to the dignity of commissioned officers—yea, you may yet get to be brigadiers if the rebellion be not too hastily crushed. We'll give you, on the whole, a soldierly welcome, and thank you for filling our thinned ranks, and the memory of our brave brothers who have fallen on many bloody fields will endear to us those who stand in their places. You will bring to us the fragrance of home and friends, the fresh zeal of northern patriotism and courage; and we will lend to you the benefit of our experience and the steady valor and confidence acquired and proved on many battle fields. You can make us wearied veterans twice as valuable by imparting to us your ardor, and we can make you twice as valuable by imparting to you our steadiness and experience. And we'll soon go home together, rejoicing in a saved country, found to be tenfold more prosperous than ever before, with a flag waving over our heads that henceforth neither home traitors nor foreign foes shall dare insult, and a 4th of July to celebrate on which children and children's children shall name us with the same honor that we have been accustomed to name the glorious fathers of our republic. Yes, come on, even copperheads, and if there is the least spark of true patriotic life left in your wretched breasts, we'll kindle it with the snap of percussion caps into a healthy flame, and brace up your system with the wholesome tonic of whistling bullets and bursting shells till we can send you home recovered and in your right minds; with a leg or an arm less than now, perhaps, but what there is left at least loyal, and not a nuisance and a disgrace to the community.

A WORD ABOUT ARMY MATTERS

I haven't any special army news for you. We have now succeeded, in three weeks' hard, incessant labor, such marching and countermarching as no army during the war has done before, in losing all the advantage in position and other respects that we had over the enemy on the 4th of July. We are not rusting away in inaction, that is some comfort. We are here, there and everywhere, putting ourselves in the way of being attacked by the enemy. If he will only be fool enough to attack us, as at Gettysburg, we shall utterly destroy him, that is if he continues to attack us long enough and often enough. Let us hope he will.

Great is Meade. But the Napoleon hasn't risen yet. We make gods of our generals or curse them as fools. Gen. Meade is a good general. The army is satisfied with him on the whole, thinks that he has undoubtedly erred on the side of too much caution ever since Gettysburg, but believes in him as a competent, faithful, patriotic officer, of very fair abilities and good moral character, which is a great deal to expect of a general—a very great deal. Don't let us be unreasonable. Yours truly,

DUNN BROWNE

In these weeks after Gettysburg, Captain Fiske was serving in a somewhat ambiguous position attached to Carroll's brigade of the Second Corps. Colonel Carroll himself and two of his regiments had been sent to New York to put down the draft rioting, and the remainder of the brigade was temporarily under a cavalry colonel, Joseph Snider. In Fiske's account here of his experience of court martial, his unnamed accuser was almost surely Colonel Snider, an outsider and by implication a martinet who was (by the testimony of Fiske's witnesses) rather neglectful of duty himself.

Court-Martialed

Elkton, Va.
August 4, 1863

A NEW EXPERIENCE

Dear Republican: I thought I had been through nearly all the varying experiences of military life, but there was one thing that had been omitted, sure enough, come to have it brought to my mind. Which omission, I am able now to inform you, has been supplied. I had been on picket and in skirmishes; in battles great and small; in all sorts of marches and bivouacs and encampments; on duty on foot and in the saddle; in the regular line, and on staff and various detached service among friends and a prisoner in the hands of the enemy. But I had never been court-martialed.

I had, to be sure, been detailed to sit as a member of such a body; I had acted in the capacity of witness before such an august assembly, but in the most interesting character of all, that of the accused party, I had never had opportunity to appear. In future I need not plead ignorance of the feelings of a person in such a position. And say what you please about the matter, dear Republican, one can enter into the real spirit of a court or trial of any kind in no other capacity whatever as he can in that of prisoner at the bar. Talk of being a judge or a juryman or a solicitor for the plaintiff or defendant, or a spectator, or a witness, or a sheriff. Pooh! All these parts together are nothing to that of the prisoner at the bar. He is the principal personage in the drama, around whom the interest must center, on whom the crisis of the plot must hinge. The next time you are listening to the eloquence of some distinguished counsel, and admiring his exquisite taste and influence with the jury, just try to realize your emotions if your life or fortune or reputation hung upon his eloquent lips. The next time you see the judge put on his black cap and long face to sentence a prisoner, imagine that you are the doomed individual for whose especial benefit the ceremony in question is to be gone through with. And the next time you see an anxious, crowded court-room awaiting the verdict of a jury, consider in what spirit you would enter into the scene were yours the verdict on which they were deliberating. However it may be with you, dear Republican, and many other virtuous people, I acknowledge henceforth to be able to have a very lively sympathy for the man who is on the wrong side of the bar in a criminal court.

COURTS MARTIAL IN GENERAL

However, if you infer from these remarks that there is any great resemblance between a court of *justice* and a court martial you will have a very erroneous notion. Why, just think of the preposterousness of such an idea. Take a half dozen officers, who have been marching all day, perhaps, and want to rest their weary bones or write a hasty letter to wives and sweethearts at night, dragged into a little hot tent and obliged to sit till midnight, hearing the details of some frivolous case of a man who went to fill his canteen without orders, or an officer who neglected to make his report at the proper hour, or on the right-sized sheets of paper—details of a case in which all the questions and answers of the witnesses must be in writing, and where everything is conducted in the slowest and most old fogyish style. Why, who could be expected to decide right, to do justice, or even to keep awake, acting on such a court? Of course, a court martial on a serious case, convened with propriety and conducted with its appropriate dignities and formalities, is a respectable, a venerable institution, and perhaps as apt to do justice as any court in the world. But the way we have had them in our army of late, the multiplying of cases (often of the slightest possible consequence) before them, the catching a few occasional spare moments for their sitting between the marches, and the very inadequate consideration able to be afforded to the cases tried, certainly tend to make the whole thing seem a farce to a man with a naturally rather strong sense of the ludicrous in his composition.

THE COURT MARTIAL IN PARTICULAR

For myself (not to speak more lightly than I can help of what should be a serious matter), after remaining in arrest some days, and after three times appearing with my witnesses at times and places appointed to find the trial postponed, at last one very rainy evening, when I had about concluded the whole thing was an *ignis-fatuus* destined to elude forever my eager grasp, I caught it sure enough in the judge advocate's little tent. Five tired officers had been gotten together and the case came on, while my witnesses, in rubber overcoats, stood outside in the rain till they were wanted. The court and judge advocate were duly sworn "to well and truly try"; the charge and its specification, "neglect of duty in not preventing the straggling of such division of the army on such a march of five days," was duly read, and the accused entered his plea of "not guilty." Then the single witness for the United States (who was also the one who preferred the charges) gives in his evidence that he did not see the defendant using any efforts to prevent straggling during the whole march of five days, although he had himself issued to him the most stringent orders to that effect, and the case for the prosecution closed.

Then the witnesses for the defendant, two of whom, however, had ingloriously "skedaddled" back to their quarters out of the rain, testified that the probable reason why the prosecutor had not seen efforts on the part of the accused to keep the men in their places, was that he was himself not there to see, none of them having seen him along the column in more than one instance during the five days; also, that the straggling of the command was comparatively very small, and caused by the excessive and needlessly rapid marching, the exhausted soldiers falling out in spite of efforts to keep up. Then a few words from the defendant, interrupted by the yawnings of the court, and the case was closed, the trial over, and the prisoner very soon sleeping in his own tent the sleep of conscious innocence, uneasy only from the fear that as several guilty persons had been recently acquitted, he might be the other thing, or, if acquitted, might be considered on that account guilty. But when a few more days had rolled away, a big document came down from headquarters, informing your humble correspondent that the honorable court had found nothing against him, unless it *were* an acquittal, and so ordered his release from arrest. So endeth this episode of his career.

REFLECTIONS OF THE ACQUITTED

Am I foolish to tell you of all these little personal matters? Not at all. Am not I a member of your family, dear Father Republican? And shall not the child prattle in the ears of his fond *parients* of all his daily experiences, even to the whippings he gets at school? Oughtn't I to be ashamed to acknowledge having appeared on a criminal charge before the authorities of my country? Not at all. Isn't it all a part of the experience, a part of the things for which we put down our names. Shall we receive good at the hands of our lesser governmental Providence, and shall we not receive evil also? Is it not through much tribulation, some starvation, and a vast deal of vexation that we shall enter into the rewards and honors that our good Uncle Samuel hath to bestow? Must we not lose legs if we would entitle ourselves to pensions? If we get promotion from his paternal hand, shall we grumble if there be mingled therewith an occasional court martial?

Let us be reasonable, my friends, whatever we are, and not allow any unworthy prejudices to get possession of our minds. "But a patriot-soldier's honor ought ever to be bright as his glittering sword, and his reputation above the breath of suspicion." That looks very well in print, to be sure. But as a matter of plain fact, the brightest sword is apt to get rusty at times, if you are not careful to wipe off the blood with your pocket handkerchief every time you stick a rebel; and as for reputation, who ever was above suspicion? A person may be so low and small as to be beneath suspicion, but above it never till he gets above this world and all that is therein. The great and pure father of his country was not above suspicion. Nay, the blessed Redeemer of mankind was not himself above suspicion. So it is all nonsense to use that kind of talk. A mean man can suspect anybody. The more virtuous, the more apt to be suspected. With which scraps of morality, commending them to your kind attention, and asking you to be as easy with me as the court martial has been, and honorably acquit me from all charges of neglect of duty to you-ward, I remain, very respectfully, your obedient servant,

DUNN BROWNE

This is Samuel Fiske at his thoughtful, amusing, perceptive best. As the Republican's *editor noted, Dunn Browne does indeed try his "mental range" here, and the* Republican's *readers were no doubt the wiser for it. With the army marking time, Fiske had found leisure to catch up on his reading—including notices of John Hanning Speke's book on his exploration (with James Grant) of the Nile; the state of silver mining in the West; and the political commentary of Warrington, the nom de plume of the Boston correspondent for the* Republican. *In a private letter, Fiske explained that he was boarding with a local family, "where there are three pretty young ladies, bitterly secesh, but very polite & they don't poison our tea." He expands on this arrangement in his letter of August 20.*

Dunn Browne Writes the Blues Away

Camp near Elk Run, Va.
August 4, 1863

METEORS AND PRETTY WOMEN

Dear Republican: If you should notice anything brilliant in my style of writing of late, you may attribute it to the inspiration of the shooting stars that have abounded in the heaven of these latitudes for a little while back; also, perhaps, in some measure to the sparkling conversation of three pretty secesh young ladies with whom I dine every day. (You needn't mention to my wife, though, this latter circumstance.) I was riding along our eleven-mile line of pickets the other night, when the meteoric shower was so profuse that I involuntarily longed for an umbrella to shed it off from me. On the right, on the left, in front and in the rear, down came the streaming rockets through the sky till I could have imagined the enemy shelling us and my ears grown deaf to the noise of the explosions; till it actually seemed as if the next sky-missile would hit me. I'd been under all sorts of musketry fire, and whatever infernal contrivances are belched forth from the mouths of cannon, but it did seem a little odd to get into the center of such a lively discharge of shooting stars. I wonder if anything like this is alluded to in that Scripture passage in the song of Deborah, "The stars in their courses fought against Sisera." They all struck pretty wide of their mark though in my case, and I suspect must have been random shots most of them, perhaps just Dame Nature trying her guns a little to get their range.

Dunn Tries His Mental Range

But however this may have been, as I said above, these heavenly spectacles may have made me a trifle meteoric in my style. And until this tendency has had time to subside, you must give me a good deal of latitude in my subjects and allow me to be somewhat erratic in the treatment of them. I shall not confine myself to the draft. You needn't expect me to give a full *resume* of Uncle Sam's system of courts-martial. Perhaps I shall leave for a time this low, scorched Virginia soil entirely, and all thought of the small contest between Meade and Lee, and take my flight through higher regions, liable to burst out upon your astonished view from any part of the horizon of science, literature, or philosophy. What should you say to a geographical paper one week, showing the reasons for supposing Captains Speke and Grant entirely mistaken in their views about the sources of the Nile, and then in the next number a serio-comic political rhyme, resembling (in its spelling) James Russell Lowell, or a sharp, bitter, politico-gossipy literary letter like one of your Warrington's?

Suppose I give you a short political tract upon the extension of the French "liberty of suffrage" to regenerated Mexico; closely followed by a few philosophical observations upon the prospects of the Washoe silver mines, as affected by Secretary Chase's manufactory of greenbacks. Suppose I descend to a little trifling with puns and conundrums, commencing with one upon our delightful situation here along the banks of the Rappahannock, with a flowery lea upon one bank and a grassy mead upon the other.

By the way, can it be true, dear Republican, that we are to have yet another change of commanders in the Army of the Potomac? Is one battle apiece all that our commanders are any of them to be allowed to fight? Ah, well, my turn is coming then all the sooner, and if my battle happens to be the last one, then I'm the next president to a dead certainty. Is there any little fat Liverpool consulate, or New York collectorship you could be prevailed upon to accept, patriotic Republican? Meantime I am going to ask the secretary of war for permission to recruit my company from the deposed major generals. There are just enough of them (with a few conscripts that have recently arrived) to bring my number up to the maximum. After I had drilled them a little no doubt they would do good service: only I'd have to be pretty careful in distributing them into groups for tent-mates, to preserve the harmony which I always insist upon in my little military family.

How Nature Covers Up Battle Fields

Did I tell you ever, among the affecting little things one is always seeing in these shifting war times, how I saw on the Second Bull Run battle field, pretty, pure delicate flowers growing out of emptied ammunition boxes, a fine rose thrusting up its graceful head through the head of a Union drum, which doubtless sounded its last charge (or retreat as the case may have been) in that battle, and a cunning scarlet verbena peeping out of a fragment of burst shell in which strange cup it had been planted? Wasn't that peace growing out of war? Even so shall the graceful and the beautiful ever grow out of the horrid and terrible things that transpire in this changing but ever advancing world. Nature covers even battle ground soon with verdure and bloom. Peace and plenty soon spring up in the track of devastating campaigns, and all things in nature and in society shall work out the progress of mankind and the harmony of God's great designs.

The Meteor Theory Again

Are the points of this epistle somewhat miscellaneous and unconnected? They are all perfectly consistent, I believe, on the meteoric theory advanced at the outset. Have I written considerable nonsense? "Am I volatile?" as little Miss Moucher asks in "David Copperfield." Well, it is owing to the heat, which is enough to evaporate anything. If you will believe me, this very letter, kept until midwinter or suffered to condense a few hours in an ice-house, would settle down into a few lines of very good sense. Perhaps as a beverage, though, it will be better to drink it before the effervescence subsides. No, really, Mr. Editor, I had a good many weighty things on my mind to-night, was a little vexed and worried, and have been trying to write myself into good spirits, "regardless of expense," to you and your readers. Good night. I think I can sleep. There goes another meteor. Yours truly,

Dunn Browne

Conscription in the North, it has been said, raised more discontent than soldiers. Drafted men, if they passed the physical (and if they reported at all), might hire substitutes to go to war for them, or pay the $300 commutation fee exempting them from that call. Just seven percent of those called actually served. The evils of the system were manifest, and Fiske's accounting of it, drawn from newspapers, was not exaggerated. To reduce the draft quotas, communities and states (and the federal government) offered bounties to volunteers, all too often resulting in a soldier of the sort Fiske describes so vividly.

The Draft and the Drafted

Bivouac near Elkton, Va.
August 8, 1863

Dear Republican: Do you want to know what the men of the great, free North seem to me to be now saying in loudest, most emphatic voice to us poor fellows in the army? "You are a set of mean, contemptible scoundrels, not fit to be associated with decent people. We have a perfect horror of your society. Far from accepting the president's very general and pressing invitation to join your ranks and work by your side for a time, we will pay any sum of money, we will try all sorts of excuses and evasions, yes, will descend to the meanest tricks to keep out of your hateful society. We hold nobody to be your proper companions but shoulder-hitters, plug-uglies, dead rabbits and all manner of vile vagabonds, the refuse of our cities, the ruffians from our penitentiaries, whom we are accordingly caressing, coaxing, and bribing to go to you in our places. Nay, you are such a nuisance that we won't even leave our indignation to be expressed by mere individual acts toward you. We will combine our efforts to spite you and isolate you. We will put our heads together as communities, we will meet in our public capacity and vote as towns and cities, to turn our backs upon you, to help men who would otherwise go to you to stay away and leave you alone. We'll take advantage of your absence to lay taxes on your property to raise money to keep decent people away from you and (if any must go) to buy murderers, thieves and other villains to go to you in their places, men who will be more likely to cut your throats than those of the enemy."

And is this what you really think of us, oh dearly-beloved people of New England, after whom our hearts yearn with an unspeakable affection, thoughts of whom keep up our spirits in long and toilsome marches, visions of whose dear faces comfort us in every hardship and amidst wounds and even in the agonies of death? Are our ranks, thinned so sorely by disease, wounds and death, only fit to be filled up by ruffians imported by your money from the dens of New York? Shall our battle flags, bearing which our best and bravest have gone down on fields of glory, and whose staffs are yet stained with the blood of their dying grasp, be left to the protection of mercenary wretches who care neither for country or reputations, who have sold themselves to you only in the hope of deserting to sell over again in endless succession, and who reach the field only because pistols and bayonets have stood between them and flight?

But putting us, your brothers in the army, out of the account, how are you treating your country, your own government, the embodiment of *your own* royal sovereignty? As an enemy whose interests are hostile to yours, with whom you are to drive sharp bargains, who is to be outwitted in every possible way! You ought to volunteer in numbers more than enough to fill our ranks now so speedily as to make the shortest kind of work with this hollow and collapsing rebellion, which nothing but your unpatriotic apathy can keep alive three months longer. But you refuse even to come where the fairest of all possible methods of designating citizens for defense has pointed you out and called you to the field. Your country, all that in our institutions which is most hallowed with sacred associations, which claims your truest allegiance, calls for one grand, indispensable, personal effort from you, and you respond with a handful of paltry greenbacks. The birthright you have boasted of all your life, in the face of all the nations, is in peril, and you grumblingly offer $300 to a Five Points' pimp and gambler to rush in and save it for you.

I am ashamed to read, in your newspapers, an account of the draft in any place and its lame and impotent conclusion. A hundred draw prizes in the lottery of glory and patriotism. Sixty-five of them obtain exemption on account of some physical disability, and the variety of diseases invented for the occasion exhausts the medical vocabulary and gives more desert of praise to the doctors for ingenuity than for patriotism. Twenty-one pay over their undesired tribute of $300 into Uncle Sam's treasury. Eight furnish substitutes, and five patriotically answer the call in their own persons. A hundred of those thus actually enrolled into the military service of their country start for the place of rendezvous. Fifteen mysteriously disappear before reaching the point in their state designated for that purpose. Twenty break out of their bounds and escape before the details leave to join their respective regiments. Seven are killed or wounded in attempts to do and go likewise. Eight of the remainder are claimed as deserters from some regiments already in the field, or some other rendezvous of recruits. Again, taking one hundred of these last remainders for a third "attention," to speak homeopathically, they embark in a steamer for the seat of war. Fifty-five of them are among the missing at the port where they are landed. Eighteen more elude the vigilance of their guards, or are killed and wounded as above, before they reach the field, and the rest—are they not indeed veterans already to have passed through so much before they have once put musket to shoulder?

Faugh! Is this the way in which the loyal people of the North show their patriotism, while the disloyal engage in riots and bloodshed in open resistance to the government? Is this the spirit in which you pay the price demanded for all that you hold dear in your country's civil and political institutions? Is this the opinion you deliberately wish to express of us, your own neighbors and friends, whom you sent out at the beginning of the war with your prayers and blessings? If so, then please stop talking about our victories. Don't be heaping praises on the courage and devotion of your armies. Don't speak of the glory of the old flag, the sacredness of our cause, or the value of our institutions. It appears that they are altogether worth—a begrudged and reluctant three hundred dollars.

Here's to the flag of our Union! Long may it wave. And if three hundred dollars will carry it deep into the ranks of the foe, here's your money. Down with this cursed rebellion, with cannon, musket and bayonet. And if three hundred dollars will send a bayonet, there are the greenbacks. To arms, to arms, my countrymen! All you hold most dear is in jeopardy. Rush to the rescue. Take with you my blessing and—this small roll of $300 in treasury notes.

I have done, my dear Republican, I can't pursue the subject any farther. What need? I've performed my example in simple addition, and the sum total is—$300. Yours affectionately,

DUNN BROWNE

Perhaps no more eloquent appeal to patriotism issued from the seat of the war to the home front than this, and perhaps none reached a wider audience. The Springfield Republican *liked to think of itself as the voice, or conscience, of New England, and Samuel Fiske here borrowed that voice for his secular sermon. The eminent Edward Everett, of course, would deliver the other address at Gettysburg in November. In his references to the ancients, Fiske meant the legendary Roman hero Marcus Curtius, who leaped into the chasm in the Forum, sealing the fissure; Cornelia's jewels were her two sons. His targeting of college profes-*

sors was pointed—he told his brother that four professors at Amherst, his alma mater, had been drafted, "& I suppose they will pay their $300 & discharge their duty to their country in that cheap & quick method." Again, Fiske is basing his appeal in part on his belief that the rebellion was in near collapse, needing but one more finishing blow.

Enlarging Further on the Draft

Camp near Elk Run, Va.
Aug. 12, 1863

MR. EVERETT'S PATRIOTISM DISCUSSED

Dear Republican: I noticed the following extract from the Boston Journal, somewhere lately, in reference to the appearance of Hon. Edward Everett with his two sons, both of whom had been drafted, before the board of enrollment of his district:

"Mr. Everett, with the manly patriotism which has distinguished his course since the commencement of this war, would not claim exemption for his sons—*except by the payment of commutation money.*"

And the Journal proceeds to speak of this as a "significant act, proving that Mr. Everett fully meets every responsibility growing out of the war for the Constitution and the Union." Whether the fact concerning Mr. Everett and his (two) responsibilities be as stated I haven't the slightest idea. But the question occurred to me that if this was a striking example of a patriot's coming fully up to "every responsibility growing out of the war, &c.," what would the Journal speak of as a mild, moderate, praiseworthy but not brilliant instance of meeting such responsibility? Would getting an exemption certificate for "myopia" (I have not my dictionary with me and am not certain of the spelling and haven't the slightest idea of the meaning of that recently conscripted medical term) meet the Journal's views of the case suggested?

If the (repeated) course of Mr. Everett in the case be an instance of exalted patriotism worthy of record among the noble examples of history, worthy of the honored governor, senator, foreign minister and pre-eminent eulogist of Washington, I was wondering what might be taken as the standard of duty for the ordinary, every-day rank-and-file patriots who haven't even risen to be writers for the New York Ledger? I should judge skedaddling to Canada would be about the "figure," wouldn't it? Shades of the ancient Romans and Greeks! I suppose Quintus Curtius, if he had lived in these times, instead of plunging with his gallant steed into the yawning gulf, would have pitched in a bag of brazen asses and—avoided the draft. I suppose Cornelia, the mother of the Gracchi, would have clasped her "jewels" to her breast and sent out to the defense a couple of jewels from the Emerald Isle as substitutes!

If a citizen worth half a million of dollars, more or less, and many millions of reputation and position and honorable influence, is worthy of especial mention for patriotism because he didn't, perhaps, instigate his sons to take the underground railroad for the British provinces, but advised them to come down with their $300, and came along personally to see them do it, or even it may be in a burst of paternal generosity footed the bill for them out of his own pocket, why, when I should suppose—however, it don't make much difference what I suppose. I don't live anywhere near the great hub of the universe, am in fact nothing more than a fly lighted on one of the felloes. And this army life, short rations and gunpowdery atmosphere may tend to confuse one's notions of patriotism, more or less.

The Opportunity Of Folks At Home

But seriously, my dear friends at home, you have been accusing us of the army of losing several glorious opportunities of overthrowing our enemies, and I think justly. We have lost several. But who is losing this opportunity now before us? We have wasted a good deal of time. Who is wasting these most precious days of all, when the enemy is exhausting his last desperate energies in preparation for one more gigantic struggle? We might have crushed Lee's army on the 4th day of July, you say. So do I. But it would have been a pretty serious responsibility to have ordered an advance against the enemy's strong position that morning, nevertheless, for Meade's army all told numbered just about 48,000 men for duty on that morning's report. And they had been fighting tremendously for three days, after one of the most fatiguing marches an army ever made and were almost entirely out of provisions. Shall not flesh and blood have a little allowance made in their behalf? We ought to have destroyed our foe at Williamsport. Yes, we ought. We did lose an opportunity there; but if you had been along those crests and seen the lines of works we ought to have stormed, and knew that our numbers were scarcely equal to Lee's, perhaps you would have lost that opportunity by an equally cautious approach. But however it has been with our blunders and mistakes in driving Lee back into Virginia instead of capturing him altogether, in only beating and not destroying him, and however much better you would have done in our places—the simple fact is now, that we cannot wisely advance upon the enemy in his own country with our present forces, and if you do not come to our help, and speedily, then it is you and not we that are losing the noble opportunity of striking the final crushing blow at the rebellion.

A General Exhortation

Come on nobly, self-sacrificingly, taking your country's call as to yourselves personally, and a few short months must accomplish the work in hand. Take the call as one upon your pockets, or as not meaning you but somebody you can buy and send on in your place, and who perhaps will occupy the service of one good man as a guard over him while he is with us, and finally be shot as a deserter, and it may be the Boston Journal will consider you as "patriotically meeting every responsibility growing out of the war for the Union," but it doesn't appear to us out here in that light.

We must see some of the best class of our citizens answering the draft in their own persons, some who find it very inconvenient indeed to leave their homes and business, some who have excellent reasons for not coming, or else the draft is a failure, the war indefinitely prolonged, or perhaps even dishonorably ended. And that, too, when the work is so nearly done, when such a small effort, compared with those the country has already repeatedly put forth, would surely soon give us an honorable peace.

And this is your own law you are annulling. Talk about the

arbitrary enforcement of a hated conscription act! Why, it was your own chosen representatives that passed it, and with public opinion overwhelmingly in its favor. It is your own chosen way of designating who should go to the field to serve your country. It is your own deliberately formed and expressed will you are nullifying, your own sovereignty you are abdicating and resisting, your own institutions you are periling, your own homes you are refusing to defend, your own brothers you are leaving unsupported in the field. The conscript wheel, turning out your name among the favored ones, is just exactly the voice of God and of your country saying to you, "Thou are the man!" and the "thou" is a personal pronoun, a *very* personal pronoun under the circumstances, and doesn't mean Michael O'Callaghan from a "substitute" office in New York, doesn't mean a bit of your land sold or a subscription paper circulated among your friends to raise $300; but it means—you.

And the call to you is a call not to a disgrace and burden, but to a glorious privilege and the exercise of your birth-right; to the noblest service you have ever had opportunity to engage in, or ever will have while your life lasts! Let the professors of our colleges who have thus been providentially selected leave their Greek roots and fossil footprints, drop tropes and metaphors and take up pistol, sword and bayonet for a time. Even though their classes should be left untaught, they would be teaching larger classes better lessons; they would make all colleges evermore more honorable and the cause of liberal learning more sacred. Let bar and pulpit and legislative hall send forth their brightest ornaments. No decorations too bright or costly to adorn the arch of our country's liberties. Let the sons of an Everett or any of our most honored names go out as cheerfully as our poorest artisans or laborers, and the blood that has coursed through the veins of hundreds of venerated ancestors be poured forth as freely as water, as indeed it has already been on scores of battle fields; and the work is accomplished. Let the draft be the occasion of a noble and manly volunteering; accept it as the call of God and your country to glorious, enviable service—and the end is indeed near, sure, triumphant. God grant it. Yours truly,

DUNN BROWNE

To this point, Fiske's complaints about the Northern conscription plan had been largely theoretical and speculative, although very perceptive. Here he has actual evidence of its workings, seen with his own eyes, and his report is devastating. To be sure, his sampling is small, consisting of the substitutes sent to the 14th Connecticut, but his statistics were probably typical. Some 74,000 substitutes were hired for the Northern armies, and overall their soldierly qualities were abysmal. Fiske again takes aim at New York governor Horatio Seymour, who during the recent draft rioting had addressed the city's disaffected as "my friends." This same issue of the Republican *carried notice of a New York City appropriation of $3 million to be paid indigent drafted men, who might use their $300 to hire a substitute.*

Dunn Browne Indignant About Substitutes

Camp near Elk Run, Va.
Aug. 17, 1863

Dear Republican: Rode up to see my regiment a day or two since. Being an inspector, shall I report to you on one point? The first thing I heard on dismounting was, "Only ten gone since last roll call." "Ten what?" do you inquire? No, dear Republican, you are not so dull as that question would imply, not even in dog-days. You know that "ten conscripts" were meant, the "substitutes" rather. Three thousand dollars worth of New England's purchased heroes had vanished within the two hours previous to my arrival; $18,000 worth in the three days previous. Sixty out of two hundred and ten in one regiment, and the ratio increasing constantly. The most of the missing are in New York I presume by this time and ready for another campaign equally short and remunerative with the one they have brought just now successfully to a close. One of them boasted that he had already made $1800 in the substitute business. Several others had sold themselves twice. Another who had just gambled away the most of the $300 that constituted his prize, in order to get himself in funds again (temporarily till the next sale), stole $75 which one of our good boys had just had paid him, on the night he left. Three hundred passed our headquarters last night—all substitutes—at

least one-third of them scoundrels who had been engaged in the
New York riots, and found it convenient to retire a little while
into the country, took the $300 to pay their expenses, and ex-
pect to be back to their old haunts as soon as Gov. Seymour
has hushed up that little affair between his "friends" and the
authorities.

Some of them won't go back. Two were killed and several
wounded on their way here from the station, seeking to break
guard. We can, probably, by letting the enemy go unwatched,
and turning our whole attention to these our northern friends,
be able to catch some of them as they are deserting, and by
shooting save ourselves from any further trouble from those particular individuals. But our patriotic brethren at home will soon
supply their places for us with equally valuable materials for our
armies. Still a better plan would be, as soon as the substitutes
are regularly accepted and mustered into the United States service, to send them to the several state penitentiaries for three
years or during the war, as they could be guarded more cheaply
and safely there than here, and our army will be likely to have as
much other business on hand as we can attend to, without the
extra duty of guarding your criminals.

I see some of the northern newspapers are blaming the drafted
men who pay the $300 commutation money and praising the
patriotic ones who furnish substitutes instead. This is a great
mistake so far as we can judge by what substitutes have already
arrived. The $300 that the drafted patriot pays over to the gov-
ernment doesn't in itself damage the country any; though it isn't
a man, yet it isn't a murderer or rioter. Lock it up in a safe and
it won't run away. The ruffian who comes to make good the place
of the citizen, on the contrary, does more damage to the country
and the government and the cause than an armed rebel, on the
average. Let us hope, therefore, my dear friends, who can't think
of coming in person to strike one final blow at the rebellion, in
accordance with a law that you yourselves made and designated
in the fairest of all possible ways—let us hope that you will pay
over the money instead of the other thing. Especially in those of
our own towns which have voted to raise money (partly by taxes
on *our* property) to buy substitutes for those who are indisposed
to come and help us—let our voice at least be heard in this—that
you will give our money to the government and not send us with

it that which we can make no use of except by hanging or shooting. Please don't make us even in the most indirect way responsible for these fellows. Not that we will object to your sending us
substitutes, if you will take men that you know and that can be
trusted. Not that we will object if you will warrant them for a
year, as is usually done with any purchased article. You make a
carriage or a clock for me. You expect to warrant it to run a year.
Why not warrant your soldier not to run for the same time? And
bind yourself to come in his place if he skedaddles? You wouldn't
want your name on an article of merchandise or manufacture
that was a cheat or an imposition. Do you want your name to be
represented in this great transaction, whose object is to preserve
your liberties and institutions, by a man who comes to desert
and whose best possible use to his country is to hang him? It is
just the simple fact, and within the truth, that a large portion of
those who have yet arrived as substitutes for conscripts are of
this class, and that *you had good reason to know them to be so*
before they came, and did put them under the strictest kind of a
guard to keep them from plundering your towns and houses, before you sent them on to be let loose among us *with arms in their
hands*.

So here are our forces reduced to mere skeletons of military
organizations—the war almost finished, so that one-fourth of the
men asked for by the government would enable us to move on to
decisive and final victory before winter—and the whole country,
even patriotic New England, so far as at present appears, is just
forming itself into one vast mutual insurance company against
the government which is only their own agent and representative—one grand, ingenious combination to prolong the war, encourage the rebels, and leave the armies of their brethren to
disgrace. Is it the same North that spoke when Sumter fell? now,
just as it is ready to fall again, back into our hands? Yours truly,

DUNN BROWNE

*Sweet reason—or perhaps it was hope—replaces indignation in
this letter, written after a day's reflection on the first results of
conscription that Captain Fiske had seen arrive in camp. Describing the draft law as essentially "a fair law, as fair as can well be*

*devised," must have caused Fiske no little pain to write; surely
he saw the law, and especially its various evasions, differently.
His hope of appealing to the better nature of drafted men—do the
right thing rather than hire a substitute or buy your way out of
your obligation—must have struck him privately as a forlorn
hope. Congress would repeal the $300 commutation "blood
money" in July 1864, but the growing bounties paid drafted men
to volunteer soon produced uncounted "bounty jumpers" every
bit as notorious as the skedaddling substitutes.*

The Draft Still Haunts Dunn Browne

Camp near Elk Run, Va.
Aug. 18, 1863

THE PEOPLE DID NOT COUNT THE COST

Dear Republican: There are reasons for most things, though
women and diplomatists don't always give the true ones. There
is a reason doubtless for the change of countenance of the northern people towards this war we are waging. A reason which
doesn't involve a real change of mind or principle. The people
have not lost their patriotism. They still cherish the Union and
the Constitution. They still desire sincerely the overthrow of
Davis and his whole rebellious dynasty. But they had not counted
the whole cost beforehand of a long war. They find it especially
hard to make allowance for the waste of war. They know they
have furnished over and over again men and materials enough,
under proper management, to have brought the war to a successful close. And the cost of experience, of learning how to do
things, the cost of schooling, they hadn't taken into account.
That it would take from ten to thirty thousand lives and unnum-
bered millions of money to make a test of the qualities of a major
general and find out that he wouldn't answer the purpose; that
whole armies must be squandered in attacking the enemy in
wrong places and ways, in order to find out the right ones; these
were matters they didn't consider beforehand. That when the
right way did appear, plain as the nose on a man's face, their
stupid official servants would often refuse to walk in it; that in-

stead of sharpening the ax of vengeance against the public foe they would oft-times be grinding their own little private axes; be scheming for places and spoils in some coming political campaign, instead of carrying out energetically the military campaign in hand; these are thoughts that didn't enter into the innocent people's noodle.

And now they have allowed themselves to get into a sort of apparent opposition to those who are only their own representatives and the cause which is their own cause and in fact as dear as ever to their hearts. They have forgotten that an act of conscription, the enforcement of which must, from the very nature of the case, be always unpopular, is in fact their own act; and instead of cordially acquiescing in it as under the circumstances indispensable, are exercising their best ingenuity in evading the provisions and rendering it utterly null and void. Our inveterate, incurable habit of boasting has also worked to the same end of wearying the people. That which has been promised over and over again so confidently and has not been performed, they will not believe in now that it is really approaching so near.

WILL THIS APATHY CONTINUE?

I cannot believe that this present apparent apathy of the people to the issue of a war in which they have sacrificed so much is going to continue; that they are going to let the results of the struggle in which they have poured out such oceans of treasure and blood escape them at the last moment, when one more good blow would finish the work. I do not believe the people really want this same conscript law to fall through. They are intelligent enough to know that it is now our only hope of getting sufficient troops soon enough for our purpose; that it is essentially a fair law, as fair as can well be devised, erring only on the side of being too easy, and especially that it *is* a law of our land and so must be executed if we care for those institutions we so vaunt. Each drafted man for himself has paid his money or bought his substitute, thinking there would be so many others who would go that his alternative choice would make little difference. But now, seeing that this course is really defeating the whole object of the draft, and endangering so seriously the final issue of our cause— seeing that all are doing the same, and learning what is the character of these substitutes they are sending us—I really believe that this sort of thing will not be allowed to continue; that hereafter men will see their duty differently and meet the crisis in a new spirit. I have seen only one real "drafted" man out of 500 substitutes, and he was a right good fellow. All the men who meet the draft in their own person will be received by our boys in the kindest spirit, and honored as true patriots and worthy comrades. Those who come as substitutes for others will be received and treated as they shall show themselves to deserve.

There, dear Republican, this is prose I have been writing today, so I'll make it short. Yours truly,

DUNN BROWNE

On August 8 Fiske wrote his brother that the army was marking time and waiting for a reinforcement of conscripts, and "I don't believe we shall do anything more through Aug. at least unless we are attacked." His prediction was correct. The Army of the Potomac lay north and west of Fredericksburg and caught its breath after the rigors of the Gettysburg campaign. At the home where he was boarding, he wrote, "we supply them with commissary stores to support their table & on the whole we are of mutual benefit to one another, as I decidedly prefer their corn cakes & coffee to our hardtack & coffee." Fiske told brother Asa that it was almost twelve months since his enlistment, and he felt he should honor his promise to his wife and to his Connecticut parish that he would return home after a year's service. If his resignation was not accepted, "I shall take it as an indication of Providence for me to stay."

Dunn Browne Has a Boarding Place

Camp near Elk Run, Va.
August 20, 1863

THE ARMY IN SUMMER QUARTERS

My dear Republican: This is one of the pleasantest places for an army to lie off in, during the heated term, that can be selected, certainly in poor, old, forsaken, ravaged Virginia. Beautiful groves of oak and pine to shade us from the heat. Pleasant grassy lawns on which to spread our blankets and take an after-dinner siesta. No mosquitoes to buzz and sting and bite, as in the most of your cities and watering places; a truly simple arcadian shepherd's life for us to lead, except that our flocks and herds are rather limited, our crooks are rifles and swords, and our pipes tobacco pipes. It is the happy lot of your humble correspondent to have his regular boarding place, quite like civil life, going three times a day to get his meals at a real house, sitting down at an actual table with a cloth on it, live young ladies sitting round it, a landlady to pour his tea, and positive board bills to settle. He resigns himself to civilized habits with his usual philosophical fortitude, chats with the young ladies and plays with the babies, throwing off the sternness of the warrior and enjoying the amenities of social life as if carnage, cannon and conscripts were not in all his thoughts. There is a sort of pleasant excitement in sitting down to a table where you have pretty good reason to think that your hosts would be glad to put "pizen" in your coffee if they dared; in conversing familiarly with these ladies whose brothers, husbands and lovers are shooting at you at every opportunity they can get, and having little after-dinner conversations with people, all of whose views, wishes and opinions are the antipodes of your own.

SECESH TAKE THINGS PHILOSOPHICALLY

I must say that these secesh show a great deal of good sense in their adverse circumstances. They take the spoiling of their goods with quietness and good nature, see their crops thrown down, their pigs and calves stolen, cows milked and hen-roosts robbed, hay carried off and stables torn down, with more equanimity than I should exhibit I fear in similar circumstances. They have become used in a measure to the losses of war, and know that where soldiers are, there chickens, dairies and kitchen gardens do not thrive. The women, unable to make any purchases in the dry goods line, are cheerfully imitating their old Revolutionary dames and manufacturing their own dress materials, with a good deal of success. These families have been without tea, coffee and sugar, months together, and only feel reduced to extremities when the salt at last gave out. The negroes having all run away, the ladies take to the household duties bravely; hands that have never washed a dish or made a "pone" of bread, go into those unaccustomed duties with energy, mix up the hoe-cakes, wield the broom and rub the skin off their knuckles at the wash-board, with commendable cheerfulness.

A GENERAL WISH FOR PEACE

But none can realize the actual meaning of war like these border state people whose homes have been right in the midst of the armies for nearly three years, between the swaying tides of friend and foe—their property stripped first by one side and then by the other, the hail destroying what the locusts didn't devour—and never lying down to sleep in security, liable to momentary attacks from marauders and stragglers from both armies, planting what they know not who shall gather, and sowing where another will most likely reap. They are tired of war. They will accept almost any settlement that shall re-establish peace. I believe this is a sentiment that is become universal through the South, and if we only hold on stoutly a little longer, we shall have a right peace with a restored Union. Yours truly,

DUNN BROWNE

It was before the spring elections, particularly that for Connecticut's governor, when Dunn Browne was last inspired to open fire on the Copperheads. While he offers no specific reason for this renewed assault, no doubt he was looking ahead to the forthcoming fall elections in which Copperhead candidates were running for the governorships in Ohio and Pennsylvania. There was speculation that if they won, the two would combine with Governor Horatio Seymour, the peace Democrat in New York, in a coalition representing more than half the North's population, to force some sort of a compromise peace. That prospect, of course, was anathema to Dunn Browne.

Dunn Browne Talks About Copperheads

Camp near Elk Run, Va.
August 29 [1863]

THE COPPERHEAD AS A FRIEND

Dear Republican: The copperheads of the North are certainly
the most faithful, thorough-going, consistent, persevering, out-
and-out, devoted, unwearying, undiscouraged set of friends that
any pack of black-hearted traitors were ever blessed withal. Their
southern lords and masters have despised them, spit upon them,
abused them as worse than abolitionists. That's nothing, to be
sure, but what they have always been used to. But see how they
are persevering now, in the very disinterestedness of malevo-
lence, through all possible obstacles, against their own interests,
through the blood of their neighbors and perhaps their own
sons—unto the threatened ruin of their country, to the blacken-
ing of their reputations, to the evident prolongation of all the
evils of a terrible war, to the stirring up of riots that endanger
their own property and the lives of their own households;
through the lowest depths of shame, crime and treason, through
suspicion, imprisonment sometimes and the indignation of all
true patriots and good men always, how faithful they are to their
southern friends and their southern institutions!

They have no interest in the preservation of slavery. It will put
no money in their pockets, add nothing to the glory of their
names, nor the dignity of their lives. Yet out of a pure, unselfish
devotion to that institution, they are willing not only to make
martyrs of themselves, but to sacrifice all their civil and political
institutions, consent to the dismemberment of their country,
give up all our prestige in the eyes of the nations—or, indeed,
consent to anything else in the whole world, no matter how humiliating or how wicked. Rather than to continue the war to the
overthrow of slavery, they would consent either to let the seced-
ing states go away as a separate nation now that they are on the
point of being conquered, or stay in the Union on their own
terms no matter how humiliating to us. Rather than stop the war
now, on the condition of slavery's being abolished, they would
continue it through other years of bloodshed, fighting even their

friends the slaveholders themselves, if they should agree to abandon the institution. If peace will bring the salvation of slavery, then peace at any price of shame and humiliation. If war is needful for its preservation, then war to any extent of blood and destruction.

THE COPPERHEAD AS A MARTYR

If there is a bona fide martyr anywhere in these degenerate times, surely it is the copperhead. Nay, he puts most martyrs to the blush, for while they sacrifice all things for conscience' sake, he adds conscience itself to his sacrifice. Other men have sacrificed wealth, position, reputation, to their principles. He has laid before his idol, wealth, position, reputation, principles and all. Others sacrifice to their country, he sacrifices his country. The South doesn't appreciate the exaltation of his spirit. The rebels deliberately and treacherously attacked the Union in behalf of slavery because it was with them a practical institution, whose niggers, cotton bales and profits were visible to their naked eye. They can't understand or believe in the sincerity of one who disinterestedly does the same as and more than they do themselves, without any such temptation of profit. The South boldly staked slavery on the issue of the war, and our executive has abolished it, as a war measure, and both sides will abide by that issue as a foregone conclusion. But the copperhead with no personal interest in the affair, in the great interests of our common humanity, steps in and demands the re-establishment of the beneficent institution on indisputable guaranty, to be perpetual forevermore, as the sine qua non of any negotiation. However, this is too hot weather for political letter writing or anything that verges on it, and it was only my intense appreciation of the constancy of the copperheads in their (want of) principles, that led me to try to put in a word for them, though not particularly in other respects their admirer. Yours truly,

DUNN BROWNE

Fiske, a man of the cloth by profession, was obviously deeply moved by the scene he describes here. General Owen, whom he credits with the inspiration for this Sunday service, was appar-

ently better suited for the role Fiske describes than for troop lead-
ing. Owen had chronic problems of command, and the next
spring, after Cold Harbor, he was brought up on charges of dis-
obedience of orders. When he agreed to be mustered out, the
charges were dropped. The newspaper report that Fiske men-
tions, of the capture of Forts Sumter and Wagner at Charleston,
proved to be premature.

A Sunday in Camp

Camp near Elk Run, Va.
August 30 [1863]

A RARE AND WORTHY GENERAL

Dear Republican: I believe I haven't written you on a Sabbath
day in a long time. I feel like dropping you a few lines to tell your
readers what quiet, pleasant, religious Sabbaths we have of late
in this division. Our brigadier, at present in command of the
division, Gen. Joshua T. Owen of Philadelphia, until the war
broke out, I believe a prominent lawyer in that city, is a man,
more rare than I wish they were among generals, who believes in
the Sabbath and appreciates the privilege and the inestimable
advantage of a divine service on that holy day. And he does not
just say to his command that there will be preaching at such and
such places, and they can go if they choose, but he tells his soldiers that divine service is the most appropriate exercise for the
Lord's day and they will be expected to attend as at any other
appointed duty, thus making a Sabbath service as important a
matter as the regular Sunday inspection. Inviting a regiment to
his headquarters to service, he just drops a polite note to the
commander requesting him to bring his command, officers and
men, except the needful guard details and the sick, at such an
hour, with their chaplain to conduct the exercise. Then they
come and in good order, decorously dressed, and pay attention,
and get good and enjoy it too—as I learn from testimony on
every hand.

GOING TO MEETING

At ten o'clock this lovely morning, he summoned the whole division together in front of headquarters, having issued a special order the night previous, and we had a right noble audience, in line on three sides of a square, three bands of music, all the drum corps, all the chaplains, and a right magnificent union meeting as it was ever my privilege to attend. How the old oaken arches of our living temple rang when the psalms of praise were lifted up by such a multitude of voices! What a mighty stillness, sacred and impressive, as that great assembly bowed in the attitude of attention, while the words of prayer rose up to God! What an inspiration to him who addressed the words of God's truth to that audience, in the multitude of orderly, attentive listeners, veterans of many a battle field, and who may go forth to another scene of danger and blood very likely before they are assembled thus again! Talk of the majesty of Roman Catholic worship in grand old arched cathedrals, or of the wonderful interest of the great camp meetings which still abound in many parts of our land; speak of any scenes or ceremonies of religious worship that may have most impressed you in all your varied experience, I don't believe you can recall one occasion among them all of more touching solemnity or real grandeur, than this division of bronzed and war-worn soldiers, sitting as little children at the feet of him who spake of a crucified and risen Savior in their ears. Our pulpit was a platform of rails crossed by several endboards from our big wagons, our hymn books the admirable little collection, the "Soldiers Hymns," and the bands played us the "Star Spangled Banner" and "America," and we remembered the conquest of Sumter and Wagner reported in the yesterday's papers, and mingled a little of secular patriotism with our religious services in a way that might seem somewhat incongruous at home perhaps; but we made it a good and glorious day, greatly enjoyed I fully believe by every officer and soldier present. Best of all was the good, earnest, religious and patriotic speech which our general, under the inspiration of the occasion, was "moved in spirit" to add unto the sermon, and which showed him as eloquent a speaker and earnest a Christian as he is valiant soldier. Wouldn't you like to have been with us, dear reader?

DUNN BROWNE

*Dunn Browne here renews his offensive against New York's Gov-
ernor Seymour and the former mayor of New York City, Fernando
Wood, whom he links with the recent draft riot, which he links
further with the draft-and-substitute scandal. The "scores of
newspapers" arrayed against poor Dunn is a cheerful inflation of
the complaint of the* Portland Press, *dealt with in Fiske's June
1863 letter. His Williamsport reporting, it will be recalled, dealt
with Meade's failure to bring the retreating Lee to battle after Gettysburg.*

In Trouble Again

Camp near Elk Run, Va.
September 2 [1863]

FOES WITHOUT AND FOES WITHIN

Dear Republican: I think I am the unfortunatest of correspondents. Because I hinted at a little of the truth in regard to the
Chancellorsville battle, I was attacked on all sides; various unknown military heroes stood, and for aught I know, still stand
ready—for I don't think that they are generally of the kind that
would be likely to have perished in the battles subsequent—to
challenge or shoot me on sight; scores of newspapers came down
with fury upon my poor little articles that I had scarcely hoped
would even be read outside of my circle of personal acquaintance, and my sincerest friends chided me for my injudicious
strictures. Yes, I even suspect that you yourself shook your sage
editorial head over my imprudences and doubted whether you
shouldn't guillotine me with the scissors. You are glad you didn't
though, most amiable Republican, aren't you? Then again, because I described, quite within the truth, the brilliancy of our
operations before Williamsport, it was hinted to me by some
kind friends, that inferior officers need to be careful in their criticisms with reference to the great operations of the army and
the conduct of their superiors. And now again because I have
indited several letters to you inviting as affectionately and earnestly as I could my friends who are drafted, to come out and
join us in their own persons, instead of giving that privilege to

anybody else, I have reason to fear that *they* think I meant something personal; and moreover because I didn't call the New York b-hoy and eye-smasher and orphan-asylum-burner who has just come out here as a substitute (for the second or third time) a "gentleman and friend," after the style of Fernandy and Horatio, he also, I learn, objects to my remarks, and he and his fellows will do for me, as soon as I desert so as to come within the sphere of their influence. Such are some of the trials of a poor newspaper correspondent. (There, I've put my foot in it again. Ten to one you'll think I meant to call you a poor newspaper.)

A FULL APOLOGY ALL AROUND

What shall I do then? Stop writing? Can't be done. Force of habit. Forced to carry a pocket inkhorn with me. Stop we to dinner or to battle; as soon as the dessert is over or the enemy are driven back, out comes pen and paper until my mind is relieved. No, that alternative is impossible. Will apologies be of any use? Well then, I think I've known many newspapers whose daily was poorer than your weekly. And, my dear friend with the myopia or the palpitatio cordis or the cornucopia (which implies fullness of purse, doesn't it?), I did not mean you, in the few desultory remarks I offered with reference to the draft. It would be the height of absurdity for a man of your social position, but especially of your delicate bodily condition, to feel bound to come out here as a soldier, merely because your name happened to be written on a scrap of paper that came out of a wheel. Moreover, it would be an encouragement of the lottery system that a man of your moral character ought not to give. Also, my friend from the sixth ward of the kingdom of Fernando the First, I disclaim any intention of disparaging your character as a gentleman and a citizen, worthy to be called a "brother and friend" of the governor of New York. You doubtless know your own value as a soldier and was compelled to get the paltry $300 about three times in order to obtain your full estimation. Allow me to solicit the honor of your service as a recruit in my—friend Smith's company. And in a general way and once and for all, if any member of the congregation feels hit by any portion of my discourses, I request him to understand that that particular passage refers to somebody who staid at home from meeting on that day, or that

I am only preaching on the wickedness of sin, in the abstract, or if personal at all in my allusions, am only aiming at people a great way off, firing over their heads, at very long range, entirely outside the circulation of The Republican. Very affectionately,

DUNN BROWNE

In this letter Fiske finds yet another direction from which to approach the home front and rally it to the Union cause. Brother Jonathan, the personification (and caricature) of the bumptious American, had originated at the time of the Revolution and, until superseded by Uncle Sam, served as opposite number to John Bull. The "imperial puppet show" Fiske mentions was the effort by Bonaparte's nephew, Napoleon III, to install the Hapsburg Maximilian as emperor of Mexico while Brother Jonathan was too preoccupied to enforce the Monroe Doctrine.

Dunn Browne Shows Up Brother Jonathan

Camp near Elk Run, Va.
September 7 [1863]

HOW HE CONDUCTS A WAR

Dear Republican: There is a considerable basis of truth in a very erroneous and ridiculous communication from an American correspondent of one of the London papers which I was reading a few days since with about equal proportions of indignation and amusement. The point touched upon was our national feeling of pride at the vast scale on which we conduct operations, whether for good or for evil. It is true no doubt that Brother Jonathan does chuckle inwardly, even in the midst of his misfortunes and ruin and bloodshed, over the bigness of the very row that has been kicked up in his household. As he has the "greatest country in all creation," the tallest mountains, longest rivers, largest lakes, and most extensive coal veins; as he has built the most miles of railroad, invented the greatest variety of notions, printed the most newspapers, established the most common schools, and indeed is infinitely ahead of the other benighted

nations and races of mankind in education, civilization and religion, in all the institutions of government and the arts and comforts of social life—so, of course, getting into difficulties, he
finds a grim consolation in the thought that they are the tough-
est difficulties that ever nation yet fell into. If he has a rebellion
to crush it is some comfort to know that it is a rebellion that
extends over a quarter of a continent and materially affects the
interests of every nation under heaven. If he must turn his attention to war, he glories in the thought that it is being carried on
the grandest scale that the world has hitherto seen; that he fires
the biggest guns, brings into the field the most formidable armies and feeds them with the largest piles of hard bread and
barrels of beef that mortal contractors ever yet bargained to furnish. Other nations have contracted in the course of centuries
their little public debts or gone into bankruptcy perhaps for a
few hundred million. He walks right up among the billions in no
time at all, and will soon be carrying on his broad shoulders a
burden that would crush half a dozen ordinary nations. Other
nations are slowly increasing their navies year by year and trying
occasional experiments with metallic sheathing and various new
devices of attack and defense. He is every month ordering iron-
clads by the score and gunboats by the hundred, and increasing
his flock of rams as if they were nothing but common merinoes.
Other powers think they do well if they blockade two or three or
half a dozen ports. He employs a small part of his navy in maintaining a blockade four thousand miles long, but occupies its
chief strength in grand naval expeditions, two or three at a time,
of a hundred or two sail apiece, and knock to pieces harbor de-
fences.

WHAT HE THINKS OF OTHER NATIONS

England and France are mighty nations, the voice of either
one of which would be decisive as to the success or ruin of any
ordinary government. Jonathan very coolly contemplates the
probability of both together recognizing the independence of his
revolted states, and talks with the utmost composure of facing
the world in arms, to maintain the integrity and durability of the
institutions he has founded; to prove the vast superiority of the
form of government he has so long vaunted. And notwithstand-

ing the vanity and foolishness of Jonathan's complacent thoughts, notwithstanding the utter absurdity, if you will, of the young giant's notions, the world is yet pretty well persuaded that, if the worst comes to worst, this big talk is ready to be followed up with big action. It may be the height of insanity per- haps to think that he could make headway against the navies of Albion, the legions of Louis Napoleon, and perhaps the added power of the Spanish Don, in connection with the gigantic rebel- lion raging all the while at home; but the magnates of those nations are well aware, that if need should come, cousin Jona- than would just eject a large mouthful of saliva, put a fresh quid in his other cheek, take a new hitch in his pantaloons and—try; and that such a trial would convulse the world. It may be that this upstart can have his unbearable braggadocio thrashed out of him, but those who undertake that little business are to find it no boys' play on their hands. So doubtless, notwithstanding all the rumors of French recognition, the shrewd Nephew of his Uncle will be satisfied if he can be permitted to play out his little play of imperial puppet show in Mexico, with no interference of Yankee actors; and "Perfide Albion," too, with the commerce of the world now in her hands, will hesitate long before she takes the step which will let loose an innumerable cloud of privateers upon her ships, to say nothing of the delicate complications of the Canadian question.

The Necessity Of Finishing The Contest

Jonathan will be left to ruin himself with his own family quar- rels at his leisure. And it must be confessed he is going ahead on that path with tremendous rapidity. In the mighty rush of events—in the clash of conflicting arms—we are strangely for- getful of the overwhelming burdens and responsibilities we are incurring, and of the fact that we cannot so go on long. One of our gallant western generals says, "We can carry on such a war as this we are waging for fifty years." I hope and believe he is much more of a soldier than statesman, for surely a more prepos- terous statement was never made. But to the mind that stops for a moment to reflect, the whole aspect of our affairs shows us the need of finishing up this war with a speedy and united effort. The country is, oh how weary of the bloodshed and suffering and

losses of the war. You are weary of it at home—we are more weary
of it here in the field. We shall very soon have actually accumulated a debt greater than even all the vast resources of the whole
country, and depreciation and bankruptcy must then follow.
There is a limit to our right to mortgage the resources of our
posterity, even if we could do so. And so every consideration
urges us to push on and make a finish of this rebellion—this very
autumn if it may be. Make the army of the Potomac up to a
hundred thousand men within a month, lead us on judiciously
against Lee, and with God's blessing we'll ruin him, take Richmond and finish the war (all the heavy work of it) before winter
closes upon us. Great is Jonathan. Yours truly,

DUNN BROWNE

7

CAMPAIGNING TO LITTLE PURPOSE

Learning that Longstreet's corps had been detached from Lee's army to reinforce Braxton Bragg's Army of Tennessee, General Meade pushed the Army of the Potomac forward toward the Rapidan, behind which Lee now posted his weakened army. Here, Samuel Fiske, returned from brigade staff duty to his company in the 14th Connecticut, hopes (against hope) that the generals might have learned something from their more than two years of campaigning. In the third sentence, parson Fiske recalls Jeremiah.

The Army in Motion

Cedar Mountain, near the Rapidan, Va.
September 17 [1863]

Dear Republican: The army of the Potomac is again on the move. Our little season of rest has passed and an earnest, active, hard, wearisome campaign has opened again upon us. Our "summer is ended" and our "harvest pretty much past" I suppose. This latter is a figurative expression, and refers of course to the conscripts and substitutes we have been gathering in with so much pains from every corner of our land. A mighty big lot of ground we've gleaned over, for a pretty small pile of grain, and not a few tares in it at that, and it will take a good deal of threshing to get it clean. But we ought to be thankful that our ranks are somewhat reinforced, and if our numbers are few at best compared with the great, strong regiments of a year ago, yet the most of those who do still rally round our banners are tried and proven men who have confidence in each other, and who can be depended on for soldier's manful duty under all circumstances.

The weak, the skulks and the cowards, are, to speak generally, weeded out. Sickness is comparatively a rare occurrence in our ranks, save among the new men, and the hardships of the campaign fall upon those whose shoulders are broad to bear them.

A HOPELESS WISH FOR COMMON SENSE

If we could only hope to have a little common sense used once in a while by any of our generals in marching the men, the terrible waste of life and strength in our previous campaigns might be, one half of it, avoided in the coming one. But we have learned that it is too much to hope for. Experience brings little wisdom in this respect, and I suppose the men will still be marched to death as they have been always before, and more men be expended in getting to the fields of battle than by the slaughter on those fields. We shall still be trotted along at the fastest pace in the hottest part of the day; still stop at the worst places for camping ground and for water that can be selected in a barren country; still never know when we stop for rest whether there will be time for making coffee or it must be spilled on the ground when half heated; still be called out into line in utmost haste in the morning at 5 a.m., and then wait with knapsacks and equipments on till 10 before actually moving. I have never known but one general of brigade, division or corps, who apparently took any pains whatever, or bestowed a thought even, upon these matters, whereon the comfort of the soldiers so much depends. And yet a single word passed along the lines to tell the men that they will have time to get water, make coffee and lunch, a very little care to halt at regular intervals and to select the best places, a little thought to slacken the pace in the heat of the day, to remember how much faster the rear of a long column have to march, where there are occasional obstructions, than the front of the same, a very little consideration for the comfort of the men, would make such a difference, would get men over a long, hard march so much more easily, would save so much straggling, so many sun strokes, such a number of precious lives, that I wonder some of our generals, men who do really to my own knowledge care for their men, do not think of these things.

A year ago to-day, we were getting our initiation to battle-scenes on the bloody field of Antietam. We didn't know this morning but we might celebrate our anniversary by a similar fight; but exactly what we are doing in the movement, and what our plans are, Gen. Meade knows better than I do. Perhaps you have heard from him by this time: all we know is that we are near the enemy, and that the little old second corps is in the front. They don't say a great deal about us in the papers; but they know whom they can depend upon in the field; and there is always a place of honor and responsibility and danger for the second.

DUNN BROWNE

Fiske justified this grisly scene, detailing the fate of substitutes who deserted from his own regiment, in hopes that in future such bungling would be corrected. Probably his real motive was to spread a strong word of warning to the home front, where the conscription evasions originated. Fiske does not exaggerate the wholesale abuses of the recuperating-patient system in the North, about which he learned first-hand as an inspector general at brigade headquarters.

A Shocking Execution

Bivouac near the Rapidan, Va.
September 21 [1863]

My dear Republican: Last Friday this division was drawn out to witness a most painful scene; such a one as sad necessity has made only too common in the army of late; the execution of two deserters, substitutes, from the 14th Connecticut volunteers, Elliot and Eastman by name. The necessity of this thing has been evident enough from the first moment we saw the style of recruits the draft was sending on to us. Its salutary effect is evident enough in the almost entire cessation of desertion since it has been generally understood through the army that the death penalty was sure to be inflicted. It is almost laughable to see the anxiety with which the stragglers from the various regiments have been rushing back to their commands within the last few days, and the eagerness with which they put in their excuses.

But there were some unnecessarily revolting circumstances connected with the execution of this sentence, that make it a scene to be put out of one's mind and forgotten as soon as possible. The poor boys were not informed of the fate that awaited them, did not know that their sentence was a fatal one, till 12 o'clock on the very Friday on which they were to be "shot to death" before the hour of 4 p.m.! Who was responsible for this cruel neglect or intentional withholding of the sentence I cannot say, but the result of the court martial had been published more than a week. Then the ammunition of the firing party (new ammunition, just served out, and such as we are expecting to use in the approaching, perhaps most important, battles of the war) was so poor in quality that only three out of sixteen guns went off at all, and the men were only wounded; one of them, I think, not even touched, and he slid off the coffin on which he sat, on to his knees, slipped the handkerchief off his eyes and stared full in the face of the men who came up singly and put the muzzle of their guns to his head, and—snapped caps at him. And the provost marshal in charge had to come up with his revolver to put the poor fellow out of his misery; and then more guns were loaded and more poor ammunition experimented upon, and the sentence finally fully executed, but made into such a scene of butchery that all eyes were turned away from it and all hearts shocked by it.

I would not have said a word in description, but in the hope that, if such things are to be done in future, the arrangements may be perfected beforehand so as to avoid a like bungling. Still no blame can be laid in this instance that I am aware of, upon the humane and gentlemanly officer who had the painful duty in charge. He could not be supposed to know that Uncle Sam's agents were furnishing us ammunition whereof not five cartridges in a hundred would go off. He supposed that the government departments whose business it is, and government inspectors, who at large salaries in safe places, pass upon all our supplies, would see to it that at least we were furnished with powder and ball and percussion caps, a majority of which would go off at some rate.

WHY OUR ARMIES ARE SO DEPLETED IN NUMBERS

Enough of this painful subject. I want to say a word about a most important matter concerning the efficiency of the army, and one nearly every reader of your columns, and every person in the community, can do something to remedy. Probably there is not a regiment in the field that has been out as long as a year but has its numbers reduced at least one-half and some of them two-thirds or even three-fourths. Of course this loss cannot be all a legitimate loss, neither is it very largely a loss by actual, bare-faced desertion. Very much the larger part are absentees on the plea of sickness or wounds. In our corps at the present time and notwithstanding our recent accessions, the number of "absent sick" borne upon our rolls is very nearly equal to, and if I mistake not, a trifle more than, the whole number present for duty in any capacity! And I presume the same is true of nearly every other corps. So that for this army in the field of, say 100,000 men, there is another army of 100,000 men scattered over the country, costing the people an equal, if not a greater sum, and doing no service to our cause. Of this vast number, I think I have good grounds for saying that one-half, I cannot possibly be exaggerating when I say one-third, or more than 30,000 out of 100,000, are able to be with us, and ought to be with us, doing service in the field. It has come to be a thing to be expected that those who are wounded or sent to the hospital sick, even slightly and temporarily so, are lost to the regiment for the rest of the war in nine cases out of ten. Men are furloughed with the greatest ease from our hospitals and then stay at home, sending certificates from their easily persuaded family physicians for the extension of their furloughs, or even staying without any extension, and the hospitals fail to report them to their commands as deserters. Great numbers of men convalescent are detailed for a thousand and one purposes about the hospitals and by provost marshals for guards, &c., till, as a matter of fact, scarcely any of them rejoin their companies. In many of our regiments as many as 50 men are detailed from each as nurses in distant hospitals. Now there are thousands of civilians, thousands of women throughout the North, who can supply the demand for nurses in their own states and cities, without keeping thousands of able-bodied soldiers from duty in the field to attend to such things. The surgeons and those in charge of hospitals are much in fault for the permission of such things. Every citizen knowing of a soldier able to return to duty and not taking measures to have him sent back is failing of his duty to his country. All provost marshals and their assistants who fail to take the needful measures to send back all those loose men to their duty are wanting to the first obligations of their office.

I hear of men walking the streets of our villages in Connecticut and Massachusetts, and even at work on their farms and in their shops, who belong to the United States, and will be back to their companies by and by with some sort of fixed-up certificates, and draw their back pay, and then staying in the service a few weeks, will again fail in their health, get sent to a hospital and try the same over again. I know many men who have never been in a battle, nor done a month's service, who have drawn one and two years' pay from Uncle Sam, and are still in good and regular standing. These men who have been discharged for disability or over age, and who are utterly unfit for soldiers, are coming out again as substitutes for drafted men. I cannot believe that the exemption boards, who find such a large proportion of drafted men unfit for military duty, say from 60 to 90 per cent, are in all cases equally rigid in their examination of substitutes. I have just heard of one old man, 64 years of age, who was a great object of pity for a time in the company I commanded, and who was finally discharged for disability, after lingering along and doing no duty for many months, now coming out here again as good as new as a substitute, with his cash in his pocket. Whether he dyed his hair and whiskers to pass the board, as I understand he did before, I know not, but I do know that he can never do a month's duty again as a soldier. And this is only one of many instances coming within my own knowledge. Let us all use every possible effort to get into the field at once all those who are fit to do duty and who really belong to Uncle Sam, and we shall have no occasion to send on men whose fitness for military duty is doubtful, no need to lament the failure of the draft, and no lack of men to finish up successfully this fall campaign.

We are now moving on, or doubtless about to do so, with our eight days' rations on our backs, to press up Lee from the North, while Burnside and Rosecrans push the confederacy from the Southwest, and Gillmore and Dahlgren finish up their beautiful and scientific problem before and over the city of the Palmettos. Yours truly,

DUNN BROWNE

*Meade's advance had stagnated, along the line of the Rapidan,
after he was required to send off two army corps, under the command of Joe Hooker of Chancellorsville memory, to stem a crisis
in Tennessee. Fiske's harrowing stint of picket duty must have
been tempered somewhat by having shelter and leisure enough to
complete these musings.*

Life on the Pickets

On picket, near the Rapidan, Va.
October 3 [1863]

Dear Republican: I learn every day something new, and it is
only by nature's beautiful compensating principle of forgetting
that I am saved from a fatal pressure on the brain. You understand, doubtless, Oh Republican, the working of this great theory of mental activity. We are always learning, always forgetting,
and it all depends on the selection whether we become wise or
otherwise. Gain good and lose evil, save the wheat and blow away
the chaff; get a little sense and forget a little nonsense every day,
and it doesn't make so much difference about the rapidity or
slowness of the process, you are in a good way, and just as certain
of becoming a prodigy of wisdom and virtue at length, as I am of
becoming senior major general of U.S. volunteers, if I remain in
the service long enough. On the whole I think my forte lies in
forgetting. Not for ten thousand worlds would I have forced back
upon my mind the vast, unspeakable load of rubbish, wickedness
and folly that this happy faculty has enabled me to throw off.
People that don't forget, or that forget unwisely, making a bad
selection, go mad, get into insane asylums, commit suicide, or
become criminals, committing moral suicide, or merely grow
foolish and imbecile, getting into a second and worse childhood.
But aside from the forgetting out and out of the useless and
unpleasant things, there is the faculty of forgetting the unpleasant part of disagreeable things and transforming that which was
extremely painful at the time into a positively agreeable memory. For instance, it would require a very powerful imagination
to make a man actually enjoy at the time being out on picket in
the rain, forty-eight hours without shelter or fire, with very little

save hard tack to eat, and a very bad lookout for getting any sleep at all. On the contrary, it seemed a very rational remark that one of my green substitutes made, looking up into the sky yesterday morning, to the effect that there was prospect of such dirty weather that probably we wouldn't be able to go out picketing till the storm was over. Poor fellow, he has found out his mistake by this time, I reckon, for I see him yonder on his post now shivering and dripping under his rubber blanket and carrying his gun at the queerest "right shoulder shift" that you ever saw at a militia muster. But when fifty years hence I shoulder my cane to rehearse for my grandchildren the wonderful campaigns of the great war of the rebellion, doubtless I shall make very light of such little privations, and laugh at the degeneracy of my effeminate descendants who think there is anything wonderful in enduring such hardships.

Bang! goes a gun close on our left to interrupt my philosophical speculations. "Steady, boys. Spring to arms and be on the alert while I go out and see what's up. I don't believe it is an attack, for there are the enemy's two cavalry pickets on yonder hill as quiet as ever." Sure enough, on moving down cautiously, pistol in hand, to my left post, I found the sentinel, mouth and eyes wide open, staring in amazement at his still smoking gun, while his comrades, over whose heads the bullet had whistled, were poking all manner of fun at him. "Sure and I was but changing the cratur from one shoulder to the other to aise me a bit, and she went off herself with the divil a touch of my finger." He had his gun at a full cock, I suppose, instead of at half cock, and so knocked it off in one of his clumsy movements. I need not say he was another of our new men.

THE NEW RECRUITS IMPROVING

But I am glad, dear Republican, to be able to tell you that I am pleasantly disappointed in the behavior of these new recruits taken as a whole. There are some rough characters among them, and some state prison birds, but the larger part of those that are left (the worst deserted in the first few days) are doing their duty with a good will, and will make good soldiers. I have forty-five of them in my company, and am getting to be right proud of their drill and general appearance. There are just enough scrape-

graces in the regiment to make the tenure of property very inse-
cure. Watches, money, knives, shirts, rations, guns, every species
of mortal property that is capable of being transferred, gets con-
veyed away with more celerity and skill than legality. You don't
know when you lie down at night but that your shelter-tent roof
will be stolen from over your head before morning, or the minia-
ture of your lady-love from out your breast pocket. Well, this
is productive of one good effect. It keeps us reminded of the
transitoriness of all earthly things.

Speaking of stealing, I should like to make the acquaintance
of that man who has stolen my Republican out of the mail for
the last three months. He has manifested a perseverance and
thoroughness of performance about the work in hand worthy of
a better cause. He has never left me a single number since he
commenced his process of abstraction. Still, dear Republican,
though I see not your friendly face, I continue to remember you
with affection and wish you all sorts of prosperity.

I don't know what we are doing here army-wise—except maintaining a long line of pickets along the Rapid Anne. Haven't seen
a newspaper for four days, and only know that the world goes
round from taking an occasional observation of the sun. Yours in
a state of benighted (perhaps blissful) ignorance,

DUNN BROWNE

P.S. Can't you send a copy of The Republican to somebody else
in my vicinity and let me steal it in accordance with the military
lex talionis?

*Dunn Browne had last advocated a temperance crusade in the
Army of the Potomac in his letter to the* Republican *of June 21,
1863; obviously, conditions had not improved in the meantime.
His calculation of the benefits of abstinence being worth 100,000
men to the army was of course literary license, but, interestingly
enough, General McClellan had claimed, when he was general-in-
chief, that total abstinence "would be worth 50,000 men to the
armies of the United States." Fiske was certainly right to point
out the particular danger of officers over-imbibing. In virtually
every battle there were instances of operations gone awry due to
drunken generals.*

Whisky in the Army

Camp near the Rapidan, Va.
October 4 [1863]

Dear Republican: An army is a big thing, and it takes a great many eatables and not a few drinkables to carry it along. Have you any idea how many barrels of "commissary" (that's a gentle euphemism for whisky) it takes per week to run the machine? I don't know exactly, but I do know that it would be better to Uncle Sam than 100,000 volunteers to his army, if he would shut off entirely and absolutely the supply of intoxicating liquors, from officers and men, from surgeons, hospitals, and everything and everybody connected with the army. On what ground is the present vast supply of whisky furnished? Is it that an occasional ration may be issued to the soldiers when returning from picket or after an exhausting march? Why there hasn't been a whisky ration issued to a single regiment to my knowledge for many a month, and I am certainly within the truth when I say that not ten a year are issued to the troops on an average. It is as good as a total abstinence society to be a private in the army. Cause why? The use of liquor has so increased among the officers that none is now left over to be issued to the men! Three gallons a week are about the present usual allowance of a brigadier general, and inferior officers in proportion. A major general who is liberal and reasonably hospitable is expected to spend at least his pay in various liquors. Every time every general or staff officer calls on a comrade, the bottle is expected to be produced. Every time an officer is promoted, he is expected to "wet his commission." Every occasion of a sword or horse presentation is improved for a big drink all round. It is not considered yet quite reputable for an officer to be helplessly or crazily drunk, when actually engaged on some special duty, such as officer of the picket or judge advocate of a court martial, but at other times it is nothing against him, and even if caught in such a case it is rather his misfortune than his fault. Poor fellow.

In short, the army is getting badly demoralized as to habits of temperance, and hundreds of young men who came out with fair characters and most correct habits will go home, if they go at all, poor bloated inebriates, and led into their evil habits, I am sorry to say too often, by the bad example of those who are older and of higher rank than they. We no longer wonder, as we used to at the beginning of the war, that battles are lost and expeditions fail, on account of the drunkenness of those who are in command, but the rather we thank God, in grateful wonder, when any undertaking gets successfully through, unruined by such drawbacks.

Oh, if the president and war department would but have the nerve to issue a prohibition of all intoxicating drinks in the army on any pretense whatever! It would need more moral courage than to issue an emancipation proclamation, and the suspension of this alcoholic habeas corpus would be a deal tougher job and attended with more odium than the suspension of the legal process of that name; but then it is also a more necessary act and likely to be more beneficial to the country. It can be done. Liquor is kept from the privates of the army on the whole with almost perfect success. It does more injury among the officers than it could do among the men. Oh, Father Abraham, if you will set your honest foot down on this point, and save the officers of your Union army, I, Dunn Browne, will take it upon me, "humble individual that I am," less than the least of your military servants, to warrant you a victory over the enemy, invariably, whenever the odds against us are not very great indeed; and so will your petitioner against the deadly rum barrel, as misdirecting the gun barrel, ever pray.

DUNN BROWNE

This letter in the Springfield Republican *for October 17 was datelined September 8, but that is clearly an error, either by Fiske or by the paper's editor. The events related here make October 8 a more likely date. Fiske's barbed remarks on Northern military efforts reflect his continued disappointment at the failure to exploit the great victories at Gettysburg and Vicksburg. At Charleston, Quincy Gillmore's efforts to bombard Fort Sumter into surrender did indeed prove futile; in Greek mythology, Antæus, like Sumter, was invincible so long as he touched the earth. William S. Rose-*

crans had come a cropper in Tennessee; after his defeat at Chick-
amauga he was besieged in Chattanooga. Fiske (and most of the
Army of the Potomac) held the Eleventh Corps responsible for
Chancellorsville, and the corps had done little better at Gettys-
burg. William B. Franklin, sent west after Fredericksburg, came a
cropper at Sabine Pass on the Texas coast on September 8, losing
two gunboats.

Dunn Browne a Military Critic Again

Camp near Culpeper, Va.
[October 8, 1863?]

THE WORK OF A LIFETIME

Dear Republican: I see it is settled on all hands that the taking
of Charleston is only a question of time. A question of a lifetime
I presume is meant. I think it is very fortunate for the prospect
of Gen. Gillmore that he is a young man. I see some surprise
is manifested that Fort Sumter holds out so long against such
repeated, severe and persevering attacks. Do you know my theory on the subject? Why it is as plain as daylight. All engineers
now acknowledge that a sand-battery or earthwork is stronger
than a fort of masonry. Well, Gillmore has knocked Fort Sumter
with his mammoth shells from a regular work of masonry back
into its original clay and dust, made an earthwork of it in short,
and of course it is stronger than ever, and if he continues to
pitch his 300-pounder shells into it till it is perfectly impregna-
ble whom will he have to blame but his own foolish self? Like the
giant Antæus, the more you knock it down the stronger it rises
again.

THE BONE OF CONTENTION REACHED

"Old Rosy," too, has run his knife across a bone somehow in
cutting the rebellion in two and dulled the edge a little. Let us
hope he will find the joint yet the next time he tries, and make a
clean cut across the spinal marrow between the vertebræ. We
hear that our 11th and 12th corps have gone to help him. It is a

very safe and even thing to do, sending them, our boys think. For we hold the 11th as about equal to another corps for the enemy, and so the 12th, being a very reliable corps, would just about balance it. If this consideration should seem to lessen their value as a reinforcement to Rosecrans, on the other hand it would lessen to an equal extent our danger in sparing them from the army of the Potomac. Beautiful is the great principle of compensation!

Just As One Might Suppose

Turning our critical glance to the Southwest, we (that is not the editorial "we," but I and another growler, corporal in my company, one of the funniest specimens of exaggerating, complaining, unreasonable humanity that you ever saw) don't wonder that the vessels of Franklin's expedition stuck fast in the Sabine Pass and were captured. The general that "co-operated" with Burnside in such fashion as he did at Fredericksburg last December, would be enough to make any eight-feet boats draw nine feet of water at the very least. That's *our* opinion. But the corporal is here called away to drill "an awkward squad," muttering that if he was to attend his wife's funeral at 3 o'clock, he supposes he would have to keep on his equipments and drill in the manual of arms up to 2 o'clock and three-quarters. So I can continue my critical observations no longer, not having sufficient support to fall back upon. Yours rather cynically,

Dunn Browne

What Fiske describes here is the Bristoe campaign, and its chief action, at Bristoe Station, on October 14. Learning of the detachment of the Eleventh and Twelfth Corps from Meade's army, Lee seized the initiative and pressed the Federals well back from the Rappahannock along the line of the Orange and Alexandria Railroad. At Bristoe Station, however, the Second Corps ambushed A. P. Hill's Confederate troops, who then (as Fiske put it) "made themselves generally scarce." Lee's loss came to some 1,900, but he once again had checkmated the Federal army.

Dunn Browne Exercises His Right to Grumble

On picket, near Bull Run, Va.
October 17 [1863]

MARCHING AND COUNTER-MARCHING

My dear Republican: We have been having some more "strategy," some more awful marching and a small sprinkling of lively fighting of late in the army of the Potomac. Last Saturday week, being near Culpeper Court House, we (the 2d corps) made a circular movement to the front and right, of a dozen or fifteen miles, to see if there was any enemy there, and encamped in the rain about five miles from the camp we left in the morning. A little after midnight we were roused out of our profound slumbers (I should have said that we were kept up nearly all the previous night drawing 8 days' rations and 60 rounds of ammunition) and drawn out into line ready for a march. We thus remained with knapsacks on, shivering in a raw October night, till 6 a.m., when we began to move. Probably some strategist more skillful than myself can tell the object of this night performance. At six we moved and made a long and hard day's march of some 18 miles, back across the Rappahannock, and encamped this side of Bealton station at 4 1/2 p.m. On Monday, feeling that we hadn't done up the other side of the Rappahannock sufficiently brown, we marched back to Rappahannock station, recrossed the river, and after advancing two or three miles by the flank, spread out into a line of battle, or rather six lines, extending say 3/4 of a mile each side of the road and advanced through woods and over fences, across ditches and hedges, up hill and down dale; tangling our legs alternately in high grass and deep mud, tumbling, staggering and trudging along, stopping every few minutes to dress our lines, till about 6 p.m., not scaring up anything more formidable than a few rabbits (I had a rabbit stew for supper), we halted, cooked our supper with about 4 miles of fence rails and retired to rest.

SOME MORE MARCHING

Just in the middle of our first slumber, our intelligent general having learned that while we were performing these various strategic evolutions in the front, the enemy had quietly passed round our flank and were nearly between us and Washington, at midnight our tired boys were started out again and pushed as rapidly as possible back to the Rappahannock, crossing it the fourth time within a few weeks, and right on along the line of the road past one station after another till we had made about twenty-five miles at 7 p.m., and bivouacked in a beautiful grove not far from Warrenton Junction. The boys' feet were blistered, and legs chafed, and their shoulders ached, and they were pretty effectually used up. The rations also had begun to run short but the improvident ones begged of the provident and some sort of supper was obtained and the army rested. At 4 a.m. we were roused again and at a little after five were on the march. Scarcely were we on the road when the enemy's cavalry attacked us on both flanks, and a battery or two opened on us, but as their attack was not in great force we soon put them to the right about, charged upon the battery and came near capturing it, but by putting their horses to a gallop they succeeded in getting off, and we resumed our march with skirmishers on each flank.

A Sharp Fight

About 4 p.m., as we were marching quietly along by the railroad near Bristoe's station, minding our own business and expecting everybody else to mind theirs, a very lively and spirited attack of cavalry, artillery and infantry was opened upon us across the track very suddenly. It would have done your heart good, dear Republican, to see how coolly the old Second took it, facing to the front (we were marching by the right flank, as usual) and charging across the railroad to repel the attack. The issue wasn't in doubt for an instant. Their fire cut down a good many of our brave boys at first (for instance, five out of my company) but they couldn't hold their ground for a moment. Across a deep cut in the railroad into the thick pines and over a burned field our boys double-quicked, and the enemy double-quicked before them—abandoned a battery and some 500 prisoners to us, and made themselves generally scarce. We returned to the line of the road and held it until 10 p.m. when we moved again (we were the rear guard of the army and of course could not remain to hold the position), marched all night, forded Bull Run creek, two and a half deep, just before daylight, and lay down on the grass in the rain for a few hours' sleep after our fatigues and dangers.

AMMUNITION AND RATIONS

Later in the day we got into a more regular camp, and though expecting to move at any moment, we remained holding this strong position and skirmishing a good deal every day with the enemy in our front. Just as I am writing I see our cavalry, who have passed over the run on a pontoon bridge (we infantry had to wade it), charging the rebels and driving them into the woods about a mile ahead of us. They say soldiers always have a grievance. We have two: eleven day's rations just served out, and sixty rounds of ammunition. Forty rounds is all that a soldier ought, or indeed can be made to carry. That fills his cartridge box, and the rest is either spoiled in his pocket or thrown at once away, to be replaced again by order in a day or two. More is thus actually wasted than is expended in battle, as can be proved by the reports of ordnance officers. And for the rations, three days' is all the haversacks will hold, six as much as any emergency ought to compel men to carry, and eleven—why you might as well issue out the whole three years' provender at once and have done with it. It is half of it wasted, and then the last days the men are starved, and about three days before the time is up, the government is obliged in spite of itself to issue some more—so nothing is gained and a great deal lost by it every way. Eight days' rations have never been made and can never be made, when issued all at once and on a march, to last the men the full time, and yet we have now eleven days' on hand—and I suppose the same cruel stupidity will be persisted in to the end, angering and embittering the men, and accomplishing no good whatever. We hear various rumors of Lee's advancing into Maryland, &c. &c., but know not much of the truth of them. Yours in haste,

DUNN BROWNE

This is an inspired characterization of the fall campaigning, from September into November of 1863, of the two armies. Thinned

by the Gettysburg struggle and weakened by detachments, they sparred and maneuvered to little strategic advantage.

The Great Virginia Express Line

Second Army Corps, Virginia
October 21 [1863]

Dear Republican: If you have any business in the transportation line, or anything connected therewith, let me solicit your custom for our

GREAT POTOMAC AND RAPIDAN THROUGH ROUTE!

PROMPTNESS AND DISPATCH!

Meade & Lee's Through Express, weekly line, between Alexandria and Culpeper; connections with principal points North and South (especially Old Capitol and the Libby prison).

The subscribers having completed their arrangements and gotten their line into running order, will hereafter, until further notice, run their machines (the "Army of the Potomac" and "Army of Northern Virginia") every week through from Culpeper, Va., to Alexandria, Va., and vice versa, giving their personal attention to the running of each train, Lee preceding Meade at a proper interval on the out trains, and Meade preceding Lee with similar regularity on the in trains. The perfect familiarity of these old stagers with the whole route in question, and the frequency with which they have traversed it, enable them to calculate with perfect accuracy the time of arrival at the indicated points. Having gotten up all their locomotives and rolling stock regardless of expense, and putting them through night and day alike, they are enabled to disregard the ordinary drawbacks of weather, state of roads, &c., as those who do a smaller business cannot.

Patronage respectfully solicited.

G. G. MEADE,

R. E. LEE

P.S. The line through Pennsylvania has been discontinued in consequence of a painful collision which occurred there in July last, but as such things have been carefully avoided ever since, and every precaution taken for the future, it is hoped that an indulgent public will not remember that unfortunate occurrence to the prejudice of the company.

DUNN BROWNE, Secretary

In the absence of military activity, Dunn turns his hand to poetry of a highly patriotic stamp, and then invokes Dickens's Sam Weller (The Pickwick Papers) *to explain any shortcomings. The 75,000-man call, overtaken by more current events, was the number Lincoln had asked for after Fort Sumter. The elections weighing on Governor Seymour is a reference to the October balloting that went heavily against the Copperhead candidates, especially in Ohio and Pennsylvania.*

Dunn Browne in Poetry and Prose

Camp near Warrenton, Va.
November 5 [1863]

Dear Republican: I have recently taken up the following lines of march and of battle:—

CLOSE UP

Marches the soldier along the rough road,
Fording the river or climbing the hill;
Crossing the meadow, or through the thick wood:
Comes the stern order, pressing him still,
       "Forward, close up!"

Weary his limbs with the terrible marches,
Burning the heat that his thirsty throat parches,
Blistered his feet and throbbing his breast,
On still the column, denying him rest.
       "Move on, close up!"

Lingers he a moment to gather a flower,
Or fill his canteen at the wayside spring;
Tempt him the clusters of a grape-lined bower,
Sharp in his ears the chiding words ring,
   "To the ranks, close up!"

Tears through the ranks a terrible shell,
Sweeps us half down the musketry fire;
Charge the foe on us with murderous yell,
Through the fierce din swells higher and higher
   The cry, "Close up!"

"Steady, boys, on!" The foe gives way: charge!
Forward! Fix bayonets! Double quick! March!
There flies our flag. Yon's the traitors' rag.
What patriot foot this day can lag?
   "On, boys, close up!"

Falls the captain: warm on his lips the words of cheer.
Fall the brave boys, some on his left, some on his right.
Stops not the column to shed o'er the heroes even a tear,
But tenderly stepping o're the dead and the dying, on to
 the fight
   The living "close up."

Thinned are our ranks of their bravest and best.
Scarce a home not in mourning all over our land.
But a nation's behind us, glad to offer the rest
Of her sons to the cause. Brothers, come. Hand in hand
   The war we'll "close up."

The end is slightly abrupt, very likely is the criticism you offer
in reference to the above effusion. But then you know, your readers will wish there was more, as Sam Weller observed to his father
in justification of his valentine, to which the ancient Tony was
objecting that it "pulled up rather sudden."

PERPLEXING QUESTIONS IN POLITICAL ECONOMY

Perhaps there is a trifle of poetic license also in the last two
lines respecting the readiness of the nation to send the rest of

her sons. Or the nation may be more ready to send them than the sons are to come. We shall know when we see the answer to the new call for "300,000 *more*" as a national New Year's present. Father Abraham isn't over modest in his calls upon us, is he? It's strange how our officials, having once gotten their hand in, rejoice to deal in big figures. It's like rouge et noir and all sorts of gambling. The play naturally gets deeper and deeper, and the small stakes put up at first do not long answer to keep up the excitement of the game. How absurdly ridiculous and contemptible we should all now consider a call for 75,000 men! What a pitiful driblet of a national expenditure would a million dollars a day now be held! Yet time was when we thought it quite a respectable sum. That was a year or two ago, when we were spending only our own, our children's and our grandchildren's money. Now that we are upon our great-grandchildren's, and still more remote unborn descendants, or rather still greatly beyond that, spending what we have no idea anybody will ever pay at all, it goes as easy as running water. There are some rather curious questions in political economy. Did you ever devote yourself particularly to that science, dear Republican? When a nation has spent three or four times all that it is worth, is it really a great deal richer than it was before? Especially if it is mainly shot away in powder and various military projectiles? Does the fact that it is spent mainly at home, and that the people at home have furnished the money alter the case? As for instance, if a man spends his money in sinking a shaft for a coal mine into his own corn field and doesn't find any coal?

GOV. SEYMOUR TO THE RESCUE

But I leave these deep speculations for the present. Neither need I concern myself in the least in reference to the forthcoming of those 300,000 volunteers. With the utmost confidence I repose upon the assurances of the honorable governor of New York, and the other statesmen and patriots of his stripe, who objected to the draft on the ground that it was so easy to raise volunteers. Now the pressure is removed, and two months are left for the people to rush to the rescue of their own accord. I expect to see the valiant Horatio resigning his office as governor and coming on at the double quick at the head of the New York quota and a few over for good measure, just about Thanksgiving time. And then our country's safe. Perhaps the result of the elections through the North may have slightly deranged his patriotic combinations however. More anon. Yours truly,

DUNN BROWNE

This secular sermon, pleading for rationality and understanding in the midst of civil war, is once again directed toward the minds of those on the home front. The "eminent English divine" that Fiske quotes was the Reverend Augustus Campbell, rector of Liverpool, who, in rejecting an invitation to hear Henry Ward Beecher lecture on the American war and emancipation, thundered that Beecher advocated "a fratricidal war accompanied by atrocities which Christian times have seen nothing to equal, and at which the whole world stands aghast almost to incredulity."

In a Forgiving State of Mind

Camp near Stevensburg, Va.
November 12 [1863]

FALSE REPORT OF BARBARITIES IN THE WAR

Dear Republican: I see by an eminent English divine, that the "atrocities of (our) northern army" in this "war of extermination" we are waging, "reach almost the point of incredulity." Why not quite that point, oh most sapient dean or bishop, I forget which? They are absolutely incredible. No man of common sense believes a word of said atrocities. They have no existence save in the imagination of excitable narrationists, or those who willfully desire to excite the passions of both sides to fury. I don't believe a squad of confederates every drank the commissary whisky out of a Yankee skull, or that either South Carolina or Massachusetts regiments ever bayoneted each other's wounded any more than I believe that the English blew their Sepoy prisoners out of the mouths of cannon. I have known a good deal personally of the treatment of prisoners by both parties, and of their conduct on the field in many and great battles, and I not only never saw an instance of barbarity on either side, but on diligent inquiry I have never substantiated on reliable testimony a single instance. On the other hand I could relate to you hundreds of instances of the most touching generosity and kindness and self-denial on the part of brave antagonists towards each other, on almost every field where they have come in conflict. Scores of times I have seen rebel soldiers, guards of prisoners, give the very last of the three days' hard bread issued to them, to the hungry prisoners, when they knew full well the penalty they would have to pay for their generosity; for a rebel camp is the very last place where you will find hard bread lying round loose, as you may well suppose; and similar instances on our side, so many as to show that kindness, delicacy, and generosity are the rule and not the exception. The wounded are treated with the most tender consideration, the prisoners with true courtesy and chivalry, women and children when their homes fall within hostile lines, with delicate kindness.

Shame on those who would make the brave of America deficient in the noble qualities that characterize the brave of other lands. There is evil and suffering enough necessarily attendant upon war; horrible scenes enough that cannot be avoided; without telling cock-and-bull stories to inflame the minds of antagonists to retaliation barbarities. I regret as much as possible the sufferings of our brave soldiers who were brought back from Richmond the other day, and so many of whom have since died, but I shall not, without the strongest evidence, believe that they have been willfully neglected, starved or otherwise abused. I know the prisoners in Richmond have always had the same rations as the confederate soldiers, and good in quality though very small in quantity. These men of ours, it must be remembered, were the *sick men* from a large body of soldiers, and the deaths in their number must be great accordingly. Moreover we know how terribly destitute the rebels are of all kinds of medicines and delicacies for the sick, and remembering all these things, let us not be hasty to call our enemies barbarians and urge acts of retaliation in kind, or do anything tending to increase the necessary horrors of war. Let us send whatever we may be able to relieve our suffering prisoners in Richmond. Let the government take every practicable measure to make their condition less pitiable, but let us at least make some excuse for our enemies for the lack of many needful things in the great extremities to which they are, as a people, reduced, and not accuse them of more than that of which they are actually guilty.

PEACE AND GOOD WILL TO ENGLAND

And if we must endeavor to treat our "erring brethren" of the South as honorable enemies as long as we can, much more must we avoid abusing our real friends the English. Nothing can be more foolish, nothing is more groundless, than the hostile feeling that has arisen in our country, during this war, against the English people. We have some few things to complain of as towards the English government, though on the whole it has maintained a pretty fair neutrality, and that was all we could ask or wish. But the English people on the whole have always been on our side, and more and more as they have better understood the principles at issue in the contest. It is our interest, our duty, our policy, our privilege to keep on the best terms, to maintain and cherish the most friendly intimacy with the only other really free people in the world and that speaks English. We must and shall be allies. There's no use in growling at each other, and it's utterly absurd to talk about fighting each other. It's the English-speaking race and the liberty-loving race against the world, and they together, and only thus, are strong enough for the contest and will gain the victory and establish the true principles of constitutional liberty over the earth. So mote it be! So will it be! Yours truly,

DUNN BROWNE

This is a curious letter. It gives the impression that it was written in sections, with Fiske in a succession of moods. He begins with a straight-from-the-shoulder appeal to the patriotism of his readers, urging them to respond to Lincoln's recent call for 300,000 men. "Phernandiwud-ims" refers, of course, to the Copperhead-isms of Fernando Wood, which the fall elections seemed to reject. He then turns to the morale of the Army of the Potomac, presenting valuable evidence of the lasting impact the Gettysburg victory had in motivating the troops. Finally, Fiske turns a bitter eye on the war profiteers and stay-at-homes of various stripes, which seems almost to negate the tone of his opening appeal.

An Appeal for Volunteers

On picket, near Stevensburg, Va.
November 14 [1863]

A BEDSTEAD SACRIFICED FOR BREAKFAST

Dear Republican: I have just burnt up my bedstead to cook my breakfast with, to such extremities am I reduced. Fortunately our furniture hereabouts is not very costly. My bedstead above mentioned consisted of seven three-cornered rails from a Virginia fence, laid down side by side in the mud near the fire, on which my lieutenant and myself spread our blankets and slept very sweetly, with a rubber blanket over us, through the steady heavy rain that improved the darkness of the night to come down upon us unseen but not unfelt. This morning, ashamed to look us in the face after such deeds of darkness, the rain has entirely disappeared, and the face of nature looks on us as smilingly and rogueishly as if the dripping doings of the night were an exquisite joke. Well, it seems to us much more like a joke now than it did, as the creases made by the rails are getting rubbed out of our sides and legs and the clothes are mostly dried.

A LITTLE PLAIN TALK TO THE STAY AT HOMES

Picketing is pretty good fun after all. How many of you are coming out here to try it, oh my dear readers of the Republican? There are at least one full thousand of you, a strong able-bodied regiment among you, who certainly ought to be here, who can't possibly get an exemption certificate from your own conscience. You know it perfectly well. It is a great deal easier to decide on a man's duty in reference to this point now, than it was when I came out a year and a half ago. Now every man who is able-bodied, or nearly so, and between the limiting ages of military service, may presume that the call is to him. When I came the question was, "Can you afford to go to the war?" Now, in the final, serious call of the government upon our remaining resources, to finish up the contest, which, so evidently to the simplest comprehension, only needs a little more perseverance and steady persistence on our part to issue rightly and establish the value and permanence of our glorious institutions; now the question is, "Can you afford to stay at home?" This is about the last opportunity. Can you afford to feel, after the war is over, that your hand did not help to achieve the glorious result that will follow? This is an especial crisis also, in the history of the war. Can you afford to contemplate the contingency of this so costly war's becoming in some measure a failure, issuing less gloriously for our republican institutions and the future welfare of our nation, because you turned your back upon it? A magnificent national history is creating itself now, that shall be written in letters of gold on the records of all generations to come. Can you afford to leave your name off the roll, to be counted out in the record of the nation's defenders?

We don't look at the matter so clearly now as we did at the commencement of the war. It has become a matter of business and selfish interest with us. A man considers whether he can make more money in the war or out of it. He looks on the government as an employer, out of whom he is to squeeze all that he can, and in whose pay he is to do merely a hireling's service, instead of feeling that the government is merely his agent and that of the citizens, and that its cause is his own cause. We must return to first principles, remember our old patriotism, read over the old-time Fourth of July speeches, which the conscription act and Phernandiwud-isms and peace-democracy have somehow temporarily driven out of our minds. The same old truths that we used to declare so often and with much gusto when patriotism didn't mean anything but talk, remain just as true now when patriotism means real sacrifice and noble action, and perhaps the pouring out of life blood.

More Patriotism Required Than At First

It requires more patriotism to enlist now than it did two years ago. To be sure it does. The novelty of the thing has worn off. The floating population, those whom a community can most readily spare, have been used up; indeed, we who are already out in the field flatter ourselves that we are not entirely "surplus population" whom you willingly spare. We see now, far more than at first, the magnitude of the work in hand, and we know more (oh, by what a serious experience) how hard and practical and wearing and toilsome and bloody a thing war is. So the volunteer who goes forth to join his country's defenders now, goes with few visions of martial glory, and with a realizing sense of the hardships and privations that are before him. And it is better so. I would not bring one recruit to our ranks by misrepresenting the case to him. Soldiering *is* a hard business, the best you can make of it. I have laid a good deal of stone fence, dug many a rod of ditch, worked at carpentering and all sorts of farming, been a bookbinder, set up type, sawed a cord of oak wood three times in two, split and piled it, besides getting my lessons and reciting them (after a fashion), all in one day. I've taught a big district school of little urchins of the Yankee "persuasion," which is harder than any of the above, and I've attended three "sewing societies" and made five and twenty "calls" of an afternoon, which is hardest of all. But of all the different kinds of manual labor that I ever attempted, the business of marching with an army, "in heavy marching order" and on rations of "hard tack" and pork, is the most exhausting. There is very little poetry and a great deal of hard work about an active campaign. It is hard to be a private, hard to be an officer, hard to march, hard to fight, hard to be out on picket in the rain, hard to live on short rations and be exposed to all sorts of weather, hard to be wounded and lose legs and arms and get ugly scars on one's face, hard to think of lying down in death without the gentle hand of love to smooth one's brow. But there is just one thing that makes all these things easy, and that is the spirit of Christian patriotism. And I do not believe that that spirit is dead in our land. I don't believe that the nation is *so* tired of this wearisome, wasteful and bloody war as to be ready to give up the principles in whose defense we first engaged. The recent elections through the North do not speak with that voice.

THE PLUCK OF THE ARMY

And if the spirit is dying out through the land at home, I assure you it is not in the army. Never was there a better and firmer tone of patriotism in the ranks. I hardly know a man, officer or private, who will acknowledge that he regrets having given his services to his country, who would if he could rub out his record of hardships, privations and dangers, passed through in the field; who is not prouder of these years than of all his previous existence. This is the best thing I know of about the army of the Potomac. The spirit of patriotism and the confidence in our cause and in our final and speedy victory, is a perfect contrast to the feelings of discouragement and impatience and growling that prevailed a year ago, and so later, after Fredericksburg. The army is going to do up the work, whether you reinforce us or not. It is for you to say whether you will come in to share the glory of it. We have worked for Uncle Sam's thirteen dollars a month, and spent that to eke out our monotonous rations and replace the clothing we have been compelled to throw away in battle or drop in wearisome marches, till the worship of the almighty dollar is driven out us any way. And if you prefer to stay at home on your farms and with your merchandise, and trade in oxen and marry wives, and revel in luxuries, and clothe your wives with laces and diamonds paid for with the profits of shoddy contracts at the expense of the brave soldiers who are fighting your battles, why be the money and the ease yours. Save your precious legs and lives, add house to house and acre to acre. Pay commutation money and avoid drafts; wrangle over party politics and settle yourselves in the fat offices. And be the hardships ours; ours the wormy crackers and the rusty pork; ours the marches, the hard blows, the wasting sicknesses; ours the longings for the dear loved ones at home, the wives and little ones who are watching and waiting for our returning steps with unutterable anxiety; be it ours to fight all the longer because you refuse to help; be it ours to come home all the fewer, that you may stay at home the more and the merrier: still will we not murmur at our share, nor willingly exchange it for yours. We will hold it a proud privilege to go home poor on our country's pay, to carry on our person the scars of our country's service, to point to the marks of our blood on our country's torn but triumphant banner, to have it written on our headstone, "He was a soldier of the Union."

Yours truly,

DUNN BROWNE

*Fiske here returns once again to issues raised by the President's
call for 300,000 new recruits. The problem for the states was
finding that many volunteers before another federal draft took effect in January 1864. As Fiske notes, the Massachusetts quota
was 15,000, and Governor John Andrew had called the legislature into special session on the matter. The bill it finally passed
was a compromise between bounties and extra pay for the new
men. Massachusetts volunteers were offered a choice: a bounty
of $325 (in addition to the $300 federal bounty), or a bounty of
$50 plus a wage supplement of $20 a month. On the principle of
a bird in the hand, editorialized the* Republican, *"it is not difficult
to tell which the most will adopt." The lawmakers evaded the
question, raised here by Fiske, of equal pay for men already in
service, leaving the matter to the 1864 legislature. The nine-month
men Fiske mentions were state militia drafts, especially those
called out for the Antietam and Gettysburg crises. Artemus Ward
(Charles Farrar Browne) was a noted humorist of the day and a
particular favorite of Mr. Lincoln's.*

Old Soldiers on Big Bounties

Near Stevensburg, Va.
[November 1863]

Dear Republican: I suppose it has never occurred to any of
our sapient legislators, who are now in extra session, anxiously
debating whether to give the new volunteers $500 apiece at the
outset, *and* then from seven to twelve dollars a month extra besides Uncle Sam's pay and bounties, or only to adopt one of those
measures—I suppose it has never entered one of their innocent
heads that the old soldiers, who have fought a dozen battles, and
borne the heat and burden of a couple of years' terrible campaigns, are entitled to any consideration. While you are lavishing
your millions freely as water to buy recruits whom no sentiment
of patriotism can induce to volunteer, no man rises to suggest
that any drop out of the ocean of your bounty should fall upon
the brave men now in the field, who sprang to arms at the first
for patriotism, and not for lucre. We don't expect that any such

measure of even-handed justice should *pass* any of the honorable
bodies now assembled; but it would be agreeable to our feelings,
we acknowledge, to have some honorable member just suggest
that the extra seven or twelve dollars a month might be paid to
the old and new men alike. We don't object to the laborers who
come in at the eleventh hour getting their penny the same as we
who have worked all the long twelve hours; but it does seem a
little tough that they should get their shillings and dollars and
guineas while we must be content with our original penny. "Shall
we not do what we will with our own?" Yes: but you are voting
away our own as well as your own; you are taxing us as well as
yourselves; you are taking something out of the pocket of every
one of the old soldiers to pay these extra dollars a month to the
new recruits who come in to fight by their sides.

Have all the necessaries of life risen so much in price as to
make additional pay necessary for those who are recruited into
our armies? I wonder where the prices are any steeper than out
here in the army, where the soldier's thirteen dollars a month
will barely purchase him an occasional potato or onion (I've seen
often ten or fifteen cents apiece paid for them) to change his
monotonous diet of pork and hard tack, to save him from scurvy,
and keep him in tobacco; and, at home, don't his wife and children, who have been left to their own resources a year and a half
already, need the help to be derived from the extra dollars a
month pay as much as the wife and children of the new man, who
can leave behind for them from two hundred to five hundred
dollars of his bounty? We have stood still and seen men come out
here for nine months, and go back again (having, a good many
of them, stopped to guard some point in the rear while we came
ahead to do the fighting) with larger pay, and their bounties, for
their three-fourths of a year's service, than all that we shall receive for the entire three years; and we have borne it from the
love we have for the good cause. We have seen the public sentiment of the North, almost the whole influence of the newspapers, and the vote of hundreds and towns and cities united to
favor the buying and sending-out to us as substitutes the lowest
and vilest classes of your population to stand by the side of your
brothers and sons as companions; and we have borne that too,
proud in the thought that we had virtue and discipline enough in

our body to keep in order even such an unruly addition. Whether, beyond all these things, we can bear the additional outrage of seeing an extra monthly wages paid out before our eyes every pay-day to the men who are now to join us, I do not know. I hope our patriotism will endure even such a test; but it will be a little different from any thing that has befallen us yet, because the bounties have been paid at home, out of our sight, while this extra wages will be a present, gratuitous, and constantly repeated insult.

To cut the matter short, and have my grumble out, if, for instance, old Massachusetts must raise ten millions more or less to put into the field her quota of 15,000, and doesn't care for the inequality and injustice done to those already in the field, let us hope that she will use some common sense in the distribution of the greenbacks. One-half of the 15,000, however she raises them, will be, in less than six months, deserters or *dead-beats*, hangers-on in hospitals, or discharged for disability—a disability, in most cases, not incurred from any service rendered the government. Let her, therefore, not give the recruits, say, more than a thousand dollars at the outset, and another thousand after at least one year's faithful service, or proof that they have been in one battle without running away; and then toss them another thousand when the war is closed and their service finished. If you will get any good service for your money, we will be better satisfied than to see you squander it away on those who come out with no idea of fighting, and who will be back at home on one plea or another almost before an ordinary railroad excursion-ticket would lose its validity. The men that stay and complete their service are the ones who ought to get the pay. Put an extra five or ten dollars a month (if you don't know what to do with your money) on the pay for the second year's service, and another increase for the third year, and there will be more sense in your expenditure.

At present, it looks to us, at this distance, as if the whole Northern people were so frightened at the possibility of the conscription wheel's giving you the patriot's privilege of serving your country in arms, as to be able to think of nothing but the getting round the present emergency at any cost. No matter how much money, if it will induce no matter whom to put their names down, and make out the state's quota. You are obliged to pass stringent laws to prevent your towns and cities from utterly ruining themselves in the extravagance of their bounties; and all that the law accomplishes is, apparently, to reserve the state legislature the privilege of making a general, universal, and so, of course, equally distributed bankruptcy. I never knew such a readiness to impose taxes before. It beats Artemus Ward's willingness to sacrifice his wife's brother to put down the rebellion, this readiness on the part of our Northern people to burden their children and children's children forevermore with enormous taxes. You can afford much better to draw lots to see which of you shall come out and help us finish up the work that is so nearly done, than to raise such extravagant sums to bribe mercenaries to come out and do your work for you. It is a freeman's privilege to vote, and to defend his government, not by proxy, but in his own person; and a nation is in a bad way when its citizens are ready to give up that privilege, and put money, instead of their own right arms, to the cause. There! I've growled my growl: now pass your bounty-acts. Yours truly,

DUNN BROWNE

Dunn Browne, in just six weeks' time, brings reform to the army, or so his Republican *readers must have thought. On October 17 he called for reducing the soldiers' burden of rations and ammunition, and now the War Department has listened, and acted. General Quincy A. Gillmore and Rear Admiral John A. Dahlgren commanded the operations against Charleston. "Litulmak" is of course "Little Mac," General McClellan, not one of Fiske's favorites. This approbation of General Meade is somewhat surprising after Fiske's brusque criticisms of Meade for failing to counterattack on July 4 at Gettysburg, and subsequently for letting Lee escape across the Potomac. Perhaps the flattering view of Meade, and the expressed optimism about the rebellion "gone up," were part of Samuel Fiske's continued efforts in these fall months to raise morale on the home front and especially to encourage enlistments.*

Almost Incredible Reforms

On picket near Stevensburg, Va.
Nov. 23 [1863]

THE RATION AND AMMUNITION QUESTION

Dear Republican: I'm greatly encouraged: more reconciled to not being commander-in-chief of all the armies in America than I have been for a long time. For there are actually some glimmerings of sense beginning to be perceptible, even in the management of our war department. An order has come down, I am informed by a credible witness who says he has seen it, has actually come down and is to take effect immediately, that the men are not to be compelled to carry on their backs henceforth more than five days' rations at any one time. I had utterly despaired of the thing; had seen the eight days', the ten days', and, in one or two instances, the eleven days' mule burden piled on the men's backs, over and over again, cruelly, wastefully and uselessly, never once accomplishing the purpose, never in any single instance lasting over six days, till I had about concluded the administration was in some way politically committed to the arrangement, and that I might be unintentionally committing high-copperheadism by grumbling about it.

And another thing. You won't believe me this time, dear Republican, I know. You needn't. It's too much to ask of you certainly in the same letter that mentions the above reform. But it's the positive fact nevertheless that only 40 rounds of cartridges are required henceforth to be carried by our soldiers. I am afraid Secretary Stanton and General Halleck aren't going to live long, they are getting so good and considerate all at once. But they couldn't die in a better cause. Why, more cartridges have been wasted during this war by compelling the men to carry sixty, eighty and even a hundred rounds when their cartridge boxes won't hold but forty, than would carry on for ten years a small "scrimmage" like that of England and France in the Crimea. And besides the relief from the burden, the boys will no longer be liable to drink gunpowder coffee from a cartridge in their haversacks bursting into their sugar or coffee-sack, or to be blowed up by a match setting fire to an extra package in their breeches pocket. The government may as well cut down the manufacture of fixed ammunition say a couple of million rounds a day, for the principal use to which cartridges have been put hitherto has been to throw them away out of their knapsacks, haversacks and pockets. The saltpetre speculators will fail most likely. Oh no! There's Gillmore and Fort Sumter to save them. If Q. A. G. could only be put upon an allowance of 40 rounds for his 300-pounders, the Sumter dust-heap defenses wouldn't be continually strengthened by the addition of so much broken iron-ware. But the bomb-shell manufacture must be encouraged, I suppose. Has it never occurred to Gillmore though, that, as the ship channel passes so near Sumter, a few more months of his bombardment will fill up that channel with more formidable obstructions than those the rebels have laid, even a mountain heap of shot and shells? Admiral Dahlgren probably perceives this danger to the passage of his iron-clads, and hence the mysterious source of the rumored estrangement of those distinguished men.

THE POTOMAC ARMY AND ITS LEADER

But to return from Charleston to the army of the Potomac. We are lying here as quietly and comfortably almost as if in winter quarters, all sorts of rumors prevailing about us and among us, but not a soul knowing what will be the next step. I doubt whether even George and Abraham are decided what is best to be done. But when they do decide, we shall lie down at night thinking of putting on an addition to our house the next day or of raising the chimney one pork-barrel higher, and in the morning at reveille, say half past five, the word will be passed round, "Breakfast, boys, pack up and off at seven." And we shall be off at seven and twenty miles distant at night, charging somebody's rifle pits, laying a pontoon bridge, or perhaps building our fourth log house for the season, to be plastered up or burned up or abandoned according to circumstances. Never was an army better in hand. Never a leader who could put it "twice in three places" quicker or more neatly. If Meade, or Halleck, or Stanton, or the president, could decide on the right thing to be done, or Providence would specially postpone the approach of winter till some two of them could agree on a plan, you might rely on the execution of it with a trust I should never have dared place in the army of the Potomac under any of its previous leaders. Before "Litulmak" would have gotten his Hd Qr tents down, and his staff and escort adorned for a start, our George would be at the end of a forty-mile expedition, just starting off his prisoners for Washington, and Father Abraham's "well done, boys!" would be flashing down to us on the telegraph wires. Pity a machine so efficient, with an engineer so careful and skillful can't be put upon some one of the routes to Richmond before the mud shuts it off.

THE REBELLION GONE UP

But the rebellion is practically "gone up" whatever is done or left undone. The longest purse decides a modern war. The party whose resources will hold out a day the longer of the two wins. Uncle Sam's wind is the best. He can strike the last blow. And down the proud, wicked rebellion goes. I grieve most sincerely, even now, in anticipation, over the vast amount of suffering and starvation which must come this winter in the rebel states; suffering of the poor women and innocent children, of thousands whose hearts have always been with the old Union and the stars and stripes. Sufferings of hosts of Union prisoners, who will have to share in a measure at least in the destitution which prevails in the land, notwithstanding all that our government can do to alleviate their condition. Yes, I acknowledge to a little compassion for what the rebel soldiers themselves will have to endure. Yet I can, with tolerable resignation, contemplate the taming influence that a little wholesome starvation will exercise over rebels in arms, and be complacent over almost anything that promises to end this dreadful contest, with success to us and a happy return to our homes. Affectionately yours,

DUNN BROWNE

Long celebrated in New England, Thanksgiving was declared by President Lincoln's proclamation a national holiday in 1863. Fiske's account of how Company I, 14th Connecticut volunteers, noticed the occasion is good-natured and cheerful enough, yet it

reveals an attitude in the army that is much changed from the year before. Fiske's letter of November 29, 1862, to the Republican recorded an elaborate plan for a real New England Thanksgiving, carried off amidst vast complications but with ultimate success by the regimental officers. Things are decidedly different after a year of war; now the only effort made to celebrate Thanksgiving is to try and imagine it.

The Soldiers' Thanksgiving

Camp near Stevensburg, Va.
November 25 [1863]

D. B. ORDERS HIS THANKSGIVING DINNER

Dear Republican: Wishing to celebrate with due festivity the national Thanksgiving to-morrow, I have just sent in the following requisition upon our brigade commissary:

Required for Officers' Mess of Co.—, ——Regiment:
One turkey,　　} dressed
Three chickens, } dressed
Eleven mince pies,
Two hundred oysters (on the half shell),
Five gallons new cider,
Two bushels winter apples (Nonesuch),
One pumpkin, 8 dozen eggs, and 1 gallon milk (for pies),
Ten lbs. hard crackers,
Four lbs. pork.

D. B., Capt., &c.

So you see we mean to render all honor to the proclamation of the president and so many worthy governors of loyal states, and lay in a stock of creature comforts, to minister to our physical wants, while not neglecting I trust the intellectual, moral and spiritual exercises appropriate to the occasion. My requisition, as above given, is not so much to furnish forth a grand dinner and gratify our relatives, as by varying somewhat from our usual bill of fare and approaching in some measure the styles of edibles that will load your tables at home, to bring ourselves the more into sympathy with you, our far off and much loved friends. We shall, through the associations connected with the various luxuries set down above, bring ourselves into a closer *rapport* with our families and kinsmen and friends, who will be sitting down to tables loaded with such like articles, only more abundantly. Partaking of these comfortable viands our thoughts and hearts will soon pass over the hundreds of intervening miles and we shall be with those we love best, enjoying the feast of reason and flow of soul that are the best portion of Thanksgiving festivities, satisfying our appetite for social converse and friendly intercourse, the greetings of affection and the words of love. Dissecting artistically the noble turkey furnished us (in answer to the above requisition) by our provident Uncle Sam, through the medium of his faithful commissary, I shall think of the many boards at which I should be heartily welcome, where the same process will be most likely gone through with at about the same time, and it will be a little as though I were really there. Helping myself to a delicate morsel of the poultry provided as above, I may be borne, so to speak, upon the wings of a chicken, to the bosom of my family, break a wish-bone with my hopeful four-year-old, sitting with bib under his chin on a high chair by my side, and ask the partner of my joys and sorrow, who sits opposite, if I may help her to a little more of the dressing. While making out my requisition I was thinking how gladly our good friends at the North would answer a requisition from us for a grand Thanksgiving dinner to the whole army of the Potomac, yes, to every one of your sons and brothers who is in the field in your cause, anywhere in our land. If we could only start an express line straight from your living hearts and hands to our mouths, what a spread would we have to-morrow! Well, we have the never-failing, lightning line of imagination, of kind wishes and deathless affection. We'll try to be well satisfied with this, and to render with some sincerity the thanks due to our kind Father above for the many good things—the infinitely rich blessings—he has bestowed upon and continued unto us the past year.

What The Dinner Really Was

I am here interrupted by the return of my messenger to the commissary. All the articles on the list are crossed out except the last two—the pork and the crackers! As a heartless joke upon my misfortune the word designating the kind of apples is left standing also. None such. Ominous designation indeed. Well, I trust, as I am baulked in my intention of sympathizing with you in my style of dinner to-morrow, that some of you will have considerably forestalled me and set forth your festive table with a big chunk of fat pork and a plate of hard bread to sympathize with a soldier's Thanksgiving dinner. Yours truly,

Dunn Browne

P.S. Orders are just in to march in the morning. So we may celebrate our Thanksgiving by a long march in the mud, or even possibly by a conflict with the enemy. Having little present cause for thanksgiving than ourselves, as far as the comfort of the day is concerned, may we at least be doing that which shall give the country some cause of lasting thanksgiving.

D.B.

The "late campaign" is that of Mine Run, November 26–December 1, and it did indeed conclude campaigning in Virginia in 1863. Fiske captures the operation in precise shorthand, and his explanation of the tactical dilemma facing the generals in this third year of war is equally valid—and notable for being a contemporaneous analysis. Writing the same day to his brother, Fiske described waiting anxiously with his men that Monday morning "& though I said nothing to anybody, I knew we could never carry the works & should lose at least half our force in making the attempt." He added, "you may imagine my relief" when the generals "looked & were of my opinion." Lee's matching offensive was the earlier Bristoe campaign. The rumored success of Grant that Fiske mentions was of course the overwhelming victory at Chattanooga.

What the Soldiers Think of the Late Campaign

Camp near Stevensburg, Va.
December 3 [1863]

Dear Republican: We have just returned from our little excursion over the Rapidan, and as one might expect from such a miserable, barren, wasted and desolate country as we have visited, we have returned no whit richer than we went away. Why, we find that not even laurels grow here at this season, and so didn't pluck one, so far as I can learn. We have just dropped over unceremoniously to call upon Lee, and found him making so much fuss to receive us, overdoing the thing in fact, that we wouldn't stop, but retired in disgust. We don't want too much parade made on our account. When we found that he was cutting down all the trees in his front dooryard to make an uncommonly high fence, and even digging up a large part of his farm into mounds and ditches and such like ornamental works over our arrival, we wouldn't countenance the thing, and came away before putting him to still more trouble.

The fall campaign in Virginia may now be considered as closed, I should think, and as a pretty even thing on the whole. They have made us a visit, and we have made them a visit. There has been a see-saw game across the Rappahannock, in which each side has gone up and gone down, and nobody can say which has kept the longest end of the plank.

The simple state of the case is this, that both the Virginia armies are now so well disciplined and experienced that they are very hard to beat. One side must make some serious blunder to meet any serious danger: and they don't make any great blunders. They have grown cautious over the experience of Fredericksburg and Gettysburg, and they have learned the value of even slight and hastily thrown-up breastworks. With the formidable rifles now in use, a single line of veteran soldiers, behind a three-foot breastwork of earth and rails or a stone fence, can drive back and almost destroy three similar lines approaching to attack them, and we have all learned this truth, and even the most pitiful coward and sneak in a regiment knows that his safest place is to stay by and not get shot in the back as he runs away. Give either our army or the rebels twenty-four hours notice of an approaching attack, and they will select a good position and throw up entrenchments which it is folly for any but overwhelmingly superior numbers to attempt to carry.

We went over the Rapidan, hoping to get at the enemy in some spot where his superiority in position would no more than balance our superiority in numbers. But he set his men to chopping and digging till, in their high and commanding position, we should have only made another Fredericksburg by trying to storm them. The order was given, and the hour was fixed (8 o'clock Monday morning), knapsacks were piled up under guard, the men were cautioned as to all the particulars of the advance, and every officer and soldier made himself ready, at the first note of the bugle, to advance on that short road to death or victory. And had the bugle sounded that line would have moved steadily up and done what human valor and endurance could do towards planting our battle flags on the crest of those bristling works. They might perhaps have done it at the sacrifice of half or two-thirds of their number. But it was a very serious "perhaps," and the hour passed, the bugle sounded not, the charge was not made—and we are safely and perhaps a little ingloriously back again in our old camp. We have met with no serious losses so far as I have learned. Our retreat was very skillfully conducted, and few stragglers fell out and few prisoners were taken.

If, deciding not to attack, we had moved at once back to Fredericksburg, and occupied the heights in the rear of that city for our winter quarters, we should all have felt that a good thing had been done, and our labor not wasted. But we waited from Monday morning till Tuesday night, and then (Lee having, I suppose, anticipated us by throwing a force into Fredericksburg) we were obliged to return the way we went, and couldn't even save our credit by saying that we went over, not particularly anxious for a fight, but just taking that route to Fredericksburg, and paying our respects to Lee in passing. However, I may be just talking nonsense and folly, as perhaps it was no part of our plan to get to F. at all, and not desirable for us to change our base thitherward. I am just telling you what the troops say about the movement among themselves. And moreover it seems as if the position back of Fredericksburg was a good deal better one to hold for the winter than our present one.

We have heard nothing from the world since we went away, and are confidently expecting to-morrow lots of letters and papers to post us up in respect to our friends and the state of the war. We don't even know what Grant has been doing or how true were the rumors of his victory that we heard just as we were moving on Thanksgiving day.

There, somebody says orders are come to be ready to move at

a moment's notice. What's up? Isn't our fall campaign ended yet? Yours in haste,

DUNN BROWNE

Meade's Mine Run campaign involved a crossing of the Rapidan and an attempt to turn Lee's flank. After corps commander William French fumbled an opportunity, Meade was left in a direct confrontation against Lee's army drawn up on good defensive ground behind Mine Run. Fiske here details the army's subsequent pull-back to recross the Rapidan at Germanna Ford.

The Withdrawal

Camp near Stevensburg, Va.
[December 1863]

Dear Republican: It is a very nice operation to withdraw an army from the immediate front of a strong enemy's line. It takes but a moment to write the newspaper item, that "Gen. So and So, finding the position of the enemy too strong to be forced, retired without loss"; but to do the thing neatly and safely, without loss of men or stores, is one of the most delicate of military operations. It is easy enough to be repulsed, and rush back helter-skelter, "every man for himself, and Gen. Stuart take the hindmost"; but to insinuate an army out of a tight place voluntarily as an unforced military measure—that is another thing.

I suppose two great armies are rarely drawn up so closely and squarely in front of each other, and lie face to face so quietly, and then separate so cleanly, as the two armies of Meade and Lee in the recent operations across the Rapidan toward Orange Court House. In that part of the line occupied on our side by the second corps, under Gen. Warren, the distance between the advanced skirmishers on either side varied from fifty yards to thirty rods, perhaps. Men could easily talk with each other across, could hear the orders given, observe the relief of sentries, and be aware of almost every movement going forward; and the problem was, to withdraw the supplies and trains, the ambu-

lances with the wounded, the troops and all the artillery, the
pickets, and even the very foremost line of skirmishers, from before that near and most formidable line of vigilant enemies, without their knowledge if possible, certainly without injury from
their attacks.

Monday morning we lay two hours in lines of battle, my regiment in the foremost, expecting, at the concerted note of the
bugle, to move forward in desperate assault upon that long line
of works, bristling with cannon, and defended by sharp abatis
along its whole front; but Tuesday evening the movement was to
be in the opposite direction, to put as great a distance as possible between us, and as silently as might be. Stealthily as a cat
might be supposed to withdraw from some too dangerous prox-
imity, on velvet toes, and with claws and teeth and watchful eyes
ever toward the enemy, so take we up our retrograde march, the
strongly guarded trains foremost, the artillery—all but a light
battery or two for emergencies—next, and the main body of the
troops following, a select regiment or two to bring up the rear,
and strong cavalry escorts all along our flanks; none left behind,
save the devoted pickets to hold fast their position till the army
be far on its way, and themselves perhaps to pay in death or
captivity for the safe departure of the main body. The usual
camp-fires are left burning, and even men to keep them up till
the withdrawal of the pickets. At 9 p.m. the grand movement
began, save that of the trains which were dragging their slow
length some hours before us along the road. Artillery rumbling
heavily stretches itself out on the turnpike. The heavy masses of
troops prolong themselves into one seemingly everlasting column, moving by the flank, in files of four, well closed up and in
excellent order, in the same direction. Tramp, tramp, tramp
along the frozen road, with occasional tinkle of a tin cup and the
low voice of comrade to comrade, or the clatter of a horse's hoofs
as an aide gallops along the column with a message; with the
gleaming of musket-barrels, and now and then a glare of light
from some wayside camp-fire, upon the moving array; through
the endless thicket of the great "Wilderness"; now among tiny,
thickly growing pines, now through groves of noble oaks, and yet
again penetrating tangled bottoms of I know not what varieties
of trees and shrubs, all matted together with vines. So make we
our way to and then along the plank-road and toward Fredericks-

burg; horses and their armed riders looking out of the trees upon our column the whole way, and casting huge, fantastic shadows in the light of the hundreds of fires kindled on either side as if to guide us on our right path. It was a right romantic spectacle, a night to be remembered a whole life long.

But you are not forgetting, I hope, the poor pickets and the rear guard still confronting the grim lines of the enemy, and upon whose faithfulness depends the safety of the whole moving body. Listening anxiously to the movements of our forces behind them; peering watchfully into the obscurity before them to see if the enemy show any indications of knowledge of our maneuver; dreading lest a premature discovery on the part of the enemy should induce them to sally out in force; and yet determined to hold their ground with steady valor, and prove themselves worthy of the trust reposed in them, though knowing that even a wound would throw them into the hands of the enemy, where the greatest sufferings and destitution would be their lot—slowly pass the anxious hours of watchfulness and piercing cold. But three o'clock in the morning comes at last. The reliable veteran officer selected to withdraw the pickets, and bring up the rear, passes quietly along the line; the advanced sentries creep back on hands and knees to the outposts; the outposts steal away to the reserves; the reserves form into column, and pass rapidly over the road, arousing every straggling sleeper from the main body who may have escaped the notice of the provost-guard, and sweeping him into their column; and the cavalry hovering along our flanks fall in right and left as the picket column passes, and are ready to check any too-sudden pursuit and skirmish along the rear of our column, till the whole army has accomplished its weary but successful night movement, and is safely across the river barrier. So nicely are the calculations made, so delicately is the whole complicated machinery of the withdrawal managed, that not one of the hundred things that might have marred the whole does actually occur; and the retirement is a successful maneuver; the retreat becomes no disaster. Discipline, steadiness, and valor have accomplished it so quietly that nothing is thought of what is indeed a more difficult feat than to fight an ordinary battle.

Dawn breaks upon the old encampment. The advanced pickets of the enemy, who had been chopping and digging and strengthening his defenses by busy details the whole night, discover that the little detached breastworks of rails over against them have no blue-coated occupants. A cautious advance of the gray-backs shows our whole line of pickets withdrawn, and our camps with their still smouldering fires deserted. A rapidly organized pursuit finds only traces of the direction in which we have departed; and Stuart's cavalry, hastening on our track, gets up just in time to see the last of the Union pontoon boats drawn up from the waters of the Rapidan upon the hither shore.

Yours truly,

DUNN BROWNE

"Lee has rather outgeneralled Meade this time," Fiske told his brother of the Mine Run campaigning, "& we have had our awful tough march for nothing." It is that march that Fiske focuses on in his third letter on the aborted operation. The withdrawal took Fiske back to his old quarters at Stevensburg, halfway between the Rapidan and the Rappahannock.

Trials and Perils of the Late March Back and Forth

Stevensburg, Va.
December 7 [1863]

Dear Republican: I told you in my last of our safe but inglorious return to our camp this side of the Rapidan, but I did not tell you what a sweet time we had during our foolish little campaign of a week. It is all very well to talk of a campaign in December; and it is a good thing to take part in, too, if something of national importance is to be accomplished. We will march and fight up to our knees in mud or through drifts of snow if we can really see anything done towards finishing up the war. But to be put through such a week as the last one was, and see absolutely nothing come of it, is a bit discouraging. Nevertheless it is better than running our heads against a stone wall and getting them broken. That is some consolation to be sure.

But I was going to tell you a little what it is to march and fight (or even to march and not fight if you think that more appropriate to our recent expedition) at this season of the year. Imagine yourself carrying all that you shall have to eat, drink, wear and sleep under for five days on your back, and your weapons of war and ammunition besides, and then march, not independently and at your leisure, but in column, where you cannot dodge the ditches and puddles and other bad places, rapidly and through the warm portion of the day, say, at a moderate estimate, fifteen miles, till you are thoroughly saturated, as to all your clothes, with perspiration, as you surely will be even if the day be quite cold. And then at dark or an hour after, as the cold night comes down around you, turn out from the road, stumble across a field or meadow, thoroughly wet your feet and legs in crossing a slough or brook, spend fifteen or twenty shivering minutes in dressing the lines and stacking arms, and find yourself dismissed for the night. You know nothing where to seek for water for your coffee, or wood to cook your supper, and dry your soaking feet, but must go running round the country until you have supplied yourself in abundance, and that, too, when several thousand other soldiers are in competition with you at the same market. Then you must kindle your fire, get out your little cup and make your coffee over a smoking, out-of-door fire, eat your hard crackers and pork, and dry off your clothes and persons as best you may by the fire, and exposed most likely to a chilling wind. Then you must select your place on the freezing ground, spread out your rubber blanket, and if you have a chum as every good soldier should, lay one of your woolen blankets under you and spread the other over the two of you, and the other rubber above that and lie down, overcoats on, to the warmest sleep you can command. If the heavens above contain themselves, you can possibly get through the night comfortably, if your circulation is first rate, for "where two lie together there is heat," even on a December night, with your feet to the fire. But if the clouds shed their rain upon you; if the cold, drizzling sleet come remorselessly down upon your so thinly protected person, then farewell sleep unless you are so exhausted with the march that sleep you must, even at the risk of its becoming the sleep of death.

But at the best estate of the soldier's bivouac, he is by no means sure of lying down in peace, under the open firmament. About once in four or five days, in his regular turn, comes guard or picket duty to give him a night of watchfulness after a day of weariness, before another day of weary marching. But this is not all. The camp is no sooner in sound repose, perhaps, than, the trains coming up, or if we are at the extreme front, coming as near as is considered safe, the order comes round to rise and draw rations. Then a detail of six or ten men from a company must go away in the darkness to the wagons, and bring the rations, and cut them up, and the sergeants must distribute them; the whole business occupying frequently all the first part of the night. Twice out of the six nights of our recent expedition, the men were disturbed till midnight in this business. Then in the morning is the same routine of wood, water, cooking breakfast, packing and preparing for march in the frosty morning air, and most likely long before day, as the order is usually to march at daylight, and off we go to another day of hard marching, or to an advance in line of battle or a charge upon the enemy. Saturday morning, November 28th, we marched over two miles in line of battle, that is ranks two deep, the line extending according to our numbers, miles perhaps, and advancing without reference to the road, and turning out for no obstacles, over ditches and sloughs, through woods and fields, sweeping everything before us. Then it rained a cold, sleety rain the whole day, and we stood shivering in six inches of mud, and at night could hardly pick out a dry spot in the woods to lie down.

Then came our movement round the enemy's flank on Sunday and the array for the expected attack on the exceedingly frosty Monday morning, &c., &c.; but the crown of the whole for a test of a man's endurance was the retreat on Tuesday night. Twelve hours of steady marching we made from 9 p.m. till 9 a.m., with only one little rest of perhaps twenty minutes. And after two or three hours to get coffee and food, we started off again and marched across country for a short cut, through woods, ditches, swamps, bushes and briars that certainly lengthened our journey at least half a dozen miles, instead of shortening it. I thought sure I should be obliged to leave one poor *played-out* officer of Uncle Sam in a big ditch that he at last stumbled into after dark. He didn't seem really worth picking up and carrying along any further. But finally, for the sake of the good cause, I pried and rolled him up the bank, clapped the hat a little firmer on the top of his head, and pushed him on across the plowed field covered with long, tough briars that tangled his legs at every step, and succeeded in emptying him into his old hut, bundled down in a heap like a parcel of limp, creased, dirty clothes, awaiting the pains of the washerwoman. But I was glad the next morning that I took the pains, and hope you are so too, for otherwise the lucubrations of your correspondent would have ceased evermore— for the man was the veritable D.B. himself. I never experienced more delicious sensations than when I laid these tired bones on the old bunk, and drew the blanket over my head for the long delayed sleep; for I had been on guard and picket duty two out of the six preceding nights, and marched the whole of the night immediately preceding. Every limb and muscle and nerve of my tired body sent up murmurs of thanksgiving for the refreshment of rest. And sleep came as the healer of all my discomforts— sweet, deep, ten-hours slumber—which, thanks to a good constitution and the health gained by sixteen months of out-door life, left me in the morning to rise fresh and young like a boy again, and ready for another similar trip.

But I have written you enough to show that a winter campaign in even favorable weather, such as we certainly did have in the main, is no mere pleasant amusement. We must have marched in that last 24 hours something over 30 miles. May our next marches amount to more than the last.

Yours, egotistically, I am afraid,

DUNN BROWNE

8

WINTER QUARTERS

The assorted medical treatments Fiske describes here suggest that his illness was dysentery, the most common of soldier complaints in this war, but his correspondence was actually absent from only one issue of the weekly Republican. *"R.W.B." was the paper's correspondent with the 10th Massachusetts, posted with the Sixth Corps in the Army of the Potomac. Fiske's complaint that a Washington press leak had compromised Meade's Mine Run operation was echoed by the* Republican, *whose editor wrote of "the official organ of the war department having given the enemy full notice. . . ." Apparently General Lee did notice; on November 25 he wrote Jefferson Davis that from "indications in the Washington papers, I infer that General Meade intends to advance." Fiske was moved to reaffirm his support for Meade (in which he paraphrases his July 27 comments) by widespread reports of the general's pending replacement.*

Dunn Browne in Winter Quarters

Camp near Stevensburg, Va.
December 24 [1863]

SICK AND WELL AGAIN

Dear Republican: Perhaps you may have noticed that I have not written you any letters for some time past. Partly, I've been sick, and a light quinine-and-whisky diet, varied with blue mass and Dovers' powders, wouldn't be likely to inspire anything very entertaining. Then I wanted, besides, to see whether you could sustain your little paper without any help from this quarter. I have been happy to see that your issues went right on as quietly and regularly as ever, with no more disturbance of equilibrium produced by a short allowance of the raw material from the second corps, than the failure of a rag merchant in Canton would affect Secretary Chase's issue of greenbacks. By the way, what has become of your pleasant correspondent "R.W.B."? I had a right good call from him when we were on our little expedition across the Rapidan and our corps were together.

I believe the people are pretty much over expecting the Potomac army to cross the country to Richmond this winter, and pretty much over grumbling at our ill success in our last attempt. Let us hope we shall not give the enemy quite so much notice next time we are about to move. There is reason in all things. It is well enough to use all the proper courtesy towards a foe. "Messieurs the English will fire first. The French guard never fires first," &c., &c. But to publish officially in a government organ, a week beforehand, the movement which ought to be of the nature of a surprise to succeed, that was laying it on a trifle thick, wasn't it? And whatever the people may say about it, it is the certainest thing possible that the army did the right thing in not attacking Lee in his position beyond the Rapidan. And Meade, knowing himself to be right on that point, won't trouble himself overmuch I hope about the howling of the people. The fact of the matter is, armies can't fight pleasantly and comfortably in the winter. The style of lying still or otherwise wasting all the decent season of the year, and then starting your grand expeditions about the 1st or 15th of December, has remained in vogue a good while to be sure, but it must, as the boys say, "play out."

GEN. MEADE AS A COMMANDER

Then, as for Gen. Meade and his supersedure, why the soldiers hereabouts think we may as well be contented with the general we have, who is certainly a good one, who has shown wonderful skill and facility in the handling and moving of an army, and has, on the whole, proved himself a pretty good match for Lee in generalship the whole campaign through, as to go further and fare—no man can say how. The country of course overrated Meade after the battle of Gettysburg, concluding that *the* great military hero had now made his appearance on the stage in the chief part, and all we should have more to do would be to clap our hands and shout "Encore!" (at each new victory) till the curtain dropped. You many not probably recollect that I wrote you a few days after Gettysburg, with an enthusiasm not quite toned up to that of the country in general, that "our new commander" was "a good general, of fully average ability, excellent military knowledge and fair moral character, which is a great deal to say of a general." "What I say I stands by." Meade is a very fair general. He has handled this army with a neatness and dispatch no other general has ever shown. Without any fuss he puts us just where we need to be in the quickest possible way. I am certain we should lose in this respect (of the mobility of the troops) by any change. And under no other leader would the men fight with more confidence. For they are sure he is chary of thrusting them into danger, is careful of their lives. And if he orders them anywhere, they know he has looked at the matter carefully, and they can probably go there. And if the order to charge those works on the other side of the Rapidan had come, as we for two hours momentarily expected it, every man would have marched cheerfully on, formidable as they looked, believing that Meade's judgment was better than his own. And still further, because he did not order the advance then, because of the hopelessness of the undertaking and his regard for their limbs and lives, the next time he tells the boys to charge, wherever it may be, those boys are going to charge, like an avalanche which don't stop till it gets there. If you had seen the cleanness, celerity and safety with which the army was withdrawn, from under the very nose of the enemy without molestation, and whisked across the Rapidan "twixt night and morning," you wouldn't supersede Meade, certainly if you suspected you might soon have occasion to advance backward out of the enemy's country. Lest any may suspect the disinterestedness of these remarks laudatory of our general, I solemnly declare that I am not on the staff of the commander in question and have no present expectation of riding a horse and wearing gold lace by his appointment. Nay, the man once actually had the impoliteness to return to me disapproved a note I sent him requesting a few days' leave.

A Smoky Chimney

We are now actually in winter quarters; about the fourth that a good many of us have built this season. Unfortunately for me we stopped at the even numbers. All my odd-numbered chimneys have drawn finely, while the even-numbered ones have smoked, though constructed with equal skill (my personal beauty renders it specially necessary to take pains with a chimney at whose fireside I am to sit), laid up with the same kinds of sods and stones and plastered with mud of the same consistency. Virginia is the most consistently muddy state that I know; always mud enough in your front dooryard to plaster up your chimney, and of the stickiest kind. Won't you come and sit with me some of these long winter evenings, dear Republican, and perhaps your— different style of beauty might counteract mine and my chimney become perfect? Affectionately,

Dunn Browne

Remarkably, in January 1864, Samuel Fiske created an island of domestic bliss squarely in the midst of his brigade encampment on the Rapidan. His wife, Lizzie, and his four-year-old son, George, on the strength of a pass wrangled from the War Department, set up housekeeping with him in a dwelling just behind the front line—and remained there into March. In this period, no doubt at his wife's urging, Fiske renewed discussion with his Connecticut parishioners regarding his leave of absence. He confessed himself torn between feelings of duty to his command and duty to his congregation. "I want to go. I want to stay," he wrote his brother. "Lizzie is decidedly rather more go than stay. . . . The Lord direct us."

A New House and Furnishing

Camp on the Rapidan, Va.
[c. January 15, 1864]

Dear Republican: Since I last wrote you, our brigade has changed its quarters. One very rainy Sabbath morning, I believe it was Dec. 27, the order came at eight o'clock, "Pack up, and move at nine." Down went our houses; on to our shoulders went all our worldly goods; and off we staggered in the pelting, pitiless storm, and through mud nearly up to our knees, about three miles, to establish a new camp on the roughest kind of a hill, Stony Mountain by name and by nature, almost on the banks of the Rapidan, and within plain sight of about a mile of the enemy's pickets. The storm continued three days, and was succeeded by a week of the snappingest cold weather that even Virginia (which has, on the whole, decidedly more bitter weather, especially nights, according to my experience, than "sunny" New England) can afford—a sweet time to build our new city, you may well imagine; that is, if you ever emigrated in the middle of winter in a storm: but it was accomplished at last, the pouring rain giving us one assistance at least—in mixing the mortar to mud up our houses. For me personally, you know, the change was all right; for my present chimney draws like a blister, and never smokes any more than my mother or Dr. Trask.

My present house has a real door, with hinges and screws and latch and bolt; an actual shovel and tongs standing by the fireplace; chairs, table, mirror, &c.; yes, positively a carpet on the floor. But, beyond all the rest of the furniture, my chief ornament and pride, which makes me the envy of all the regiment and brigade; the finishing perfection of my house, which maketh this domestic temple to exceed in glory all the former ones I have built; my polished corner-stone, my crowning cupola, my heaven-pointing spire, my portico of Corinthian columns, my statues of finest marble and brass, my—oh there's no use in talking! It isn't to be described any more than a moonrise, or painted any more than a sunset. You couldn't guess it in a month. I can't tell it to you all at once, at least not without a good deal of preparation. I doubt if you can realize it when I tell you. Indeed, I know nobody can who hasn't been a poor, forlorn, uncivilized widower of a soldier for a couple of years. But the words that express this glory of my house, the syllables that convey to your dull ears some very faint and feeble and distant conception of your correspondent's present felicity in camp, at the extreme front, on the Rapidan, are—a wife and baby! We are housekeeping on our front picket line. I have a home, like a bird's nest on the breech of a cannon.

War!—I don't know any thing about it: I am in perfect peace. News!—I haven't looked in the papers for a fortnight; but my little boy has just found a little secesh dog to play with. Writing notes of the campaign for the Republican—nonsense! Don't I ride out every morning along the picket lines with somebody in a riding habit and a side-saddle? You wouldn't have had this brief epistle if the owner of said side-saddle hadn't suddenly recalled it this morning, so that the usual ride couldn't be taken. Good-by!

DUNN BROWNE

General William French, slow-moving and dull-witted, apparently was responsible for this contretemps. The records indicate that French had trouble in this period properly meshing his picket lines with those of his neighboring corps, which produced an overlap— the posting of his pickets in rear of Fiske's brigade. Then, on January 17, came a notice from headquarters to French to tighten security on his picket lines. In a command run like French's, the result was inevitable. William French would emerge from the subsequent reorganization of the Army of the Potomac without a corps command.

Official Jealousy

Camp on the Rapidan, Va.
[c. January 20, 1864]

Dear Republican: Our regiment and brigade are at present maintaining a sort of "armed-neutrality" position between the two Virginia armies. We don't exactly belong to Lee's host; for the Rapidan is between us and certain sharp questions, and rather grim-looking musket barrels are pointed our way when we venture too near that picturesque stream. No more do we at present seem to belong to Meade's army; for the third corps, with that brilliant strategy which their commander is said to have displayed in our late (too late) operations on the other side of the river, have posted their line of pickets directly in our rear, cutting us off from all communication with our own division and corps commanders, from all our supplies, and from the Northern world generally. The officers of their picket are instructed to let nobody pass either way without a written order from the head-quarters of Gen. Meade himself, or of the general commanding the third corps; so that even Gen. Warren, our corps general, if he wishes to visit this portion of his command, must ride over and ask permission of Gen. French. A surgeon with a pass from Gen. Warren was stopped and turned back to-day, while in his regular line of duty, and going out to attend the sick in his own regiment, in cases where life and death might well depend upon his speedy presence. And last night the good chaplain of the 108th New York, coming with his wife, who had just arrived from Washington with Gen. Meade's permission in her hands, was stopped at this ferocious picket-line within a mile of his cabin home, after a long ride in the mud from Brandy Station, and confronted by an officer and twenty armed men, who expressed their readiness to spill their last drop of blood to stay the farther progress of that ambulance. So the poor lady and her unfortunate spouse were forced to turn back through more miles of Virginia mud and seek other quarters for the night.

Wagons of express-matter, orderlies hurrying with dispatches, cavalrymen going out to their picket posts, all sorts of locomotives and locomotors, roll back in dismay before that fatal barrier. The constancy of that line of pickets is really amazing. If the third corps stood before the onslaught of our common enemy with the heroic valor and determination displayed as above against chaplains and doctors and women and teamsters, there should be no more danger of hearing ill news of the army of the Potomac. Learning of these transactions of yesterday and to-day, the thought irresistibly pressed upon me, if Ewell's rebel corps, which the third corps was ordered to attack when we crossed the Rapidan, had only consisted of chaplains and surgeons and ladies and sick persons in ambulances, and wagoneers in charge of supply trains, how different might have been the result of that whole trans-Rapidan movement! After all, having a good position is considerable in warfare. These brave fellows have a portion of the second corps between them and the enemy. Woe therefore to any lady or mule-driver who attempts now to break through their lines!

Thus much of the inconvenience and disturbance and annoyance as the result of personal jealousies and pique amongst the higher officers of our army. Add in the alcoholic element, and you get to the bottom of all our troubles and ill successes very nearly.

In case this missive shall be able to pass through this formidable barrier in our rear, you will learn, dear Republican, that I remain, even in the most desperate beleaguerment, your affectionate

DUNN BROWNE

Dunn Browne's report of this affair at Morton's Ford on February 6 is both careful and perceptive. The 14th Connecticut's 115 casualties (out of the total of 255 lost in this bungled demonstration) had been exceeded only by its losses at Antietam and Fredericksburg. After all Fiske's rage at the quality of the bounty men and substitutes coming to his regiment, it is of interest that General Alexander Hays, in his report of the action, blamed the high casualties on the "faltering of two regiments of conscripts and substitutes," one of the two being the 14th Connecticut.

Across the Rapidan and Back Again

Camp on the Rapidan, Va.
[c. February 8, 1864]

Dear Republican: I see in the Washington Chronicle of to-day that the third corps came up to the Rapidan on Saturday, laid down a pontoon bridge, crossed over after great opposition, repulsed the enemy, after a two-hours' spirited contest, with great slaughter and the loss of a host of prisoners, &c.; and that the second corps came up towards night, and afforded some support to the third; and so, on the whole, things were all right, the reconnaissance successful, the object accomplished.

You know my great regard for the third corps, and especially my high appreciation of their recent operations in the rear of our own little brigade in cutting off our communications with the rest of our corps and the army, and resisting with the utmost valor and constancy the advent of certain surgeons, chaplains, and ladies to our camp, and so would be ready to read the above account of the Chronicle, doubtless, with the utmost confidence in its truth. But I am pained to say that there are one or two slight mistakes therein, nevertheless; and that the third corps, instead of crossing the Rapidan, repulsing the enemy with great slaughter, and then being supported by the second corps, is still confining its operations to our rear. Its crossing of the Rapidan, as well as the pontoon bridge on which it crossed, is "all in the eye" of the veracious writer of the above dispatch.

The pontoons were ordered up on Saturday; and if they had arrived in time to be made into a bridge, and the third corps had been ordered to cross on them, it would doubtless have done so, and done itself credit against whatever enemy appeared to resist them. But the pontoons stuck in the mud half a mile back of the river; and the second corps, being ordered to make a demonstration on the other side of the Rapidan, sent over its third division about noon, wading the river three feet in depth and icy cold (our gallant old general, Hays, set a famous example, dismounting and wading two or three times across), captured a few prisoners of the enemy's picket, and advanced, deployed as skirmishers, about a mile into the enemy's country, under fire from his batteries, and finally took up a position in front of the enemy's earthworks, but screened somewhat from their fire, and lay till night. Just at dusk, the rebels made a furious attack upon our line, evidently intending to drive us into the river: but the old third division was too much chilled by the first crossing to wish to do it again in the dark in great haste, and so turned to it with a will, repulsed the enemy's attack, and drove them about a mile farther back and to the right, exposed a good deal of the way to a flanking fire from the batteries (we had no artillery at all over the river, owing to the non-arrival of the pontoons), and cleaned out a whole nest of houses and out-buildings which were filled with gray-backs; and finally paused only when they came against a full line of battle of the enemy posted behind their works. Our boys being only a line of skirmishers, and having gotten a good deal mixed up in the darkness, and having fired into each other a number of times by mistake, halted, threw out a picket, collected the dead and wounded, and at midnight withdrew across the river without opposition; a part of our second division crossing on a temporary bridge of trees and rails to cover the retreat of the third.

Losses In The Fight

The loss of the division was between two and three hundred, one-half of which was sustained by the 14th Connecticut, which was in the thickest of the *mêlée* about the clump of houses, and fought in many instances hand to hand with the enemy; having seven officers and eighty-nine men wounded, eighteen missing, killed, or prisoners, and six killed whose bodies were brought off the field. Many others are mortally wounded. This regiment, it will be thus seen, has suffered as much as in a battle of the first magnitude, mourning the loss of many of her bravest and best. Still the affair, I suppose, must be called only a reconnaissance, and may have not a feather's weight upon the issue of the great conflict. I don't know that any thing whatever has been accomplished in this "three-days' demonstration against the enemy along the line of the Rapidan" which Gen. Sedgwick was ordered to make, but hope that it is not utterly in vain, as, in our part of it at least, it has been with a very considerable loss of valuable men. The camp of our brigade has about a dozen ladies within it, who behaved with the utmost coolness through the trying time, several of them witnessing the greater part of the fight from the hill above the camp, and having thus an experience that rarely falls to the lot of the gentler sex.

You will doubtless get a clearer idea of the operations along our line, as a whole, before this reaches you, than I have data to give; though, if the above account in the Chronicle be a fair specimen of the news you get, it will bear a trifle of correction. Yours truly,

DUNN BROWNE

Dunn Browne takes aim at the ineffable, incompetent General Benjamin Butler, political general extraordinaire. Butler's scheme, undertaken in parallel with the demonstration described in the previous letter, was to spring a surprise attack on Richmond from Williamsburg on the Peninsula, "occupy Capitol Square in that city for at least two or three hours," and release the Union prisoners held there. A Confederate force met the column on the Chickahominy, a dozen miles short of the city, blocked the road and the river crossing with felled trees, and turned it back. The historian of the Second Corps, with sarcasm equal to Fiske's, gave Butler's losses as six forage caps. According to Butler, a New York private, under sentence for the murder of a comrade, escaped and revealed the plan; he blamed Mr. Lincoln for having suspended "till further orders" the man's execution. Previously Butler had administered captured New Orleans with great notoriety. The first "hero of New Orleans" was, of course, Andrew Jackson.

Dunn Browne Still on the Rapidan

Camp on the Rapidan, Va.
February 15 [1864]

DEDICATION OF A CAMP CHURCH

Dear Republican: We had a real dedication yesterday of a house of God, built of logs and plastered with mud, thirty feet by eighteen, and covered with canvas furnished by the Christian Commission, pewed with log benches and able to accommodate 150 people with comfort. It seemed actually like "going to meeting" again, for we had a dozen ladies in the audience and good singing and a good sermon and good worship every way. When the chapter describing the glorious dedication of Solomon's temple was read, it occurred to me that there was something of a contrast between the scene at Jerusalem and our humble dedication service on the bank of the Rapidan. But "all the people said amen" I think in both cases; and if the spirit of the Lord filled with a cloud of glory that temple built of fragrant cedar overlaid with shining gold, perhaps He was equally present with us in our temple of riven pine overlaid with Virginia mud.

A BRILLIANT CAVALRY REVIEW

Religious services yesterday—a military pageant to-day. A grand cavalry review of Gen. Merritt's and Gen. Kilpatrick's divisions. It was a right brilliant and imposing spectacle, and honored by the presence of a pretty large number of infantry and lady spectators. Gen. Pleasonton was the reviewing officer and made uncommonly good time in moving down his two miles' line of troops and up in their rear, as the day was cold and bitter and a flake of snow falling occasionally. Taking our station not far from the reviewing officer's stand (just far enough not to see too plainly the dirty hats and uniforms which were mixed in with the clean), we saw the apparently endless column of riders and tramping steeds pass proudly by, till it really seemed as if we had cavalry enough to ride into Richmond without drawing rein. There is one good thing about these grand reviews anyhow. It gives a man confidence in his cause; makes him feel that he is part of a big thing, to see the ranks of steady veterans gathered together in such numbers and going through their movements with such precision. It doesn't seem that any force could resist them.

BUTLER'S GREAT EXPEDITION TO RICHMOND

We have just heard here of the trees in the road and across the ferry which stopped the grand expedition of Gen. Butler to take Richmond. What a pity it was that a deserter from our ranks informed the enemy of the danger the city was in from the vast force (of about 5000 men) of the great Yankee general! What a comfort it would have been to us of the army of the Potomac, when we were ordered to make a demonstration along our whole line against the enemy, to cooperate with an important move-ment upon Richmond from the other side, if we had but known the full amount of Butler's force! If we had had but a mental glimpse of those two whole negro regiments! If we had been cog-nizant of the fact that there were in addition to the colored troops as many as seven or eight hundred cavalry and mounted infantry! It is no wonder the rebel capital trembled in its shoes, and its 40,000 inhabitants began to think of leaving the city to its fate. It is no wonder that our army of 50,000 were straight-away ordered to keep Lee occupied so that he could not send reinforcements to the doomed capital! Our regiments need not regret the loss of a few hundred killed and wounded to afford some humble cooperation to such a promising movement upon the rebel center! Our starving boys on Belle Island have no longer reason to complain of government for neglecting them,

in their deplorable condition! Hath not that paternal government sent a force of about 5000 men to deliver them out of the
hands of their cruel enemies and captors? Is it a wonder that the
great Yankee general was exceedingly wrath with the deserter
that foiled a plan that otherwise could scarcely have failed of
signal success? Why, the enterprise recorded in Scripture of Gid-
eon and his band of 300, which was crowned with such perfect
success, was not on the whole so promising a plan, looked at
from a merely human point of view, as this over which our modern Benjamin presided, and which came to naught because of
the trees that had fallen across the road. Curses light on the
traitor hands that felled those trees, and the Birmingham forges
that turned out the axes that were used in the operation, and
the blockade-runners that brought them into Wilmington, and
the confederate shin-plasters that paid for them!

There, that is the best I can do for you, oh second hero of New
Orleans! The next time you go to Richmond I hope you will have
a clear road before you, and at least a couple of brigades with
you, so as to make even any attempt at resistance on the part of
the enemy hopeless. Yours truly,

DUNN BROWNE

Samuel Fiske sometimes reveals a trace of naïveté regarding his
fellow soldiers (excepting bounty jumpers and substitutes), and
indeed about their folks back home. The inspection of express
boxes and packages had started during Joe Hooker's regime, a
year or so earlier, when the Army of the Potomac was literally
disintegrating through desertion. It was discovered then that the
folks back home, in great numbers, were sending their soldier
sons and husbands and sweethearts civilian clothes that greatly
aided them in deserting the cause. They also sent substantial
amounts of liquor. After the inspection policy became known, the
amount of contraband (especially liquor) that was sent greatly
diminished. But the inspections continued, with enough abuses to
inspire editorials by Dunn Browne and others. Those guilty of the
abuses were by no means always provost guards; theft occurred
from one end of the express-delivery chain to the other.

Maine Law for the Soldiers

Camp on the Rapidan, Va.
February 20 [1864]

Dear Republican: Great pains are taken to watch over the habits of the privates in this army. The provost department is truly paternal in the affectionate interest it displays in the boxes which are sent on by express to the dear boys, lest they should contain liquors whereby said privates should be tempted to intoxication, to the injury of the "morale" of the army. Why, every mortal box that the hand of love directs to the soldier boys is stopped at corps headquarters, and I don't know but at army headquarters too, and goes into the vast pile that is always to be seen there awaiting the pleasure of the provost marshal and his minions to wrench off the cover, ransack the contents and confiscate—I trust the provost boys for understanding the meaning of the word—the liquor that may be found therein. Now all those occasional bottles of "bitters" and variously named medicines and alcoholic compounds, which come in the express boxes of the whole army, together wouldn't make a stream large enough to wet the whistle of one ordinary headquarters. But a great principle is involved; the morals of the army are in danger; and so the provost marshal firmly performs his duty.

The boxes may all be delayed two or three days by this process, and lie exposed in the open air through one or two soaking rains it may well be. But who shall speak of such a trifle as that in the face of this grand temperance maneuver? These driblets of liquor would do less harm, likely enough, sprinkled over the whole army, so to speak, than confined to the uses of the provost guards simply, some foolish objector might suggest. But this great temperance measure scorns even to notice such insinuations. It is true that about half the contents of the boxes and packages get broken, spoiled, lost, injured or stolen in the opening process; everything is turned topsy-turvy, the apples, eggs, and doughnuts roll out in the dirt; pickle and jam bottles coming to pieces mingle their contents with silk handkerchiefs, flannel shirts and quires of writing paper, more than the taste of the donors would probably choose; the packages of tea, and the pepper boxes, and the saleratus, and the tiny ink-bottle got into one well-mangled compound, and it becomes difficult to tell which is cow-hide boots and which is mince pies, by the time the lid is finally pressed back to its place by some strong knee and fastened by nails, of which one passes through the toe of a slipper that didn't get in quite quickly enough, and another ruins a vest that mother's hands had made to keep her boy warm this cold winter weather. But what are these little inconveniences to the private soldier before the working of this great moral, preventive, reformatory movement? I am ashamed to speak of a pair of six dollar boots coming up missing in one of my boys' boxes last week, when I think that there might have been a bottle of plantation bitters in that same box if the boots had been left in it. I did feel a little indignant when I discovered two boxes in one load entirely empty, and saw the angry and grieved faces of the boys that received them. But it was a great consolation to reflect that they now certainly couldn't get drunk on the contents. I used to worry and fret to see, as I have done, scores and hundreds of times, boxes more than half empty, and what was left in them all shaken into one indistinguishable and valueless mass—clothing, crockery and cookery "in one red burial blent."

But I have become more enlightened now, and can take wider views, having frequently heard the remark made, "Well, it would be a great deal better if these privates didn't get any boxes from home. Uncle Sam provides for them well enough." Then another, "Yes, and if great care wasn't taken they'd smuggle liquor into the army that way and get drunk." At this stage of the conversation I have noticed that the bottle is usually passed, and the interlocutors take another drink and a slice of "that pudding," and proceed perhaps to give their orders to the caterer of the mess what things to send for from Washington.

Oh, private, when will you appreciate the kind care that watches over your morals so closely and takes such pains to preserve your temperate habits and keep you in the way wherein you ought to walk? Oh, sister, packing with such tender care the warm flannels and socks and needlebook and sundry goodies to eat in the tight, strong box for the darling sojer brother, mixing prayers and loving wishes with every package, wrapping each keepsake in sisterly affection and tissue paper, and anticipating the delight with which that brother shall unpack every article; don't trouble your gentle breast too much at the thought of the rough hands of the provost guard unpacking your treasures (they are practiced hands, very), for, though you may fail to see it, there is a great principle involved, and the moral welfare of the army depends upon your overcoming your scruples. It is probable that you have put a bottle of "old rye" in the lower right-hand corner of that box, next to the Bible with the marked passages in it, and the temperate habits so carefully cultivated in the army must be guarded from evil home influences. Oh, father, nail not up so grimly, with iron bands around each end, that box with Christmas turkey and mince pies and sundry comforts and luxuries that mother's hands have prepared for the boy at the war. You cannot bind so fast that provost's axe may not loose, nor ensure that that turkey shall not be a "gone goose" before it reaches its intended destination. No matter what freight you prepay upon it, the uncertainty that proverbially attends all martial matters doth not leave your missive exempt. Grumble not overmuch. The ways of provost guards may be very mysterious to you, and this precautionary temperance measure not fully appreciated by our dull intellect; but that the interests of the country somehow demand it, and the army would be straightaway ruined through the medium of Adams express company, without this check, take the word of yours, affectionately,

DUNN BROWNE

There actually was a rather grand Second Corps ball, held on Washington's Birthday, February 22, in a 50-foot by 150-foot "ballroom" erected for the occasion; but alas for Dunn's "bit of very small gossip," the president's son was not present. The newspapers of the period were full of speculation about presidential hopefuls in an election year, and Fiske lists the principal ones. Confederate conscription in North Carolina had run afoul of the chief justice of the state's supreme court, who ruled the draft law unenforceable, and thus North Carolina troops were more likely than most to desert.

From Dunn Browne on Picket

On the Rapidan, Va.
February 26 [1864]

BOB LINCOLN ON HIS DIGNITY

Dear Republican: Do you want a bit of very small gossip, and a trifle malicious withal? Well, I heard that at the great second

corps ball the other night, in the crowded supper room, an officer with a lady, in the back row, touched a well-dressed fellow in
front of him and asked him to pass a plate for the lady for some
tongue or an ice, or whatever the article required might be. "I'm
not one of the waiters here, sir," was the polite rejoinder; and
"You had better go back to school, my boy, and try to improve
your manners," was the well deserved rebuke of the officer,
whose elbow was touched a moment after by some one who whispered, "Hush, that young fellow is Bob o'Lincoln," I trust this
story of the snobbishness of our heir apparent is a slander, the
invention of some disappointed fair one who didn't get an opportunity to dance with the prince. It is bad enough to be a president's son anyway without being gossiped about.

PRESIDENT AND EX-PRESIDENT

But the least desirable thing in the whole world, it seems to
me, is to be an ex-president. Why don't these honorables who
are moving heaven and earth to get the presidential nomination,
scheming, intriguing, bribing, promising, lying, ready to sell
their souls to attain the desirable goal: why, in the name of common sense and experience, don't they reflect upon the end that
is before them? That after the presidency comes the ex-presi-
dency? Who would be what Pierce, what Buchanan, is now, for
all that a four years' residence at the White House could possibly
involve of honor, power, or pleasure? Can it be possible that
Chase, for instance, would be willing to exchange his present
position and reputation for the worry and risk and weariness of
the presidency, to be followed by the extinguishment of the ex-
presidency? For McClellan, now, the case is different. It might
be a comfort to him even to become an ex-president. It grieves
me to see the papers so filled with talk about the machinations
of cabinet officers, president and generals to oust each other
from, and secure for themselves, the chances of nomination to
office. Can it be true that those whose hearts, heads and hands
ought to be full of the one great work of carrying the nation
through this terrible crisis and crushing the hopes of rebels in
arms, are occupied instead with the petty prospects of personal
ambition and even oft times sacrificing the welfare of the nation
to their private piques and jealousies? The curse of the soldiers

in arms, and the burdened people behind them, will be on all such. The curse of God, who hath given them such opportunities and such responsibilities, will be on them. But I cannot believe such things of men like Chase, and Lincoln, and Grant, and Banks. At least the man who shall devote himself most earnestly and successfully to the ending of this rebellion, who shall work with an eye and a heart single to that great end, forgetting self in his country, he is the one whose name shall be in the hearts of our children and his praises on their lips. He shall be greater and better than a president. He could even afford to be an ex-president, like the glorious Washington, and Adams, and Jefferson.

REBEL DESERTERS AND THEIR STORIES

There, my reflections are interrupted by the approach of a corporal with two butternut-colored prisoners who have just deserted the enemy's picket post here at the ford, and waded the cold deep stream to take refuge within our lines. They are men of some 40 years of age, with families in North Carolina, conscripted six months since, and apparently overjoyed at the successful opportunity of escape which they say they have been long watching for. They report the one uniform story that we hear every day from such stragglers into our lines, of discontent in the rebel camps, especially among the North Carolina troops. Every camp is most carefully guarded, they say; no man allowed to leave on any excuse; rations very short and precarious; sometimes many days without any meat, and then a tiny bit of bacon or fresh beef, their staple article corn-meal. I take it there must be something to all this talk, but we haven't noticed much diminution in the spirit with which our enemies fight as yet. Yours truly,

DUNN BROWNE

The ascension of U.S. Grant to the office of general-in-chief of all the Union armies, with a new broom to sweep clean, had not yet penetrated to the Washington bureaus, as Dunn Browne ruefully discovers.

How Not to Do it in Washington

Camp on the Rapidan, Va.
[c. March 15, 1864]

Dear Republican: The clerks in the various departments at Washington ought to have something done for them; they ought. They are a much-abused, overworked, under-paid, and ill-appreciated community; they are. You have some influence with some members of Congress, I doubt not. I hope you will try to do something for them. I wish I could adequately represent their case to you, and, through your columns, to a sympathizing public.

I can't say, to be sure, that I have a very thorough personal knowledge of any of them; in fact, I have only had a passing glimpse of one or two: but I have wandered a good deal within a day or two along the outer halls and passages, and about the doorways that lead to their official sanctums, and even in the ante-rooms of a few of the more condescending of them (standing, of course, and with my hat off). I have had a good deal of conversation with their doorkeepers and orderlies and errand-boys. I have seen many of their overcoats, the pegs on which they hang their hats; even, in a few instances, the very desks and arm-chairs whereat and wherein they perform their arduous labors.

Yea, I believe, upon second thought, that I am too modest in speaking of my acquaintance with this class of public functionaries. I have actually stood in the august presence of quite a number of specimens, and been permitted to admire the curt, abrupt, and very decisive answers they give to questions which foolish people, interested in matters pertaining to their various bureaus, persist in asking them. It is interesting to observe the brevity and authority with which they dispose of impertinent questioners, and the audacity and presence of mind with which they baffle the attempts constantly made by a meddling public to get information from them in reference to matters pertaining to their various departments. In a few instances, it really seemed to me that one would have to impart some useful information, and answer a question, so as to afford some satisfaction to the asker. But no: the difficulty of the situation only afforded a more brilliant opportunity of success in extrication. The genius of "how not to do it" in each case gloriously triumphed over the temptation to do it, and the locution always became a circumlocution. If they dispose of all the public business intrusted to them as summarily as they dispose of all such individuals of the public as have the impudence to intrude upon their official hours on pretense of important matters, I am sure the public would have no reason to complain, though their five or six daily "business-hours" should be curtailed to two or three. The fortress of official dignity is well defended. If you break the outer line of skirmishers that defend the extreme walls and the great gates of entrance, it is only to find an inner picket-guard posted before each successive door, and numerous ditches and abatis of formality to impede your every step of progress. If by patience and perseverance you penetrate at last into the very recesses of the fortress, you find, most likely, not the great man himself, but only his factotum, the clerk of the clerk, the shadow of the shade; and if he can not bully you into giving up your object, or persuade you that you have come to the wrong place to transact your business, and the very last door is opened to your importunity, and you fancy the garrison must surrender at discretion, you find to your disappointment that the hand-to-hand attack is a greater failure than the battle afar off. Your foe has had the experience of years to aid him in resisting such attacks as you are making upon him. You have but one plain thrust for the attack: he has a thousand cunning parries familiar to his hand for the defense. You quickly retire discomfited from the presence; and every janitor casts a look of malicious triumph after your retiring steps.

How Things Go At The Dead-Letter Office

I had a number of matters to attend to in Washington, and so saved a day from a very short leave of absence to accomplish them. I will only trouble you with one or two of the milder instances of the way I accomplished them. One thing was to hunt up in the dead-letter office a package of important papers, directed to me in the mail, that had somehow gone astray. Nothing easier than that; certainly not, if there were anybody in the proper office to attend to my case. But I called at the noble post-office building; after some inquiries, found the office of the po-

lite Dr.———, who attends to that branch of the business; was
ushered into a fine apartment, elegantly furnished; and sat down
by a cozy fire to wait for the officer, who happened to be out for
the moment. It was right in the middle of the official day; but
there I sat and waited five minutes, ten minutes, wondering
whether the head of the dead-letter office was a dead-head or no.
After about fifteen minutes of impatient waiting, for my business
pressed me (foolish fellow! I might just as well have waited there
by that pleasant fire all the day), I rummaged round in the adjoining rooms, and asked various clerks for information of the
good doctor. "Oh! he will be in in a few minutes."—"Well, but
isn't there any one else who can attend to my business?" No:
there was no one else. I must wait a few minutes. Twenty minutes, twenty-five minutes, passed, but no Dr.——— came; and I left
to fulfill an appointment in another part of the city.

Well, it was a small matter that a man should be out of his
office for twenty-five minutes. Yes; and it was a small matter that
I was attending to anyway. It was only some documents for half
a dozen dead soldiers killed at Gettysburg, which, if I could obtain, I might draw the back pay due to the widows and mothers
and orphans. I doubt much if I should have gotten the pay, however (in one day), if I had found the papers, judging from the rest
of my experience. Here was one case of failure because a clerk
wasn't there when I wanted him. Most of my failures were because a clerk was there.

At The Adjutant-General's Office

Judge of this other case I will relate; about a fair specimen of
my experience. An errand at the adjutant-general's office. Went
up at ten o'clock. Found a fat doorkeeper. Asked him if I could
see any of the assistant adjutant-generals or their clerks. No:
couldn't see anybody on business till eleven o'clock. Departed.
Came back at eleven. Found a long string of people passing in
slowly to one of the rooms. Took my turn. Got a word at last with
a clerk. Found it wasn't his specialty to answer questions of the
sort I asked him. Was referred by him to another clerk who perhaps could. Went to another room. Stopped by a doorkeeper. At
last, permitted to enter, after some other people had come out.

Stated my case to the clerk at the desk: "Pay of certain officers of my regiment stopped by order from your office near four months since. No reason assigned. No notice given. Come to you for reason."—"Why don't you send up your request through the proper military channels, sir?"—"Request was sent up eight weeks ago, enclosing a precise copy of the order issued from your own office to the paymaster. Instead of looking in your own office to find the reason for your own order, you sent our request over to the paymaster-general, asking him why the order was issued. He sent it back endorsed with the statement, that no such order of stoppage was recorded in the pay-department. This you sent back to us 'through the regular channel' as eminently satisfactory. So it would be, only the paymaster, having your positive order not to pay us, and no order countermanding it, refuses to come down with the greenbacks. Another paper came up to you from us several weeks ago, and has not been heard from. This is the progress of eight weeks through the regular channels."—"Why don't you ask the paymaster to find out about the matter?"—"We have done so. He says he has been repeatedly to your office, which, of course, is the only place where information can be obtained, and is unable to get any satisfactory reply."—"Why don't you go to the ordnance and quartermaster departments, and see if your accounts are all right there?"—"We have done so, and find it a reasonable certainty that no stoppages against us have been ordered there. The order came from you. You had a precise copy of it sent you with our application. Where could we apply for information as to the reason of your acts save to you?"—"Very well: we'll try to look it up."—"But, sir, if you would let a clerk look at your orders of that date, and answer us to-day, we can perhaps get our pay; otherwise we shall not have access to the paymaster again for two or three months."

The clerk, utterly disgusted at such pertinacity, dismisses us with an appointment to call again at two o'clock. He will see what he can do for us. Call again at two o'clock. Doorkeeper refuses to let us in. No person seen on business after two o'clock. Finally work our way through with the plea of the special appointment. Find, of course, that nothing has been done. "What shall be our next course?"—"Oh! send up another paper through the regular channel."

PROMPTNESS AT THE PROVOST-MARSHAL'S

This is just a fair specimen of my luck through the day, only that my answers in this case were a hundred times more civil and gentlemanly than the average. The only place where my business was passed with promptness and dispatch was at the provost-marshal's, whither I went to get a pass down "to the front." Every facility is offered, I must in candor acknowledge, to him who is on his way to put himself in the path of the enemy. It was a real comfort to me to have my valise examined for whisky at the railroad station. It looked a little as if Grant was going to try to keep liquor out of the army; but my confidence in it as a temperance measure was slightly impaired when I found that there was about the usual amount of the ardent at the commissaries' and the sutlers'. An officer's carpet-bag is searched, and his private bottle of brandy confiscated; but he can order a whole case at a time brought to his quarters through the sutler, and buy whisky at a dollar a gallon of that respectable old rumseller, Uncle Samuel, at the commissary's.

I am afraid this letter is rather long; but, with so much red-tape in it, how could it be otherwise? Yours truly,

DUNN BROWNE

9

INTO THE WILDERNESS

As the Army of the Potomac began to shake itself loose from winter quarters, Captain Fiske was himself preparing for renewed campaigning. Soon after writing this letter, he began a ten-day leave, escorting his wife and son back to Connecticut and arranging for them to board in his Madison parish. His congregation, he told his brother, "wouldn't unite with me in asking for a dissolution of our connection but gave me another six months from the first of March." Instead of returning home from the wars to his pastorship, as he originally intended, Samuel Fiske committed himself to seeing through at least the spring campaign of 1864.

Prepared to Move

Camp on the Rapidan, Va.
March 24, 1864

Dear Republican: It is a very unpleasant thing about war that there can't be some comfortable arrangement whereby all the marching and fighting should be done in the daytime and in the pleasantest weather. Here we are ordered up nights to get under arms; picketing is kept up during the rainiest weather; and no regard is had to the nerves or feelings of the shakiest and most feminine of us, which by no means is identical with the ladies of our camp, who are cool as veterans in all our alarms. Now, "hired men," at home, are expected to lie around rainy days, or do merely some light in-doors jobs; but Uncle Sam's thirteen dollars a month means "rain or shine," Sundays and week days, night-work as well as day-work, and mighty uncertain about stopping for meals.

We've been on the *qui vive*, now, for three days and nights; and the air is all full of uncertain rumors. Sometimes we are immediately to cross the Rapidan, and attack; sometimes we tumble out of our bunks, and fall in in all haste, expecting a momentary attack from the enemy, who have crossed in great force to gobble us up; sometimes Kilpatrick is far in the rear of the rebels, and on the war-trail for Richmond. A few minutes later, we hear he has taken Gordonsville, and captured Gen. Lee and Gen. Ewell. Yesterday the sixth and third corps were over the river; to-day they have not crossed the river; and we expect by to-morrow to find that they have not moved at all. So we keep ready to "move at a moment's notice"; lie around, eating and sleeping at all hours of the day and night; never relaxing our vigilance, or unstrapping the ladies' trunks; taking out one teacup and knife and fork at a time; and having things so rolled and strapped up, that nothing whatsoever that we want is to be found. Everything military is mixed up, east and west and north and south, pretty much. I hope somebody holds all the threads, and will wind them up without much tangling. We get into a resigned, soldierly way of taking every thing as it comes, and not worrying over tumults and alarms and reports. We trust that somehow it is all coming out right, and so wait with patience, not even knowing what part we ourselves are performing in the passing scenes and events till we read in the newspapers a day or two after.

The Republican is getting into much more regular habits in its visits to camp, and is a comfort to very many borrowers. I procured one new subscription the other day, and am going to obtain a third when the paymaster has visited us; so that, among the three of us, we may be pretty sure to get all the numbers. So you see its prospects are good and circulation increasing in these regions.

Yours truly,

DUNN BROWNE

To ready the Army of the Potomac for the spring campaign, General Meade initiated sweeping changes. The five corps of infantry were consolidated into three, with the decimated First and Third corps disappearing from the order of battle. Fiske's Second Corps gained two divisions by transfer from the Third. His brigade, commanded by Samuel Carroll, now contained no fewer than eight regiments and a battalion, up from four regiments. Captain Fiske was himself making adjustments to new circumstances, having moved from commanding Company I to commanding Company G of the 14th Connecticut. General-in-chief Grant elected to make his headquarters with the Potomac army in the field.

Preparations in Virginia

Camp on the Rapidan, Va.
April 18, 1864

A Soldier's View of Re-Organization

Dear Republican: Re-organization is the order of the day with us just at the present. Do you know exactly what that is, most sapient of newspapers? Well, if I may use an illustration from the printing office, it's just knocking a form into pi to have the fun of picking out the letters and setting them up over again. It is resolving all creation back into chaos and starting a fresh world on a new plan. It is shaking a fair city all down into one promiscuous dustheap and then pulling out the bricks to rebuild it on the ruins. It's shaking a community all up together in a huge bag and then making a new draw for husbands and wives, familiar friends and neighbors, houses and lands, trades, professions and habits of life. In the new arrangement Mr. Jones may find Mrs. Smith a much more agreeable and congenial companion; still I wouldn't wonder if the stupid fellow had his prejudices in favor of the old co-partnership after all. Well, we all hope much good will come of the changes that have been made, and that the apple trees are in enough straighter rows now to pay for the transplanting of them. The thing we are trying to get clear in our heads is at present the numbers of the new brigades, divisions and corps that we belong to, so we can have our friends direct our letters to us without danger of miscarrying. There is a great consumption of red, white and blue flannel in changing the corps badges, and heavy requisitions are made in the quartermaster's department for paint to number over the wagons and other public property.

GEN. GRANT AND THE WEATHER

Gen. Grant has made about half a dozen attempts to review the 2d corps, but unsuccessfully as yet on account of the weather. Nature has been "re-organizing" herself here in Virginia with a general flood, very much in the same way as Grant with the army. And rivers, lakes, islands, railway bridges and corduroy roads have broken out in new spots, as well as brigadiers. I trust the good old dame and the good new general will both be rather indulgent with us till we get used to running under the "spring arrangement." They have been very successful, each of them, in their combinations hitherto. We are disposed to trust them implicitly for the forthcoming campaign. Our boys are well satisfied to have the rain come before we get moved out of our comfortable winter quarters, rather than just after. We have tried breaking camp and then getting stuck in the mud and undergoing a long cold rain in shelter tents, and it is a picnic not at all according to our taste. We prefer on the whole to have winter come in the winter and the summer confined principally within the limits of the summer.

NEEDED CHANGE IN THE CALENDAR

It appears to me, however, that the years have been growing later and later, and the seasons more and more backward in coming to time, for the last decade or two. The autumn has pushed itself along into winter's place, winter crowded out the spring, &c., &c., till the calendar quite needs another Julius Caesar or Gregory to "re-organize" it. Why should not Grant, now that his "hand is in," issue an order on the subject at once, in time to have May day come in appropriately with all her flowers and gentle breezes and sunshine and smiles. The April showers, though, have come in due season and in overflowing abundance, so there is no ground for complaint on that score. Yours nearly re-organized,

DUNN BROWNE

Although a pastor in civilian life, Fiske makes no mention, in his letters to the Republican, *of playing a leading role in such Sunday*

services as he describes here. Regimental chaplains presided over the communion, but apparently Fiske did not join Captains Haw- ley and Price of his regiment in passing the bread and wine of the Eucharist, or at least not on this occasion.

The Soldiers' Communion

Camp on the Rapidan, Va.
April 25 [1864]

Dear Republican: We had a very precious day yesterday, and the thought of it was a comfort all through the hard work of the evening; for we sat down at the Lord's table, and held sweet communion with him and with one another. Twelve men (of the 108th New York mostly, but one or two from our regiment) were baptized; and about twenty-five professed their solemn faith in, and made everlasting covenant with, Christ, to be his hence- forth. We had a short, comprehensive creed and covenant for them to assent to and take upon themselves; and then seventy- five or eighty, perhaps, partook of the sacrament.

I never had a sweeter time in my life. I have no doubt of the perfect propriety of our action in having this season; for the Lord was evidently present to bless. Mr. Grassey (108th New York) was very happy in all his remarks and services; Mr. Murphy (1st Delaware) assisted; Capt. Hawley and Capt. Price passed the ele- ments. We had just our usual soldiers' bread, and the wine in two pewter cups, poured from a brown stone pitcher; and there was no white linen to represent that which was wrapped around the Savior's body: but every thing seemed decent and in order, and we all enjoyed the season as if it were the very institution of the ordinance in that upper room in Jerusalem. It was the last ser- vice we shall have, I suppose, in our little log-chapel. The roof comes down to-day to be carried back to the Christian Commis- sion again; and we worship God in the open air for the summer. Yours truly,

DUNN BROWNE

This economics lecture by Samuel Fiske seems to have been in- fluenced more by newspaper accounts of abusers of the financial

system than by the actual facts of the case—which in any event and at that moment were not easily grasped by the layman. In fact the Northern war effort rested on a far more substantial financial foundation than Fiske suggests; certainly it was not going the way of the Confederacy's disastrous finances. As one historian has observed, "The Internal Revenue Act of 1862 taxed almost everything but the air northerners breathed"; half again as much war revenue was raised in the North by taxes as by the issuance of paper money. The "A.L.P." Fiske mentions was one of the Republican's correspondents whose articles appeared under the heading "Papers on Political Economy." The metropolitan fairs were fund-raising events held throughout the North for the benefit of the troops.

A Soldier's View of Political Economy

Camp on the Rapidan, Va.
April 25, 1864

Dear Republican: I hear a good deal said and read a good deal in the newspapers about the "treasures we are pouring out like water" for the carrying on of the war; about our "vast and unprecedented pecuniary sacrifices and expenditures," &c., &c. And it really seems to me that it is very nearly time to be taking some measures to make those statements actual facts. We have been carrying on the war over three years, and have now spent the revenues of some ten generations to come after us. Wouldn't it be well enough at last to put our hands into our own pockets and spend some of our own resources? With all our big talk on the subject, I believe the simple matter of fact is, that we have raised a national revenue for these three years about 33 or perhaps 50 per cent greater than in our previous years of peace. I haven't access to figures, and I never remember them when I do. But with our expenses twelve or fifteen times greater than in peace, we certainly haven't doubled our revenues; I am not certain if, on the whole, for the three years taken together, we have increased them at all over the old peace standard.

We have poured out treasures like water to be sure, but it has hitherto been somebody else's treasures. And as we have spent them among ourselves, as a matter of fact we have been making a good thing pecuniarily out of our "enormous patriotic sacrifices." Hence the great apparent prosperity and abundance throughout the North. We have drawn bills on our remote posterity and got them cashed, at a heavy discount of course, to pay for the diamonds of the shoddy contractors' wives, and lavish in every kind of foolish extravagance. The people have cried out time and again to be taxed, but when Congress came to consider the items of any tax bill, there has always been for every one some special reason for exemption, so that taxes haven't to any extent been laid on. A big tax has been just going to be laid on liquors for two years or so past, but the whisky dealers have bought up and fought off Congress, till I believe the progress of the thing up to this time is, that all liquors distilled after the end of the present century or thereabouts, shall pay $1 a gallon into the treasury. The bank circulation is going to be taxed, but although the profits of those institutions are far greater than ever before on account of not having to pay specie for that which they have once received specie, they have been too strong for Congress so far. And in general any interest that has been strong enough to be able to pay some revenue to the government if taxed, has also been strong enough to keep from being taxed to any great amount, leaving only the weak interests that aren't of much account anyway to catch it heavily. So that on the whole we have not yet spent anything on the war, pecuniarily, in spite of all our talk, but on the contrary have been borrowing, borrowing, borrowing, and putting the proceeds, heavily shaved to be sure, in our own pockets.

The cotton manufacturers have been making money ever since the war began with the utmost rapidity. The woolen manufacturers and wool growers have had nothing to do but take in and invest their money. The railroads never began to have such receipts, as since we have been making these "warlike sacrifices." The farmers never received before such prices for provisions. Importers and merchants generally never did so well. All corporations have waxed fat and kicked. The coal interest has had everything its own black and dirty way. Owners of real estate have hardly had pockets large enough to hold their rents. And every kind of "fancy" stock has blown its bubbles and seen them float away unbursted. Everybody is bound to make a good thing out of this great national crisis. And it doesn't seem as if we were ever going to be willing to put our hands in our pockets and pay as we go. Our finances are fast going the same way as those of the rebels. Our promises to pay are worth about fifty cents on a dollar as yet; that is we haven't cheated our creditors out of only half of what we owe them, and are only half bankrupt. The question is, shall we try at all to save the remaining moiety of our national credit, or let it quite go? For decency's sake don't let us talk about our patriotism and our sacrifices so long as we are all seeking to make personal gains out of our country's distress, and refusing even to tax ourselves enough to half pay the interest on our enormously increasing debt. England borrowed money indeed to carry on her wars, but for every dollar she borrowed she raised another dollar at least by taxation. Let us do the same and gold won't stay at 180 long. Let us refuse to do it much longer and gold will not stay at 180 either, but it will go out of sight entirely and the rest of our credit with it.

Please tell "A.L.P." that I am not intending to rival him in a series of politico-economical papers, but only to give you a plain soldier's view of the "way things are working," and to express my faith that not even spending $50 for knick-knacks at a metropolitan fair is going to discharge one's whole duty to his country in these times. Affectionately,

DUNN BROWNE

This letter was written one day before the Army of the Potomac crossed the Rapidan to campaign in the Wilderness. Captain Fiske's complaint here about army rationing was long-standing. Senator Henry Wilson of Massachusetts was chairman of the Senate's Committee on Military Affairs, and this proposal to return rationing to the old standard was to be combined with a monthly pay increase of $2. The soldier, it was said, "will value the addition to his wages in hard cash more than the rations." Fiske, alas, left no comment on that bit of congressional reasoning. The earlier Union reverses of the spring he refers to were Butler's aborted advance on Richmond, a failed cavalry raid on the Confederate capital by Judson Kilpatrick, and the bungled campaign on the Red River in the southwestern theater. In the matter of a lack of *inspirational addresses to the troops, it may be noted that Fiske was not with the army during the period of the Peninsula campaign, at which time General McClellan did indeed address his men, and in imitation of Napoleon—and thereby increased their devotion to his leadership. But now, in 1864, the Army of the Potomac would go on the offensive without a similar effort from Meade (or from Grant). It is entirely fitting that in this letter—his last—Samuel Fiske eloquently renews his faith in the cause for which he was fighting.*

Dunn Browne's Parting Grumble and Advice

Camp on the Rapidan, Va.
May 3, 1864

A Tempest In Camp

Dear Republican: Stepping out of my tent yesterday for a moment, I saw a huge red cloud sweeping over Pony mountain with tremendous rapidity and fury, and before we had half done wondering whether it was some stray aurora borealis shooting across Virginia, one of the boys exclaimed, "That's genuine Virginia mud taking to itself wings"; and sure enough, our whole eastern horizon was darkened with a tornado of dust, and we sprang to our houses to keep them from breaking their connection with the hillside on which we are located. What a time we did have, to be sure! The principle of gravitation was nowhere. The "star of empire" never took its way westward with half the velocity with which the barrels from our chimneys, the hats from our heads and the canvas from our huts started on a tour towards the Rocky mountains. We could readily believe that the earth was whirling from west to east as rapidly as the astronomers tell us, and moreover that she evidently meant to leave us behind, this trip at least. The many trees that had been left standing in and about our camp couldn't withstand the blast for a moment, but broke like pipe stems before the first rush of the tempest; and woe to the luckless log hut that happened to be squatted in the path of its fall. A huge pine made kindling wood of the stately mansion of our colonel, grinding to splinters the tender young pines that composed its walls as ruthlessly as the porcine mother sometimes devours her offspring. Well for the colonel that he was out of his hut at the time on a tour of picket duty, or there would have been a likely chance for promotion to somebody in our regiment. I have heard of nobody that was injured, at least seriously, but the "scare" was considerable, and the dust that filled our houses and covered our beds and clothes and food, something like the cloud of ashes that buried Pompeii. Our oldest sailors said they never saw anything like it. The tempest soon blew itself over, however, and the rain that succeeded it was not much more than enough to lay the dust. So we speedily repaired damages and settled into our pristine "quiet along the Rapidan."

A RAZEE OF OUR HOUSES

To-day, nevertheless, an order from division headquarters has done what the tornado didn't half accomplish, namely, has unroofed all our houses and leveled them to the ground. "Going to move," are we? Oh no, not at all. But the fact is we are getting altogether too effeminate for soldiers. Why should we lie in comfortable dry huts, on bunks raised from the ground, when thousands of acres of sacred Virginia soil lie all around us, on which (with the slight trouble of tearing our houses down) we may extend ourselves? Why indulge in chimneys when it is so much more soldierly to gather round a smoky fire out of doors to cook our food and warm ourselves? Why interfere with the providential design of these searching spring rains and withering winds by remaining behind plastered log barriers and under tight roofs, when so little work will enable us to return to nature's wild simplicity? Some of our foolish boys murmur at these orders emanating from comfortable, luxurious headquarters, and think we might as well have remained in our tight little cabins the few days we have yet to stay, as to catch colds all of us by lying on the ground before we commence our summer's marchings. But it is well known that soldiers will grumble at the kindest provisions made for their comfort, and of course we shall go on with our wholesome sanitary arrangements regardless of any such talk.

THE RATION QUESTION

Why, actually, some of these ungrateful boys object to the bill Senator Wilson is introducing, cutting down their ration to the old standard; and declare that with the present ration (marching), they used last summer frequently to eat the ten crackers allowed per day at a single meal, and wonder what they will do if it is reduced. Now it is well known (to all the people that stay at home and read the newspapers) that no man can possibly eat the whole of the bountiful ration that Uncle Sam allows his soldiers; and it is well known to the heads of the war bureaus at Washington (as we see by an order issued on the subject last year) that it is perfectly easy for the soldier to carry 12 days' rations on his person on the march, and even, in case of necessity, where the beef is driven on the hoof, and there is some green corn to be obtained, 24 or 30 days' rations. In face of these well known facts, then, how absurd for a soldier to set up the statement that he does, as a matter of fact, often eat a whole day's marching ration at a single meal and call for more, and that no soldier ever did carry on his back more than what he ate in six days! How preposterous to mention the circumstance that nineteen out of twenty of the enlisted men spend their whole pay in purchasing additions to this same extravagantly liberal allowance of Uncle Sam, and that after a three days' march, on a supply of (it may be) 11 days' rations, the usual price of hard tack is a dime a piece! I have seen hundreds of times a dollar offered for half a dozen hard breads, or for a day's ration, although of course a true soldier will scorn to take money from a comrade for anything to eat that he may happen to have over.

Does it ever occur to anyone who is thinking of the liberal rations of our government, to ask whether the soldier, as a matter of fact, gets that full allowance? It is true that if the soldier had all the beans, rice, molasses, potatoes, dried apples, pickles, hominy, &c., &c., that the regulations allow him, and time and skill to cook them properly, he would be able to satisfy his appetite very reasonably, and even often have something over. But when we come to the marches, the hard work of the soldier, his ration is ten crackers a day (a short pound) and three-fourths of a pound of pork or one and one-quarter pounds of fresh beef of the poorest and boniest kind, and nothing else except a small allowance of sugar and coffee. This hard bread is frequently spoiled by wet, and some part of it unfit to eat by reason of bugs and worms. Now I affirm, in spite of Gen. Wilson, or Gen. Halleck, or anybody else, that this is a short ration for a hearty man on a hard march, and that when the extra of "small rations," as they are called (beans, rice, &c.), are not issued, at least 12 or 14 crackers a day should be issued to make the ration good. If the soldier obtained the money value of these articles to which he is entitled, but which are not issued, as the regulations say he shall, in his company fund, the matter would be better, but in practice he seldom or never does.

THE BOYS LIKE TO BE TALKED TO

There are several things which I could suggest as measures likely to benefit the boys of our army, but as my turn has not yet come to take command of the forces, they may not be at present adopted. I think, for instance, that they ought to be talked to a little more. All the great generals of ancient times, and of modern times, too, have stirred the enthusiasms of their troops on the eve of battle by rousing speeches. Xenophon, Hannibal, Scipio, Caesar, everybody who wanted to get some great exploits out of the troops under his command, has told them what he wanted them to do, appealed to their patriotism, their religion, their love of glory, or whatever motive might most excite them to lofty action. Cromwell stirred up the religious enthusiasm of his troops till no foe of equal numbers could resist their grim onset. Napoleon, with a few fiery sentences, roused his Frenchmen to the most exalted spirit of courage and devotion. Now no soldiers under heaven ever came to war from a more intelligent spirit of patriotism than ours; none with a clearer sense of the principles which lay at the basis of the contest in which they are engaged; none more capable of being encouraged and roused to enthusiasm by the lofty enthusiasms of a generous leader. And our nation, of all others, has been a nation of perpetual public gatherings and speech makings. But our generals have said never a word (I speak in a general way) to encourage the troops, to keep alive their patriotism and regard for the cause, to cherish that living sympathy which should ever exist between a leader and his troops—have seemed desirous, on the whole, to make their men mere machines, going into battle without knowing anything where the pinch of the contest was, or precisely what was required of them—save to go forward at the order "forward" and fire at the order "fire."

I believe a good deal more might be made by a different course of proceeding, that our boys are something more than shooting machines, or if machines, that there are strings and pulleys and wheels in them that mere military orders don't reach, and yet which might have much effect in deciding battles—these great and terrible battles that are to decide this opening campaign, and probably bring the war to an end—these coming successes (as we devoutly hope) that are to atone for the disgraceful reverses our arms have this spring sustained in every quarter where they have been engaged. Oh for power to speak a word that might thrill the breast of every Union soldier and rouse in him that holy enthusiasm for our right cause, which should make every blow struck irresistible, and carry our arms victorious right into the citadel of rebellion, and conquer a right peace. One or two of Meade's modest, earnest orders, published to the army near the Gettysburg times, had a wonderfully happy effect. I trust more may be issued, and that every opportunity may be taken to inspire the patriotism and enthusiasm of our troops, and keep before their minds the great principles which first sent them forth from their peaceful homes to fight for endangered liberty and republican government, for God and freedom throughout the world.

Yours truly,

DUNN BROWNE

Back on September 26, 1862, Dunn Browne had explained to his readers that he was virtually addicted to his habit of letter-writing: ". . . even if you should read in the bulletin that Dunn Browne has fallen in a heroic charge upon the enemy's battery, waving his sword and cheering on his men, &c., &c., you may still expect one more farewell epistle written perhaps in red ink and showing the ruling passion strong in death." So it was to be. In the editorial columns of the Springfield Republican *of May 21, 1864—the same issue that carried the letter above—appeared this notice:*

"We learn by private letter from Fredericksburg, 13th, that the wounds of Capt. Samuel Fiske of the Connecticut 14th (our 'Dunn Browne') were so severe that he had been given up by the surgeons, and was likely to live but two or three days. . . ." Then, in the next issue, May 28, this notice: ". . . our 'Dunn Browne' died at Fredericksburg, Va., on Sunday, of the wounds received in the Wilderness battles. . . . Our readers all knew him, and they all loved him; and no word of ours can add to the brave record of his life, or take away the pang that his death occasions."

On the morning of May 6, the second day of the Wilderness fighting, General Hancock's Second Corps was staggered by a surprise Confederate attack. The 14th Connecticut was one of the regiments in Carroll's brigade thrown forward to stem the assault. No doubt (as Dunn Browne prophesied) Captain Fiske was waving his sword and cheering on his men when he was struck in the chest by a bullet that penetrated his right lung. He was evacuated to Fredericksburg, which his brother Asa called "this city of the mangled & dying." Efforts to extract the bullet were unavailing, and there he lingered for sixteen days, his life slipping away slowly. His family was with him when he died on May 22. He marked that last morning as Dunn Browne. "To-day I shall get my marching orders," he observed; "well, I am ready."

INDEX